HOW THE CITY REALLY WORKS

THE TIMES

HOW THE CITY REALLY WORKS

The definitive guide to money and investing in London's square mile

Alexander Davidson

KOGAN
PAGE

London and Philadelphia

Publisher's note

Every possible effort has been made to ensure that the information contained in this book is accurate at the time of going to press, and the publishers and author cannot accept responsibility for any errors or omissions, however caused. No responsibility for loss or damage occasioned to any person acting, or refraining from action, as a result of the material in this publication can be accepted by the editor, the publisher or the author.

First published in Great Britain and the United States in 2006 by Kogan Page Limited

120 Pentonville Road
London N1 9JN
United Kingdom
www.kogan-page.co.uk

525 South 4th Street, #241
Philadelphia PA 19147
USA

© Alexander Davidson, 2006

The views expressed in this book are those of the author, and are not necessarily the same as those of Times Newspapers Ltd.

ISBN 0 7494 4243 3

British Library Cataloguing-in-Publication Data

A CIP record for this book is available from the British Library.

Library of Congress Cataloging-in-Publication Data

Davidson, Alexander, 1957-
   How the city really works: the definitive guide to money and investing in London's square mile / Alex Davidson.
        p. cm.
   Includes bibliographical references.
   ISBN 0-7494-4243-3
   1. Finance–England–London. 2. Financial institutions–England–London. 3. Stock exchanges–England–London. I. Title.
HG186.G72L663 2006
332.109421–dc22

                                    2006013153

Typeset by JS Typesetting Ltd, Porthcawl, Mid Glamorgan
Printed and bound in the United Kingdom by Bell & Bain, Glasgow

Contents

The Institute of Chartered Accountants in England & Wales (ICAEW) is the UK's leading accountancy body and the largest in Europe, with over 127,000 members working in business and public practice in 143 different countries. The ICAEW has a number of prestigious qualifications and awards for potential and existing chartered accountants including:

The ACA – the Associate Chartered Accountant (ACA) is the premier qualification for business. It is a broad-based accountancy qualification that attracts the very best motivated individuals to enter training after school or university. Composed of the Professional Stage and the Advanced Stage, the qualification has an excellent reputation and international appeal.

More details are available via **www.icaew.co.uk/students**

The Corporate Finance qualification – open to established individuals working in the global corporate finance industry who wish to advance their career path or graduates who want a recognised professional qualification. It focuses on the development of practical and management skills within corporate finance. Successful candidates at Advanced Diploma receive the globally recognised CF designation.

For more information, please visit: **www.cfqualification.com**

International Financial Reporting Standards (IFRS) – this learning and assessment programme is aimed at anyone with an interest in IFRS whether from an accounting background or not. The IFRS Certificate focuses on broad knowledge and understanding of international standards; and the IFRS Diploma focuses on the technical requirements of the international standards in a business environment.

Please visit: **www.icaew.co.uk/ifrs**

The Oxford University Diploma in Financial Strategy – developed in partnership with Saïd Business School at Oxford University, the Diploma is a Masters-level course for senior accountants already in roles including chief finance officer, finance director, treasurer and controller. Its four modules cover Business Strategy, Finance and Management Control Systems, each of four full days teaching in four teaching periods – March, June, September and December.

More details are available from: **www.sbs.ox.ac.uk/diploma**

Pathways – the 'Examination of Experience' is a route to membership allowing qualified members of ACCA, CIMA and CIPFA to qualify for membership of the ICAEW provided that they have the relevant necessary experience and pass an entrance examination – equivalent to the ACA advanced case study.

Pathways information can be found at **www.icaew.co.uk/pathways**

Mr Smith is on his way.
He checked in 15 minutes ago.

10 minute check-in
Bank - 22 mins
Canary Wharf - 14 mins
24 European destinations
Over 200 flights daily

LondonCityAirport

LondonCityAirport.com

Flying but faster

WELCOME TO A NEW ASSET CLASS

"Beauty is in the Eye of the Investor"

OPEN AN OFFSHORE DIAMOND ACCOUNT AND BE ASSURED OF THE STABILITY AND INTEGRITY OF SWISS BANKING ALONG WITH THE PRESTIGE AND PERFORMANCE OF THE INTERNATIONAL COLOURED DIAMOND MARKET.

For centuries, *coloured diamonds* have been admired for their beauty and mystique. They are extremely rare. In fact, only one in ten thousand diamonds has a hue. They are also the most concentrated form of wealth in the world, achieving prices of millions of dollars per carat. As the demand for these crystalline works of art increases over the next decade, Pastor-Genève invites you to profit from the three pillars of success the Coloured Diamond Market has to offer:

LONG-TERM GROWTH - CAPITAL PRESERVATION - WEALTH DISCRETION

Pastor-Genève - Building Global Relationships

Pastor-Genève B.V.B.A. is a European dealer that specializes in rare coloured diamonds. Our Managing Director, Stephen Hershoff, has over forty years of experience in the international diamond market. Our chief consultant, Stephen Hofer, is known as the foremost expert in the field and is the author of the award winning "Collecting & Classifying Coloured Diamonds" a 742-page book considered the ultimate reference guide for coloured diamond investors and collectors.

The Coloured Diamond Chronicle- Essential Market Information

To learn more about our coloured diamond investment program, you have been selected to receive a FREE SUBSCRIPTION to our monthly newsletter, The Coloured Diamond Chronicle. Upon receipt of your application, respondents will also receive a copy of our informative Coloured Diamond Brochure.

I look forward to your reply.
Cordially yours,

Stephen Hershoff
Managing Director, Pastor-Genève B.V.B.A.

To receive the invaluable information in *"Coloured Diamond Collecting & Investing"*, simply mail, e-mail or fax your contact details: Name, Mailing Address, E-mail Address and Telephone Number to Pastor-Genève B.V.B.A. at the company address listed below.

Pastor-Genève B.V.B.A. • Brusselstraat 51, B-2018 Antwerpen, Belgium • Tel: + (0) 32 3 244 1871 • Fax: + (0) 32 3 244 1873
www.pastor-geneve.com • HRA N° 321.563   BTW N° 444.815.472

Coloured Diamonds

By Stephen Hershoff, Managing Director, Pastor-Geneve bvba

Diamonds have long been thought of as the most concentrated form of wealth – a private and easily transportable international asset. The coloured diamond market in particular, can be traced back centuries to Indian traders and European Royalty. These rare works of art have been an essential asset of the wealthy classes for centuries and have recently garnered the attention of the general public for their beauty, rarity and value.

Although coloured diamonds continue to generate images of affluence, collectors and investors now recognize the powerful investment fundamentals driving this closely held market.

In the last two years alone, 38 of the 40 highest prices paid for gemstones and jewelry at the major auction houses around the globe have been for coloured diamonds.[1]

With the biggest laboratory in the world, the Gemological Institute of America, reporting demand for coloured diamond services up 68 % in the last five years[2], the long-term potential of investing in coloured diamonds has never been stronger.

Grading Diamonds

Like any asset, the price of a diamond and its ability to increase in value is partly determined by how rare it is. The main factors that influence diamond prices are its colour, cut, clarity and carat weight, all being factors of rarity.

Colour – The single most important factor in grading and valuing coloured diamonds is the colour of the stone. The colour saturation of the diamond is measured to determine the grading, or quality of the stone. The grading standards developed by the GIA for Fancy Coloured Diamonds are: Faint; Very Light; Fancy Light; Fancy; Fancy Intense; Fancy Deep/Dark and Fancy Vivid.[3] The stones at the top end of the grading spectrum are the rarest pieces in the marketplace with the highest values.

Cut – Cut has the strongest influence on the diamonds brilliance. In a well-cut stone, rays of light entering the diamond reflect back to the eye of the observer. The cutter of fancy coloured diamonds is an artist using the coloured diamond rough material to create individual masterpieces with perfectly faceted dimensions and a vibrant colour composition.

Carat Weight – The size of a diamond has an impact on its price and is a major factor of rarity. The metric carat, which equals 0.20 gram, is the standard unit of weight for diamonds and most other gems. Coloured diamonds tend to appear naturally in smaller sizes compared to other diamonds and gemstones. In fact, very few pink diamonds from the Argyle mine in Australia are over one carat in size. At last years Argyle tender, the largest pink diamond was 2.31 carats.[4]

Clarity – Diamonds contain minute imperfections called inclusions. The majority of coloured diamonds contain inclusions because of the chemical structure and pressure required to create one. Coloured diamond connoisseurs will acquire a stone based on the colour saturation and consider clarity as a secondary issue. Instead of using a loop to examine the stone, they use different light sources as their guide. The question they ask is: How does the stone look in natural sunlight as opposed to artificial light? Coloured diamonds selling for hundreds of thousands of pounds per carat are valued for their colour first and second how the clarity affects the colour.

Understanding Coloured Diamonds

The actual grading of coloured diamonds is very straightforward and simple to understand but requires laboratory equipment and years of experience to become an expert. It is based on both colour saturation and the appearance of colour. It is important to note that coloured diamonds often appear in nature with a dominant colour and a colour modifier, or secondary colour. On a certificate, colour modifiers will appear with the suffix (-ish). For example, a coloured diamond with a dominant colour of orange and traces of yellow will be certified as follows: Fancy Intense yellowish Orange.

The term "Fancy Intense" indicates a medium to strong amount of colour saturation. Note the dominant colour orange appears last and is capitalized while the secondary colour yellow appears first and is in lowercase. To learn more about the grading of coloured diamonds, it is suggested to consult Stephen Hofer's "Collecting & Classifying Coloured Diamonds."[5]

Certificates & Reports

When purchasing a fancy coloured diamond, it is essential that the stone have an origin-of-colour report from the GIA or one of the other qualified gemological laboratories. This report will determine whether or not the diamonds colour is natural. The report will also indicate the diamond's colour grade and classification along with its weight and measurements. The primary laboratories used for grading and certification are: GIA, IGI, EGL and the HRD.

Rarity – Commercial Demand versus Natural Supply

While it is true that all natural coloured diamonds are rare, the intelligent investor knows that there are differences in rarity among different colours. In other words, certain colours are more or less rare than other colours. In addition, investors must also understand which diamond colours are "perceived in the commercial marketplace" as being more rare than others.

For every 10,000 carats of colourless diamonds mined, only 1 carat will turn out to be a fancy coloured diamond.[6] Of the estimated 120 million carats of diamonds mined each year[7], just over 2,000 carats will be cut and polished coloured diamonds.[8]

Consider the Argyle mine in Australia:
"Argyle mines 30 million carats a year, and less than 5 percent is jewelry grade. "Less than 1/10th of one percent of that are pink diamonds. Out of those, it's a minute percent that are usable for jewelry."[9]

In the coloured diamond marketplace-where buyers compete against one another to own the so-called "best" stones for their collection and/or portfolio-knowing the order of coloured diamond rarity from "least rare" to "more rare" is an important step in determining a diamond's present and potential value.

For simplicities sake, we have divided coloured diamonds into three categories of rarity:
Extremely Rare – Red, Violet, Green, Blue
Rare – Purple, Pink, Orange, Olive, White
Moderately Rare – Gray, Yellow, Brown, Black, Colourless

Investing in Coloured Diamonds

In terms of both value and growth, fancy coloured diamonds are offering perhaps the best return on investment in the gemstone market.[10] "The market for natural coloured diamonds is very strong at the moment and prices have risen by 25% within the last year," says Andrew Coxon, vice president of De Beers in London.[11]

Since 1970 blue diamonds have doubled in price every 5 years, pink diamonds have doubled in price every 6-7 years and yellow diamonds have doubled in price every 8-10 years. During recessions, coloured diamonds tend to retain their value and in stable or healthy economies they appreciate in price.[12]

While there are no performance guarantees, the consensus of coloured diamond dealers is that continued long-term conservative appreciation of 7%-10% annually is a reasonable prospect with the rarer colours appreciating in excess of this range.[13] Investors should consider starting a collection by investing 5,000 to 10,000 pounds in one or two coloured diamonds.

The following recent auction results indicate the prices achieved and the potential of the market for top-end coloured diamonds:
2004 Christie's 2.38 Carat Fancy Intense Yellow, Estimate $26,000-$31,000 Selling Price $56,000[14]
2004 Sotheby's 5.59 Carat Fancy Intense purplish Pink, Estimate 1.36m USD – 1.52m Selling Price 1.85m USD[15]
2005 Christie's 0.90 Fancy Blue, Estimate: $35,000-$50,000 Selling Price: $71,760[16]

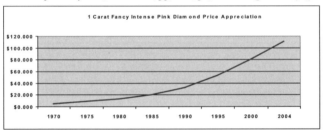

1 Carat Fancy Intense Pink Diamond Price Appreciation

Average prices of a highly saturated 1-carat fancy intense pink diamond since 1970, eye clean stones

There are five main reasons why investors purchase coloured diamonds:
Privacy – Most countries do not require the ownership of coloured diamonds be disclosed to any government authority. The certificates are in bearer form, there are no names or serial numbers and there are no registration requirements for coloured diamonds.

Portability – Coloured Diamonds are considered the most concentrated form of wealth in the world. A multi-million dollar portfolio can be discreetly placed in a small envelope.

Estate Planning – Consider the purchase of a small selection of coloured diamonds that can be discreetly passed from one generation to the next. Depending on the number of heirs, more stones with less unit value may be needed.

Price Stability – The majority of the important coloured diamonds are in strong financial hands, whether it be the dealers/jewellers or the investors/collectors who own them. Even in a severe recession, owners of fine coloured diamonds who need money will sacrifice or discount their common merchandise or other assets first. Fine coloured diamonds are so hard to substitute that anything that can be replaced more readily will be sold first. These two fundamentals combine to lead to remarkable price stability and consistency.[17]

Long Term Growth – At a time when global demand for quality coloured diamonds is rising, major sources of supply in South Africa and Australia, including the Kimberley mine and the Argyle mine,[18] should be closing in the next two to three years. Because of these supply and demand factors, the long-term price appreciation of coloured diamond prices should continue for the next decade.

Summary

Fancy coloured diamonds have among the most liquid and highly developed markets for any collectible asset. They can be transferred quietly and legally and sold globally in most major cities. However, owners must allow time to sell their coloured diamonds; they are similar to real estate or rare art and require time to find the right buyer. Be realistic in your investment outlook; while coloured diamonds have historically been an exceptional investment, they are not as liquid as most securities investments and they are subject to higher markups.

You should view them as a mid-to-long-term investment with a time horizon of five years or longer from acquisition to liquidation. When you do want to sell, you should contact your dealer at least ninety days before expecting to achieve results. This will give your dealer the chance to accurately gauge the expected market price.

Before you buy your first diamond, research the market. Always work with a dealer that specializes in coloured diamonds. It is important to learn the subtle nuances of the market so that you can make informed decisions and plan your portfolio to realistically meet your long-term financial goals.

Author's Bio:
Stephen Hershoff is Managing Director of Pastor-Geneve bvba. He has over forty years of experience in the diamond business. Beginning in London in the 1960's, he was a dealer in diamonds and other coloured gems. Throughout the late 1960's and 1970's, he concentrated on advising a private client base of international collectors and connoisseurs through his own consulting company. In the early 1980's, he moved to North America to assume responsibility for a company that became one of the four most important gem dealers recommended by the Dow Jones-Irwin Guide to fine gems and jewellery. His company, Pastor-Geneve, is recognized as one of the most established dealers in the coloured diamond market.

Sources:
[1] GIA Publications: The Loupe "Fancy Color Diamonds catch Public Fancy." By Russell Shor

[2] GIA Publications: The Loupe "Fancy Color Diamonds catch Public Fancy." By Russell Shor, page 91

[3] http://www.gia.edu/newsroom/3720/5720/public_interest_articles_details.cfm

[4] Rapaport News, "Pink Diamonds" by Robert Genis, November 11, 2004

[5] Collecting & Classifying Coloured Diamonds, Stephen C. Hofer, Ashland Press, New York, 1998
http://www.telegraph.co.uk/money/main.jhtml?xml=/money/2003/02/19/cmdiam119.xml -

[6] http://money.guardian.co.uk/print/0,3858,4532840-110138,00.html

[7] http://www.moneyweek.com/article/515/investing/markets/gem-investment.html

[8] Coloured Diamond Price Forecast 2010: A Report Prepared Exclusively for Sovereign Society Members, by David Markum, Gemologist

[9] http://money.cnn.com/2004/01/23/pf/q_ultraluxury/

[10] http://www.iht.com/articles/104985.htm

[11] http://www.europeanbusiness.eu.com/features/2005/jul/world_diamonds.html

[12] http://www.webguru.com/investing-diamonds.htm

[13] The Sovereign Individual, June 2003, Ireland, Mark Nestmann

[14] Christie's Geneva May 2004, Lot #134 Round Brilliant

[15] Sotheby's Geneva May 2004, Lot #325 Pear Shaped

[16] Christie's Hong Kong June 2005, Lot #2543 Round Brilliant

[17] Zurich Club Communique, August 2002, UK

[18] Jewelry Circular Keystone, April 2005 "Argyle still in the Pink, but maybe not for long."
http://business.iafrica.com/company/462150.htm

Acknowledgements

In striving to produce an up-to-date text reflecting how the City works, I was overwhelmed by the generosity of many professionals who gave of their valuable time freely for the purpose of getting it right. In no particular order, I would like to thank the following organisations and people.

On banking and finance, the Bank of England gave me enormous help. The British Bankers' Association was kind enough to discuss at length my chapter on commercial banking, and to correct early drafts. The Building Societies Association, the Finance & Leasing Association, and the Factors and Discounters Association answered my questions. Egg and First Direct offered useful perspectives.

The Association of Private Client Investment Managers and Stockbrokers gave a large number of chapters a detailed reading and made extremely useful points and suggestions. My thanks are due to Compeer for releasing its important research to me. Charles Newsome, investment manager at Christows, helped me to inject balance and a healthy dose of realism into some sections.

On trading systems and many other areas, the London Stock Exchange was enormously helpful, both in arranging interviews with key executives and in supplying information, clarifying points and checking for accuracy.

LCH.Clearnet was very helpful on the clearing aspects of post-trade services. Deutsche Börse kindly provided its own broad perspective and comments. Denis Peters, corporate communications director at Euroclear, kindly read the full manuscript for me and made many useful points, far beyond the call of duty.

On derivatives, I would thank Euronext.liffe, EDX London and the Baltic Exchange for help. Jill Leyland, Economic Adviser to World Gold Council, explained gold markets to me. I thank various executives at ICAP for giving me continuous and valuable help and interviews, which enabled me to improve the coverage on money markets and derivatives. GFI Group gave me further invaluable help on derivatives. My gratitude is due to Peter Sceats, Expert Witness and consultant director of business development at TFS London, for some useful perspectives.

At PLUS Markets Group, Nemone Wynn-Evans, director of business development, was particularly helpful on all aspects of market making and was willing to read and comment at length on relevant sections of the book. Jamie Whitehorn, head of regulation, was also very helpful.

The Financial Ombudsman Service kindly gave me an overview of its services. On the personal finance chapter, Anna Bowes at Chase de Vere Financial Solutions had some valuable comments and Justin Modray at Bestinvest (Brokers) was very helpful. Kevin Carr of Lifesearch gave me important insight into protection products. Tom McPhail, head of pensions research at Hargreaves Lansdown, had some useful suggestions on pensions.

The UK Debt Management Office explained some important points about gilts. The International Capital Market Association found time to read and comment usefully on some of the bonds coverage. On foreign exchange, I am grateful to Chris Furness, senior currency strategist, 4CAST, who discussed the market with me at length over an extended period, and helped me substantially with the relevant chapter. The Bank of International Settlements was helpful in answering queries.

For help on pooled investments and other matters, I am grateful to The Association of Investment Trust Companies and the Investment Management Association. On hedge funds, the Alternative Investment Management Association read my text and made useful comments.

On corporate governance and regulation, my thanks are due to Chris Hodges, Financial Reporting Council, and his colleague David Loweth, and to David Styles, assistant director, corporate law and governance directorate, DTI. On money laundering, Chris Hamblin, my colleague at Complinet, helped me to interpret some of the PR-speak and commented on my coverage.

I thank Hill & Knowlton for providing invaluable background insights into how PR practitioners operate, which helped to put some balance into Chapter 17.

On insurance, my thanks are due to Lloyd's of London executives for patience in answering my sometimes difficult questions and checking material, to Equitas for explaining properly what it does and to Peter Staddon, head of technical services at the British Insurance Brokers' Association for reading drafts. My thanks are also due to Pam Byrne, director of financial and compliance services and others at The International Underwriting Association of London for commenting on parts of the manuscript.

Many others helped, including at the highest level in City firms and trade associations, but preferred to stay anonymous. I would like to take this opportunity to thank them all, and any whose names I have inadvertently omitted from this list. The help I received was great. The errors are entirely my own.

Know Your Risk, Know Your Options?
By Mark Greenaway

Derivatives introduction

Derivatives are financial instruments whose value is derived from underlying assets, such as stock market indices, equities or commodities and can be used for hedging or speculation.

Options to enhance income

Many investors remain wary of trading options due to the perception of high risk and volatility. However when used prudently, traded options can generate income on an equity portfolio, whilst minimising risk.

Getting started:

Options on equities are available on most FTSE 100 shares and are traded on Euronext.liffe. A full list of these options is available on their website (www.euronext.com) and provides a good starting point for private investors new to options.

So what are options?

Essentially, there are two types of options; **calls** and **puts**.

A call option on FTSE equities gives the holder the right, but not the obligation, to buy the underlying stock (normally 1000 shares) at the option strike (the buying) price at any time up until the expiry date. A put option gives the holder the right, but not the obligation to sell the underlying stock at the option strike (the selling) price at any time up until the expiry date. A buyer of a call option would be bullish of the stock and a buyer of a put option, bearish.

The key benefit for a buyer of an option is the risk is limited to the price paid for the option, but there is a potential for unlimited rewards. As with any market, for every buyer of an option there has to be a seller and *this is where investors can use options to generate income.*

For the seller of an option, the risk/reward profile is the reverse to that of the buyer. A seller's maximum profit is limited to the premium received, but the losses could be virtually unlimited.

Why would anyone sell an option and how they could possibly enhance their returns? The answer is that they must be used in conjunction with an equity portfolio or with other options in a way that can **limit your risk**.

Useful sites:

www.liffe.com/liffeinvestor
www.sucden.co.uk

Mark Greenaway is Head of Private Client Services at London based Futures and Options broker Sucden (UK) Limited.

Dedication

For Acelia, Philip, Victoria, Eleanor and Michael
This book is for you

Important note

This book aims to explain the City understandably, using simple language and generic examples. The wording does not have the status of legal definitions, and this guide is for educational purposes. It should not be used as a definitive source or, in particular, as a substitute for investment advice. The book is necessarily selective and seeks to cover only the main City activities. It may reflect some of the author's preferences. The City changes quickly and the details in this book may become out of date, but the overview will stay true.

Abbreviations

When I use the name of an organisation for the first time in a chapter, I spell it out in full. Subsequently, I usually abbreviate it. For example, you will find the Financial Services Authority referred to subsequently as the FSA, and the London Stock Exchange as the LSE.

Serviced apartments in the City

As travel is becoming an inevitable part of modern life serviced apartments are a growth market providing flexible, comfortable accommodation in the City. Serviced apartments offer more space than traditional hotel accommodation and kitchen facilities allow residents an extra option. They come into their own for stays of 1 month plus, but overall provide excellent value for money when judged on the level of comfort, flexibility and range of facilities.

The term 'Serviced apartment' is a very broad description and they range in quality, facilities and services provided allowing for everyone to meet their requirements in terms of budget and amenities. Minimum stays are generally from 1 week, 1 month or 3 months depending on the building, however there are some that take bookings from one night.

The ideal way to make your choice of apartment is to speak to an agency that specializes in this growth sector. They have an in-depth knowledge of the many serviced apartments available in the city saving valuable time going through the host of options on offer.

Late Night London (www.latenightlondon.co.uk), the capital's five star on-line guide to drinking and dining, lists a whole host of fantastic City bars showing that the Square Mile now rivals its West End sister.

Springing up across the City are a whole myriad of fantastic lounge bars complete with restaurants and private rooms. Top *Late Night London* choices include new arrivals, The Livery on Wood Street, EC2 and The Wall on Old Broad Street, EC2 as well as the hugely popular Digress City on Ropemaker Street, EC2 and Alibi on Shoe Lane, EC4.

Fashioned for the city's most discerning crowd, all these fantastic bars are seriously stylish and ideal for business lunches, after work drinks with colleagues and friends as well as private parties and corporate events, small or large.

Sophisticated and contemporary, all the bars featured on *Late Night London* offer uniquely designed flexible spaces for a wide variety of occasions, events and parties all of which can be hired free of charge. Book a booth for after-work drinks, take a private room for a meeting or exclusive party or simply reserve a table for lunch. Each *Late Night London* City bar is available for exclusive private hire at the weekend.

Whichever bar you head for, you can be assured of delicious food from weekly changing lunchtime specials and party platters to cheese boards and pâté plates. Drinkers will appreciate each bars' contemporary cocktail list, wide range of beers, both on tap and bottled, and varied wine list with many choices by the glass.

If you can't decide which bar is for you, log onto **www.latenightlondon.co.uk** to contact their corporate events team and party planning service whose teams are dedicated to finding the perfect bar to suit your individual requirements, completely free of charge.

Ideal for business or pleasure, *Late Night London* takes all the hassle out of socialising in the Square Mile – a great bar is simply a click of the mouse away – www.latenightlondon.co.uk

Stylish and flexible venues for all corporate events and parties

Our venues offer a wide range of uniquely designed spaces, atmosphere and style that can accommodate:

- ## Product launches

- ## Private parties
  (Private bar hire available)

- ## Day conferences

- ## Meetings

- ## Drinks receptions

- ## Corporate dinners
  (Function menus available. All menus are flexible)

- ## Exhibitions

- ## Fashion shows

Our Corporate Events Team can help you plan your event, catering for all your individual requirements, **free of charge** or simply help you choose the perfect venue.

Contact Samantha and the team to discuss your requirements:

T: 020 7534 5547

E: events@latenightlondon.co.uk

THE WALL
45 Old Broad Street
London EC2N 1HU
www.thewallbar.co.uk

THE LIVERY
130 Wood Street
London EC2V 6DA
www.thelivery.co.uk

digress
City Point, 1 Ropemaker St
London EC2Y 9AW
www.digress-city.co.uk

alibi
18 Lime Office Court
Hill House, Shoe Lane
London EC4A 3BQ
www.alibi-bar.co.uk

The City of London – A World Leader

The City of London, situated at the heart of the Greater London metropolis, is firmly positioned as the world's leading international financial and business centre.

Key to the City's success on the international stage is its openness and attractiveness to both UK businesses and those from overseas. Financial institutions are drawn to the City by benefits such as highly skilled labour, clusters of customers and of course large financial markets with globally competitive rates of liquidity and high levels of specialisation. Everything global financiers need to do business is to be found on their doorstep. It is this high concentration in such a small area, that makes the City unique, and puts it ahead of financial rivals such as New York and Tokyo. This is why more foreign banks locate in London than anywhere else and its foreign exchange market is the largest in the world.

Whilst the City's reach is truly global in nature, it is extremely important to the UK economy. The City contributes approximately 3% to the UK's GDP, and 13% to that of London.

As Europe's financial capital, the City is also vital to its European neighbours. Research shows that European Union GDP would reduce immediately by 33bn (with 23bn per annum permanently lost in the long term) if London's financial services cluster did not exist. This would mean a loss of 100,000 jobs across Europe. If the City were to lose its European pre-eminence the EU would pay a high price.

Liaison with the European Union is therefore a key priority for the City. For this reason, the Corporation of London opened a City Office in Brussels in 2004. The Corporation is the provider of local government services to the Square Mile, and it also has the role of promoting the City, both at home and abroad. It has been involved for many years in facilitating contact between the City and European Union institutions, and has fully supported the process of EU enlargement. The City Office is an important new venture and its establishment follows wide ranging consultation with practitioners, trade associations and other stakeholders. The Office, guided by an Advisory Group of senior City practitioners, aims to help shape new thinking about the future direction of the financial services market in the enlarged EU, and to enable the City to develop further its approach to strategic, pan-EU issues.

The Lord Mayor of the City of London, a respected ambassador for financial services, also plays a key role in promoting the Square Mile, within the EU and beyond. Over the past year, the vast majority of new EU member states have been visited by the Lord Mayor, as well as many other countries across the globe.

The City is rightly proud of its prestigious status at a domestic, European and international level, and the Corporation works hard to help maintain this position. We are very aware however, that we must never become complacent and that success cannot be left to chance.

If the City is to continue to thrive, the infrastructure and public services of London as a whole must be modern and efficient, to accommodate population growth and to sustain economic development. Transport projects are particularly important, in order to maintain London's credibility as a place to do international business.

The world of finance is fast-moving, yet London stays ahead of the pace. It is sensitive to the pulse of the international market place, because it is at the heart of it – it is in all our interests to make sure that it remains there.

Michael Snyder is Chairman of the Policy and Resources Committee at the Corporation of London

The Corporation of London – In Partnership with the City
www.cityoflondon.gov.uk

Start your Banking and Finance career at EBS London

We have designed the European Business School London (EBS-L) MSc in Global Banking and Finance with the aim to equip course members with the relevant skills and expertise to pursue successful careers in the Banking and Finance industry or Consulting located in the City. This MSc course provides a strong foundation in the principles and practice of Global Banking and Finance and is taught by well-qualified faculty staff.

This MSc is practical and career oriented, with high standards of rigour and opportunity to study in a stimulating, experienced, talented and diverse international environment. Both the faculty and student groups reflect the strong emphasis of EBS-London on international experience, which is further enhanced by our global alumni network. MSc participants come from a rich diversity of academic backgrounds, professional expertise and nationalities, bringing a wealth of experience to the programme. All

have a high level of intellectual ability, the capacity for hard work and the motivation to take on new challenges and commitments. Although most participants have previous experience in the field of finance and the programme is rigorous and demanding, no formal prior training in finance is required.

The objective of the MSc programme is to help individuals, and hence any organisation that employs them, to enhance their managerial effectiveness within the field of Global Banking and Finance by providing MSc participants with a strong foundation in the principles and practice of finance and furnishing them with analytical tools and new skills to form a sound basis for financial decision-making.

The course covers Financial Markets, Strategy, Quantitative Methods, Financial Institutions, Financial Regulation and Corporate Governance. The MSc requires all students to write a dissertation on a global Banking and Finance theme.

The course emphasises state of art teaching of important issues such as Basel 2, MifiD and Sarbanes Oxley. Seminars and visits are

organised with speakers coming from the City and policy networks in the UK & the European Union. We hope that you find your time with the European Business School London from an intellectual and practical point of view stimulating and rewarding.

Dr. John Ryan
Course Leader
MSc Global Banking and Finance

Learn the Trading Secrets of Professional Traders

More and more people are discovering how investing in professional trader coaching makes a world of difference when it comes to achieving immediate monthly income from trading the stock market.

Set up by professional trader Greg Secker, Traders University covers everything from getting started in the stock market to becoming an advanced trading expert. It is regarded as the most comprehensive training available today. The course encompasses an intensive weekend supported by professional coaching and a six month graduate support program.

To be the best you have to learn from the best, which is where Greg's track record sets the standard. He is an established industry professional who kick-started his career at 24 as the youngest ever vice president and Head of On-line Trading for one of the most volatile and well-known trading floors in North America. In 1997, he was responsible for creating one of the first global on-line dealing businesses supporting a money-market business that ran into the billions on a daily basis. Greg has set up and managed online dealing rooms for many of the largest financial organisations in North America, Australasia and Europe.

Greg now shares his expertise through his seminars and coaching, supporting delegates on their own trading journeys to financial independence. He states "If you can spare an hour a day, with a little training, you will be impressed at how much extra income you can generate. The reason we achieve such positive results, is we train people one-on-one following our immersion (2 day) training course – and it works!"

Greg has a team of full time professional traders who he personally trains and monitors weekly to ensure the graduates are receiving the best possible training. The team must demonstrate consistent monthly returns of at least 15% (though most exceed this significantly!) to remain in the team and ensure that the standard of coaching support remains unrivalled in the industry.

The full Traders University package includes a week of pre-event coaching, a two day intensive seminar presented by Greg, three one-to-one coaching sessions with one of the coaching team and six month's access to a weekly Graduate Conference Call and the Traders University forum.

To sign up for a **FREE** preview seminar and learn how you could make Immediate Monthly Income **NOW**!

Visit: **www.tradersuniversity.co.uk/times**
Call: **0870 766 5234**
Email: **tickets@tradersuniversity.co.uk**

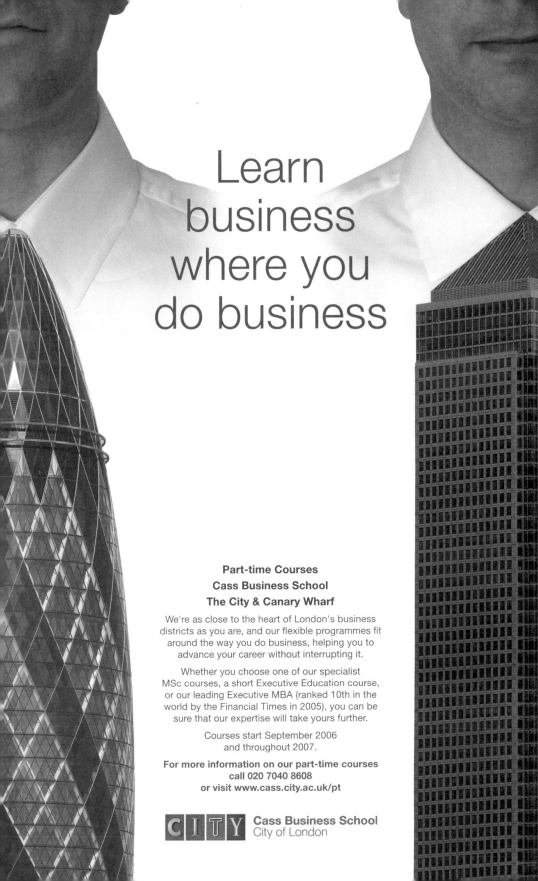

Royal Exchange

A unique grade 1 listed building in the heart of the square mile, an ideal venue to host your event

- Grand Café and Bar
- Restaurant Sauterelle
- Private dining rooms

- Breakfast meetings/reception
- Lunch and dinner – max 30 persons
- Cocktail receptions 40-700 persons
- Exhibitions/Product launches
- Weddings or Social occasions

Please contact the Events Department
Tel: 020 7628 3500
Fax: 020 7256 7435
chriss@conran-restaurants.co.uk
www.conran.com

The Royal Exchange

Recently opened, Restaurant Sauterelle completes Conran Restaurants' gastronomic presence at The Royal Exchange alongside the Grand Café & Bars. Steeped in history, The Royal Exchange is one of the City's great landmarks, its grade 1 listed columns and arches make it a stunning venue for any occasion. The Grand Café and Bar takes its inspiration from the elegant early twentieth century Viennese coffee houses. Above and all around is a series of wonderful stone-wall mezzanines housing two chic bars and a relaxed and unique private dining area, the perfect place from which to view the bustling courtyard of The Royal Exchange.

Choose from the superb selection of crustacea in the courtyard, relax with a glass of Champagne in one of the mezzanine bars or enjoy simple, classic French food in the Restaurant Sauterelle. The thoroughly modern menus include breakfast, lunch, afternoon tea and dinner. The beautiful private dining rooms host 22 guests seated and 80 for a cocktail reception. The venue is also available for corporate cocktail parties and exclusive hire for up to 700.

Wherever you settle should feel like
home

Demands for a single European
capital market have set
harmonisation in motion.

We are convinced of the benefits
of harmonised financial markets
in Europe and are committed to
removing barriers to cross-border
securities settlement.

euroclear

DELIVERING A DOMESTIC
MARKET FOR EUROPE

Introduction

The City of London is vast and complex. It is developing not just every month but every day and every minute. It has progressed even in the weeks before this book went to press. Technology struggles to keep up. New, increasingly exotic products – particularly in derivatives – grab market share in an increasingly international market place. This book aims to explain the City in language you can understand.

I am conscious that there is a gulf between how private investors experience the City, particularly the stock market and derivatives, and the way wholesale markets operate. This book aims to cover both. I have given the stock market early prominence in the book because it is the part that most people will understand. Bonds are a larger asset class than equities and we explore these too.

In the City today, derivatives have in some cases become more significant to traders than the underlying instrument, and this book gives them due prominence. I have included money markets with government bonds in one chapter, and corporate bonds with credit derivatives in another.

We will look at the highly efficient foreign exchange market, and such issues as whether the dollar will remain the leading world currency. I have provided a full explanation of the Bank of England's role in setting interest rates and of its participation in money markets. We will look at how the City is regulated, and how this is shaping its style of doing business – which is truly the topic of the moment.

I focus on the increasing role of corporate governance, and how far it is considered to help business. We look at how Lloyd's of London has constantly survived crises and the impact on the insurance market of events such as the 11 September 2001 terrorist attacks on New York. We will take a critical look at pension reform movements and other areas of personal finance. We will compare types of pooled investment.

Of the utmost importance to the City is communication. We focus on the role of analysts in this post-Spitzer era where they have lost some credibility, and examine some of the techniques. We will look critically at discounted cash flow analysis and EBITDA, explain the City's dependence on earnings per share, and attempt to throw some light on technical analysis issues.

We will look at the subtle art of financial public relations, and how far you can rely on the business press and tip sheets. The various types of investor are examined, including the powerful hedge funds, and the book delves into the perhaps more esoteric aspects of the City, including shipping and metals. In the equities world, we cover market makers, and clearing and settlement.

If you want to work in the City, or have started doing so and need to know more about how the parts fit into the whole, this book will give you a modern overview. If you are an investor, it aims to fill in the gaps that you may not easily glean from your broker or the financial press. This book will help significantly with some professional examinations but is no substitute for your course text. Our approach is practical as well as theoretical. It covers the City as it works today. The text is so designed that you may read it consecutively, or may dip into chapters – because not everybody will want to understand every area of the City all at once.

If you have had little or no exposure to the City, I hope this book will be a treat for you. I have tapped the expertise of practising professionals and aim to impart a flavour of the world in which they work. I have drawn on my own experience of working as a share dealer, as well as in financial journalism.

It is, indeed, in the throb of real experience that many text books fall short, which, to be fair, is in keeping with their aims. This book gives you an experience that is perhaps closer to the knuckle. It was fun to write, and I hope you will enjoy reading it.

The City of London

Introduction

In this chapter we will define the City of London in geographical and product terms, and see how it has developed in history from the cosy club that it was until the mid-1980s to the competitive international market place it is today. We will examine the global market share of the City and some employment issues.

A world apart

The City has an aura of mystery but much of the jargon describes buying and selling of products that are, in many cases, easily defined. The fast-moving environment of City traders has formed a background for many a movie or documentary. The City still has a reputation for being a world apart, and its workers do tend to enjoy better opportunities than may be available, for example, to metal workers in the North of England.

The flip side is that most City workers are doing mundane work, if for above-average pay, in conditions that are not always secure. The large financial institutions are constantly reconstructing themselves, and the City is famous for downsizing. To pin down what the City is, we need to consider activity type and geographical positioning. The City is a sometimes shifting combination of the two.

Broadly speaking, the City operates in or around the geographical *square mile* in the centre of London. It covers wholesale financial services, which are money and/or securities exchanges between professionals, or between professionals and companies or governments, but also some retail activity. A stockbroker dealing with retail clients is considered part of the City provided that it operates within or near the square mile. But the retail stockbroker

GATEWAY TO LONDON

The centre of economic growth within London is shifting east. In recent years London's economy has remained resilient to global economic pressures and continued to attract increased investment and play host to a growing population. To accommodate this growth we are now looking east and to the Thames Gateway London area in particular as a focus for new housing and employment locations.

Gateway to London, the Inward Investment and Business Retention agency for Thames Gateway London, is responsible for helping to deliver growth in business and jobs to the area. We do this by helping companies already established in the area to expand and grow and by actively marketing the area to attract new investment from other parts of the UK and abroad. It is a hugely exciting time with multiple opportunities and it is our job to provide business and investors with everything they need to thrive and expand.

Our offer to leading companies is the strongest in the UK. Specifically, we have:

- A highly skilled labour pool of 3.6 million people
- Access to London's 300,000 graduates a year – over a third of the workforce has a degree qualification
- The lowest overall employment costs anywhere in London and one of the lowest in Southern England
- A diverse population with over 300 languages spoken
- A thriving economic base with 28% of all London VAT registered businesses located in the Thames Gateway London area
- The fastest growing infrastructure in the UK
- The latest telecommunications infrastructure and business support services already in place
- 1,000 hectares of available development land with high quality office, warehouse and manufacturing locations and available premises from $100m^2$ to $100,000m^2$

As a result the area has become the logical choice for companies seeking a sophisticated and central location, yet one that offers a typical saving of 40-50% when compared with Central or West London.

Comparative office rental costs in key business locations

Thames Gateway London	Manchester	West London	Paris
Canary Wharf £30-35 sq ft	Prime £30 sq ft	Prime £80 sq ft	Prime £57 sq ft
Royal Docks £19.50 sq ft	Prime £30 sq ft	Prime £80 sq ft	Prime £57 sq ft
Romford £15 sq ft	Out of Town £19.50 sq ft	Out of Town £27.50 sq ft	Out of Town £40 sq ft

The area is home to a number of prestigious commercial hubs, the best known of which is of course Canary Wharf, providing world class business accommodation and already a financial and HQ centre. Other flagship sites with available premises and good transport links include the Royals Business Park, Woolwich Arsenal, the Greenwich Peninsula, White Hart Triangle, Ferry Lane and Beam Reach.

These specific locations are all within broader 'zones of change' where significant new investment will provide homes, business premises and open space together with new community, cultural and leisure facilities as part of the region's growth. These include London Riverside; the Isle of Dogs; Stratford, Leaside & the Royal Docks; Greenwich, Deptford & Lewisham; The Greenwich Peninsula; and Woolwich, Belvedere & Erith.

These areas already have developed clusters as locations for headquarters, back office functions, manufacturing & industrial, logistics & distribution and contact centres. In addition, specialist research clusters are also emerging in bio-medical and pharmaceutical R&D and the architectural, engineering, telecoms and food sectors.

With such an offer, and a wide range of financial assistance available from Government, it is no wonder that the city is moving east and at Gateway to London, we look forward to continue playing a major role in London's future.

For more information contact
Gateway to London on 020 7540 5560
or visit www.gtlon.co.uk

It's wide open

Thames Gateway London is the fastest growing and most dynamic business region in Europe and is unrivalled in terms of opportunity and investment.

This huge area is already benefiting from a transport, property and employment revolution and is set to become the destination of choice for international business.

Thames Gateway London offers:

▸ **A vast range of competitively priced high quality premises**

▸ **Excellent national and international transport connections**

▸ **Extensive business support networks**

▸ **Unrivalled access to a highly skilled workforce**

▸ **Financial assistance and grants**

Gateway to London is your single point of contact for exciting developments in Europe's largest business centre. We'd like to open your mind to the opportunities.

If you're a GROWING BUSINESS and you need more room to breathe, call us on **020 7540 5560** email **info@gtlon.co.uk** or visit **www.gtlon.co.uk**

We have the S P A C E to realise your dreams

GATEWAY TO
LONDON
OPPORTUNITIES
IN THE THAMES
GATEWAY

operating from the provinces will not describe itself as a City firm unless it has a head office based there.

Somebody who works at a City head office of a clearing bank can claim to work in the City, but a colleague working for a provincial branch cannot. If a firm only sells insurance, pensions and unit trusts, this is not in itself City activity, even if it operates in the square mile. But stockbrokers considered part of the City also offer these general financial services. Commercial insurance professionals who work in the London market are part of the City.

Over the years, the physical boundaries have expanded beyond the traditional square mile. One of the most important City locations is Canary Wharf, part of the Docklands, where some leading investment banks, including Morgan Stanley and Credit Suisse, are based, as well as the Financial Services Authority (FSA), which regulates all financial services in the UK. Schroder Salomon Smith Barney famously has an office in Victoria.

Financial markets

Financial markets give borrowers an opportunity to raise capital, making contact with lenders through banks and other intermediaries. Commercial banks take deposits and lend them to borrowers. Investment banks sell the securities of corporate or government issuers to investors. Securities may be debt instruments, such as syndicated loans or bonds, or may be shares. Following issue, securities may be traded on relevant markets.

Cash deposits and bonds are at the low end of the risk spectrum in an investor's portfolio, and equities and derivatives are at the high end. The portfolio should ideally be balanced, but as dictated by the investor's risk profile. The older investor should not take so much risk with his or her life savings as the younger one.

No gain without pain

London is a world class financial centre. It has concentrated expertise, is well placed in the time zones between New York and Japan, and its regulatory regime sets international standards. To reach this position, the City has historically taken risks.

In the 19th century, the UK merchant banks, now more usually known by the US term *investment banks*, developed rapidly but, with the advent of the First World War in 1914, some failed to retrieve moneys owed to them and almost collapsed. They survived only because the Bank of England gave them special loans. After the War, the banks became independently successful again. After the Second World War started in 1939, they started losing business.

International securities were the break that restored the City's fortunes. The Eurobond market started in London in July 1963 and received a boost shortly afterwards when the US introduced compulsory US interest equalisation tax, which drove issuers away from the US.

The fortunes of sterling have been a more broadly based factor in building up the City. In the late 1970s sterling rose sharply because of the North Sea oil bonanza and, in October 1979, the Conservative Government under Margaret Thatcher as prime minister abolished the exchange controls limiting the amount of currency that UK residents could exchange for another. It removed a restriction on the rise of sterling that had been in force since 1939. UK institutional investors started adding substantially to their overseas investments, although mostly through foreign brokers.

The London Stock Exchange (LSE) is a famous British institution that has so far managed to retain its independence in the face of recent takeover interest. In July 1983, the LSE came to an historic agreement with the Government to abolish fixed commission rates and single capacity in stockbrokers, a move aimed to make them more competitive. The changes came into force on 27 October 1986, and were known as *Big Bang*.

The jobber had been a wholesaler of stock to the broker but was suddenly made obsolete. In came both broker dealers, whose role merged the previous responsibilities of the jobber and broker, and market makers. Overseas securities firms could for the first time become members of the LSE, and trading on the floor of the Exchange was replaced eventually by a screen-based system.

The popular image of the City was as a cosy club of florid-faced ex-public school chaps with a penchant for long liquid lunches who had more bonhomie than brains and were not above bending the rules, in so far as these existed. How much truth there was in this remains the subject of debate, but the deregulation was undoubtedly a step in the opposite direction. A new type of City worker, competitive and egalitarian, was stepping into key roles.

As the City grows more complex, specialisation is the order of the day. The equity salesperson or analyst may have little knowledge of the bond market, and for bond salespeople, the relative ignorance is about equities. Neither of these specialists may know much about the commodities markets or Lloyd's insurance.

At the same time, an event in one type of market can create a chain reaction in another, and markets have some interdependence. Bonds issuance is supported by the swaps market, which enables some borrowers to swap their obligation for one that is more congenial. Hedging of derivatives cannot exist without liquidity provided by speculators. Deposit accounts and various financial instruments are affected by foreign exchange movements, which are impacted by interest rate movements, in turn driven by inflationary pressures.

The macro-economic numbers are under scrutiny by a vast army of City strategists and economists paid indecent money to sit glued to their screens and bark out their opinions and forecasts. Securities analysts harness this and other data for research. How these professionals communicate with the City is strictly regulated, but there are informal as well as formal channels.

It is the good name of the City, including its regulator, that attracts so many from abroad. Many banks in the City are foreign-owned, including many from the US, and the LSE attracts a large number of listings from non-UK firms. Managers of hedge funds, a relatively unrestricted form of investment vehicle, favour London as a location. The Lloyd's of London insurance market has kept a high reputation through some rocky times.

At the same time, individual institutions have seen their roles diminished in some respects. The Bank of England no longer supervises the banking system and its most public role is to set interest rates. The LSE now outsources settlement and it has been the target of takeover interest. The FSA regulates the City but through principles, which puts a responsibility on firms to interpret the rules. The trade bodies in the City have become a powerful lobbying voice, especially when they act together. But critics fear the fragmentation of power in the City could ultimately become a competitive disadvantage.

The City is a world leader

In volumes of financial business, the UK is behind the US and Japan, which are more domestically focused, and leads the way in Europe, according to a report *The City's Importance to the EU Economy 2005*, published by the Corporation of London in February 2005. The UK dominates global markets in six areas, the report found. They include cross-border bank lending, in which the UK has a 20 per cent global market share, and foreign exchange dealing, in which the UK has a 31 per cent share against the 19 per cent share of the US, its nearest rival.

In over-the-counter (OTC) derivatives, the UK has a 43 per cent market share, of which about three-quarters are interest rate swaps and similar products. In foreign equities trading, the UK similarly has a 43 per cent share, in this case a significant decline in recent years, from a peak of 65 per cent in 1998. In international bonds, the UK has 60 per cent of the global primary market and 70 per cent of the secondary market. In marine insurance the UK has a 19 per cent market share, and, in aviation insurance, 39 per cent.

London has a particular opportunity to build on its European dominance in OTC derivatives and hedge funds, according to the Corporation of London report. London's share of world hedge fund assets is expected to grow from 14 per cent in 2004 to 20 per cent in 2010. London's OTC activity is expected to double by 2008.

Markets are people

As the City has developed in size and international stature, it has demanded increasingly better educated entry-level workers. For bright university graduates, the City has increasingly become the first career choice. The class of degree matters to firms, and an MBA from the right institution opens doors. Many candidates for City jobs will have specialised in perceived relevant subjects such as economics or accounting.

But frontline jobs in the City also require heavy socialising and sales skills, and an ability to deal with clients and bring in money is ultimately a necessity, a criterion fully reflected in the stringent recruitment process. In the City, status comes from the size of the pay packet and bonus more than the intellectual demands of the job, although some fund managers would disagree.

The City has a small army of support staff ranging from IT professionals to settlement clerks, editors, newsletter writers, press officers, trainers and others. Some are temps. The work is increasingly being outsourced to cheaper locations such as India, a process which carries its own risks. At the end of 2004, 316,000 people were employed in City-type jobs in London, up 5,000 on the previous year, according to a report by International Financial Services, London. The financial sector, including the City, accounted for 6.8 per cent of the UK economy in 2004.

Some years ago, consumer finance journalists fondly speculated on whether the internet would plug the vast gap between consumer and industry knowledge. It has not yet happened. Professionals at their screens still have better resources, more time and superior experience and skills in their field than the man in the street. It is hoped that this book will take you a long way towards understanding what they do.

The next step

To understand the City requires you to grasp the individual activities within it and how they fit in the broader context. It is like putting together a jigsaw puzzle, and this book will guide you on what goes where. In the next chapter, we will make a start with the Bank of England.

"Your 1st Health Club in the City" since 1970

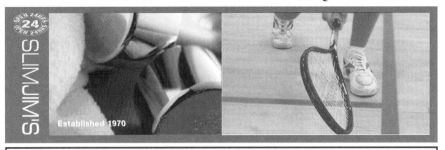

Slim Jim's was the 1st Health Club in the City and with it's home from home club atmosphere you can work out and escape office life within walking distance. Relax in our lounge in front of the wide screen TV with as much free tea or coffee as you like. Or train in our fully equipped gym without the stress of queuing.

Open 24 hrs Mon-Fri • Flexible monthly memberships
4 Free personal training sessions (for all new members) • Lockers & Laundry Service

Contact: **020 72479982**   Sales.slimjims@slim-jims.co.uk   **www.slim-jims.co.uk**

MARKET SPORTS
health & fitness health & fitness health & fitness

Market Sports have been specialist in Health & Fitness for almost a decade. Always located in the centre of the city's action, we have been asafe haven for many businessmen and women over the years.

Quality Facilities at affordable prices have been a Market Sports priority. We are sure you'll agree that Market Sports in Shoreditch provides a great opportunity to relax whilst improving your health and quality of life.

Operating Hours:
Monday to Friday: 7am to 10pm
(Gym and Pool close at 9.30pm)

Saturday & Sunday: 10am to 6pm
(Gym and Pool close at 5.30pm)

020 7739 6688

or fax:
020 7739 2002

or Email:
info@marketsports.co.uk

The Citypoint Club

An oasis of calm and luxury in the heart of the busy City…. Conveniently situated in London's Ropemaker Street, just 2 minutes walk from Moorgate station. The Citypoint Club provides an ideal escape.

The Club boasts from an extensive range of facilities including a fully equipped gym area, a stunning pool, fitness studios offering energetic & relaxing classes, squash facilities and a luxurious spa area with treatments, steam, sauna and plunge pools.

Opening times:
Mon-Fri 6am-10pm • Sat & Sun 9am-6pm   Contact: 020 79206200

Putting property into business

Choosing to put your company in the heart of London's key business district sends a strong signal to your customers, your competitors and your staff. Being "where it matters" has been a guiding principal for managed and services office company, Stonemartin plc. It has established 500,000 sqft of first class landmark office buildings for its clients in the UK's foremost business districts. Its 100,000 sqft flagship and headquarters is New Broad Street House, EC2, next to London's Liverpool Street mainline station.

But its clients gain far more than an enviable image. On offer is a modern, carefully designed space with a range of flexible workplace solutions, meeting rooms and conference facilities for businesses large and small, as well as the city's first Institute of Directors (IoD) Hub, where any of the 55,000 IoD members can touch down and use the WiFi enabled directors room for informal meetings, or simply to work.

The company has been careful to design flexibility into its workplace offer. In a climate where business agility is increasingly important, such flexibility gives its clients' the option to tailor its office requirements to fit the demands of their business. It argues that poorly negotiated lease terms, and a lack of appreciation of the real costs of the workplace tied up in elements like rates, services charges, fit out, IT, facilities management, set up and exit costs, stifle agility for many businesses and leave them carrying a dangerous hidden "contingent" liability in the event of an economic downturn.

The Workplace Performance Initiative

Taking these principals further is the Workplace Performance Initiative (WPI), of which Stonemartin is a founding member. The initiative encourages business leaders to assess the financial, strategic and human impact of workplace choices. It promotes the development of a "workplace strategy", helping businesses assess the right positioning, mix and organisation of workplace options to encourage staff retention and productivity as well as saving costs and enabling business agility.

Visit **www.workplaceperformance.net** to receive a free business issues paper entitled "Organising the workplace for profit", or to register to attend one of the many practical workshops being held up and down the country.

For further information please contact Tim Worboys, Sales & Marketing Director Stonemartin on **020 7194 7503**, or visit **www.stonemartin.co.uk** or **www.workplaceperformance.net**

2

The Bank of England

Introduction

In this chapter, we will focus on the Bank of England – the UK's Central Bank – including its history, its role and operations. We will look at its open market operations and the role of the Bank's Monetary Policy Committee in keeping inflation to the specified level. We will conclude with a glance at the Bank's international liaison.

Origin

The Bank of England (www.bankofengland.co.uk) is the UK's Central Bank. It was set up as a private company in 1694 with the aim of helping the British Government under William and Mary to raise cash to finance the war against Louis XIV of France. From the earliest years in its 300-year history, the Bank of England has been the government's banker. Since the 18th century, it has also been a bank for other UK banks. As a result of the 1844 Act, the Bank of England gained the right to the sole issue of banknotes in England and Wales. It remained a privately owned bank until nationalisation in 1946.

Until 1997, the Bank of England was both the supervisor of banks and adviser to the government on monetary policy, tasks conducted from different departments. There was a potential conflict of interests in setting interest rates. The banking crisis of 1973–75 revealed weaknesses in the informal supervisory approach, which led to the Banking Act 1979, and subsequently the Banking Act 1987, under which the Bank would authorise and, in a flexible way, supervise the banking sector.

The Bank of England's continued role as supervisor came under increasing scrutiny, particularly after the July 1991 collapse of Bank of Credit and Commerce International (BCCI). In October 1992, a report by Lord Justice

Bingham found that the Bank had not pursued 'the truth about BCCI with the rigour which BCCI's market reputation justified'. But it did not recommend that the Bank should be deprived of its banking supervisory role.

The Bank of England has statutory immunity against negligence claims, but Deloitte, the liquidators of BCCI, took a £850 million lawsuit against it claiming 'misfeasance in public office'. In November 2005, the case collapsed and the Bank was thoroughly cleared of any allegations of dishonesty in relation to its supervisory role of BCCI.

In 1995, Barings collapsed after its trader Nick Leeson had lost over £800 million through unauthorised trades in derivatives, and it triggered further consideration of the Bank of England's supervisory role. Under the regulatory regime of the time (discussed in Chapter 18), Barings, as a major investment and trading bank, had to seek authorisation from the Bank of England for its banking activities, the Securities and Futures Authority for its securities dealing services, and the Investment Management Regulatory Organisation for its investment management. The number of regulators perhaps made it difficult for any individual authority to supervise the diverse business of the bank.

Changes were inevitable. The Bank of England Act, 1998, transferred responsibility for authorising the banks and supervision of the banking system from the Bank of England to the Financial Services Authority (FSA), a new single statutory regulator for the financial services industry. The Bank has retained responsibility for the stability of the banking system.

Role today

The Bank is responsible for the overall stability of the UK financial markets, and maintaining price stability. It also manages the UK's gold and currency reserves on behalf of HM Treasury. The Bank can intervene in the money markets and, in accordance with government policy, occasionally in the foreign exchange market. It also oversees payment and settlement services under the Settlement Finality Directive adopted in May 1998. All the clearing banks keep accounts at the Bank of England and use them to settle differences between themselves in the clearing system, exchanging cheques written by each other's customers, or moving credit.

The *Court* of the Bank of England consists of the Governor of the Bank of England, two deputy governors, and 16 non-executive directors, who oversee the Bank's affairs apart from the formation of monetary policy. The executive team is the Bank's senior management team. It consists of the Governor; two deputy Governors; five executive directors who are responsible respectively for financial markets, financial stability, monetary analysis and statistics, banking services and central services; and an adviser to the Governor.

The Bank cooperates closely with the Treasury and the FSA, participating in many financial forums, but, in accordance with the 1998 legislation, the FSA now supervises banks.

Monetary policy

The Bank of England and the government have traditionally cooperated on monetary policy – the setting of interest rates. The objective is to maintain monetary stability and to support the government's economic policies, including its objectives for growth and employment. As a central bank, the Bank of England can influence money supply by its interest rate decisions, open market operations, and by changing the level of bank reserves allowed to be held interest-free with the Bank.

Traditionally, the Bank of England advised on interest rate policy, and the decision on whether to change rates rested with the Chancellor of the Exchequer. But after the Labour Government won the May 1997 general election, Chancellor Gordon Brown, to the country's surprise, gave the Bank of England full responsibility for monetary policy, which became statutory when the Bank of England Act came into force on 1 June 1998. By this move, which meant independence for the central bank, the Labour Government answered concerns that governments had a political agenda and so should not be given responsibility for setting interest rates and addressing inflation.

Inflation targeting

The Chancellor, acting for the Treasury, defines price stability and sets the annual inflation target, and the Bank has the task of keeping inflation at the target set by the government. Its tool is the power to change the *repo* rate. This is the short-term rate at which the Bank of England lends to banks for repurchase agreements. It is for practical purposes synonymous with the term *base* rate. Under extreme circumstances, the government can instruct the Bank on interest rates for a limited period.

Inflation may be defined as a continued rise in price levels that diminishes the value of money and it is a necessary part of economic development. Experts cannot agree on the cause. Some cite cost-push inflation, based on rising manufacturing costs, and others believe in demand-pull inflation, based on demand exceeding supply. The monetarist view attributes inflation to a money supply that has grown too quickly, a view currently out of favour.

Business always has an underlying incentive to increase the profit margin and so create inflation, but this is hampered by the ability of competition to move in. Markets are more efficient than they were in the 1960s and 1970s, when employees routinely bargained through their unions for high wages linked to inflation expectations. Rising commodity prices contributed to the demand spiral. When inflation is high, prices become detached from value, and the economic outcome is suboptimal. Central banks such as the Bank of England traditionally fear that the inflationary environment could become embedded.

Inflation targeting, as practised by the Bank of England, has had a clear impact across the world in helping to keep inflation expectations low. But it has encouraged the public to take on more debt, according to a February 2006 statement by the Bank for International Settlements, the Basel-based bank for central banks, an organisation which fosters international monetary and financial cooperation.

The Monetary Policy Committee

On the request of Chancellor Brown, the Bank has established a Monetary Policy Committee, known as the MPC, to make interest rate decisions. It consists of the Governor of the Bank of England, who is appointed for a five-year term by the Chancellor, and two deputy governors, also appointed for five years, as well as the Bank's chief economist, the executive director of market operations, and four external members who have been mainly economists.

The MPC conducts two-day meetings every month to determine the appropriate interest rate used for lending money via the repo market (see Chapter 9), which is effectively the market's short-term interest rate. The Bank is mandated by the Government to keep inflation at 2.0 per cent as measured by the Consumer Price Index. If inflation should rise over 1.0 per cent above or below this target, the Governor of the Bank must write an open letter to the Chancellor explaining why inflation has missed the target and what the Bank will do to bring inflation back within the inflation target parameters.

Before December 2003, the measure of inflation was RPIX, the headline offshoot of the Retail Price Index (RPI), by which the target was 2.5 per cent a year. This is still published but may not be in the foreseeable future because it is no longer used much for practical purposes, although the RPI is still used for the indexation of pensions, state benefits, and index-linked gilts. The Consumer Prices Index, known as CPI, is preferred for making comparisons between countries in the euro zone and equates to the European Harmonised Index of Consumer Prices.

Decision making

In its monthly decision on interest rates, the MPC considers a wide range of economic indicators and surveys, including the CPI, earnings growth, the

Purchasing Managers' Index, Producer Prices, gross domestic product, retail sales, house prices and the performance of sterling. It considers the reports of its regional agents around the country.

In making up its mind, the MPC looks at its inflation forecast two years ahead; a change in interest rates can take this long to take full effect. If the economy has entered a fast-growth phase and employment is rising, the Bank may look to raise interest rates in an attempt to curb inflationary pressures. If the economy is the early stages of a slowdown, the Bank may be less likely to raise rates. The MPC has kept the base rate unchanged more often than not over the past eight years, but this is not in itself a sign that the economy has been doing better or worse.

On the first day of the meeting, the MPC considers the briefings given the previous week by the Bank's economists; on the second day it considers and votes, announcing a decision by noon. The basis for decision making is a majority vote. The minutes of the MPC meeting are published 13 days afterwards and are read carefully by strategists looking for enlightenment on the committee's thinking, including, most importantly, clues about likely interest rate policy at the Committee's next monthly meeting.

The Bank of England also publishes a quarterly Inflation Report, which takes a retrospective look at recent progress and makes inflation and GDP growth forecasts. Various economists, including a shadow MPC through *Times Online* (www.timesonline.co.uk), make interest rate predictions before the MPC meeting.

Knock-on effect

Once the MPC has changed the repo (repurchase agreement) rate, the retail banks tend to change their lending rates rapidly, often setting them at a margin above the base rate. Banks will vary their margin as a commercial decision, and may occasionally lend at the repo rate itself, which means that they will be lending money at the same rate at which they borrowed it.

Higher interest rates will usually have the broad effect of slowing consumer spending. They make it more expensive for companies to borrow, and this can slow their growth. A secondary effect is that investors may move from shares into cash because they can get a higher return on their deposit accounts, which can depress share prices.

Open-market operations

The Bank of England lends money to banks borrowing and lending every day in the money markets. Through these *open-market operations*, the Bank covers any imbalance. It buys securities daily, both outright, and on a repo basis. Repo means to buy securities from a bank and later to sell them back to it at a higher price (see Chapter 9). The Bank once arranged its financing through discount houses but this route is no longer available.

Lender of last resort

If a bank encounters liquidity problems, and this threatens to have adverse impact across the financial system, the Bank of England can act as the lender of last resort. If a high street bank should fail and the public panicked and withdrew money en masse from the banking system, the Bank of England would have the power to step in to ensure that wider financial instability was avoided.

The criteria for intervention are stringent. In 1995, the Bank of England decided not to intervene to save Barings from going bust, taking the view that the event would pose no systemic threat to the UK banking system, and that a wholly market solution was more suitable to address the bank's insolvency.

In other cases, the Bank of England has intervened. In 1890, the Bank, along with various commercial banks, rescued Barings after its bad debts in Argentina were three times its capital and threatened its solvency. In 1975, the Bank arranged a banking consortium to act as a lifeboat in the secondary banking crisis precipitated by large exposures to the property sector. In 1984, it helped Johnson Matthey Bankers Limited, a London market maker in gold bullion which had got into financial difficulties from its commercial lending exposures. If the operation had been allowed to fail, other bullion dealers would have joined the creditors, which would have diminished confidence in the London gold market.

International liaison

Globally, the Bank of England liaises with such organisations as the International Monetary Fund, and the Bank for International Settlements.

So far, the UK Government's refusal to join the euro has kept the Bank of England in control of UK interest rates. If a referendum in the UK should decide in favour of joining the euro, and the transition was made, UK interest rates and monetary policy would rest with the European Central Bank (ECB), established on 1 June 1998.

The ECB is independent but must back the EU's general economic policies. It takes interest rate decisions on a majority vote, which, if applied to the UK, might not suit its economic conditions. The Bank of England, if it joined the single currency, might then conduct money market operations and foreign exchange intervention within EU policy limits in addition to providing assessments on the UK economy.

3

Commercial banking

Introduction

Banks are now authorised and supervised by the Financial Services Authority (FSA), and there are two main types: commercial banks and investment banks. In this chapter, we will look at the activities of commercial banks, which take deposits, lend money, participate in the money markets and in foreign exchange and trade finance. We will look briefly at building societies. We will scrutinise how banks raise finance, credit collection services, the issue of bad debt, capital adequacy and the Basel Capital Accord.

History

The original purpose of banks was to stash cash. The earliest bankers operated in Florence from the 15th century and conducted business from benches in the open air. The Italian word for bank is derived from *banco*, which means bench. If a bank was liquidated, its operation was broken up, hence the word *bankrupt*.

In the late 14th and early 15th centuries, some Italian merchants from Lombardy came to London, and set up as money lenders in Lombard Street, the part of the City of London where banking activities are concentrated. British banking started in the 17th century with rich merchants storing their money in the vaults of goldsmiths because these premises were secure. They were encouraged to seek the safe custody of their assets when, in 1640, King Charles I seized private gold deposited in the Tower of London to pay an English army that he was raising against Scotland, where he was also king.

By 1677, there were 44 goldsmith bankers in London. They would provide a receipt for money deposited, which was initially used to retain the full sum, and subsequently became assignable, and so a primitive form of bank note.

The International Capital Market Association (ICMA)

The International Capital Market Association (ICMA) is the self-regulatory organisation and trade association representing the financial institutions active in the international capital market worldwide. ICMA's members are located in some 50 countries across the globe, including all the world's main financial centres, and currently number over 400 firms in total.

The International Capital Market Association was created in July 2005 by the merger of the International Securities Market Association (ISMA) and the International Primary Market Association (IPMA), creating an organisation with a broad franchise across the primary and secondary international capital market, with the mandate and the financial and organisational resources to represent the interests of the investment banking industry in maintaining and developing an efficient and cost effective international market for capital.

ICMA's members are not only geographically widespread, they also vary considerably in size and type of activities. ICMA represents the very diverse interests of a large pan-European membership, from the smaller primarily retail focused private banks based in Switzerland, Luxembourg, Belgium, Italy and Germany, to the largest global investment banks based in the City of London. It provides a forum for all professional market participants to have a voice in shaping the market through its various committees, regional groupings and special interest groups.

The international capital market is itself characterised by a wide variety of issuers, issuing currencies, credit quality, and the technical specifications of the securities themselves. In this complex marketplace ICMA maintains standards of good practice in the primary markets and has developed standard documentation for new issues leading to greater efficiencies and cost savings for issuing banks.

Due to its inherent cross border nature, the international capital market is not subject to the same degree of regulation that governs domestic primary and secondary markets. In this marketplace ICMA has (previously as ISMA), for some 35 years, performed a crucial central role by providing and enforcing a self-regulatory code of industry-driven rules and recommendations which regulate issuance, trading and settlement.

The market in the 30 or more years since its inception has been a great European success story, as well as a major contributor to the increased growth and importance of the European capital markets. It has always shown an unrivalled capacity for innovation, constantly developing new financial products to meet the needs of a broad spectrum of borrowers and investors. In the comparatively short period since the introduction of the Euro there has been a spectacular rate of growth in issuance in the European market accompanied by a commensurate increase in trading volumes and liquidity to levels unheard of a decade ago. The people of the enlarged EU have benefited from this contribution to the development of a European financial infrastructure.

One of the major challenges facing the capital market in Europe in recent years has been the implementation of the EU Financial Services Action Plan, with its goal of creating a single market in financial services throughout Europe, which contains no fewer than 42 legislative, regulatory and advisory measures. Reaching political agreement amongst the 25 member states of the EU on these measures represents a considerable achievement in itself. ICMA seeks to foster the appropriate levels of regulation in the capital market and when responding to regulatory initiatives its goal is always to achieve favourable outcomes for its membership and the market as a whole. Broad engagement and support from members and other market participants is particularly important to the Association's advocacy efforts and increasingly it works with other national and international associations representing the market to achieve this.

Key initiatives at the time of writing involve commenting on the implementing measure on the Markets in Financial Instruments Directive (MiFID) which will have a major impact on almost every element of business of ICMA member firms across Europe. This will impose new regulation on areas as diverse as the management of conflicts of interest, outsourcing, suitability, risk warnings, classification of clients into retail and professional, transaction reporting to regulators, inducements and the publication of quotes and transactions by OTC equity dealers. There is also a possibility that the pre- and post trade transparency provisions of the MiFID could be extended to bonds and derivatives. ICMA with other trade associations has commissioned independent academic research into the European bond markets to inform the European Commission's review in this area.

Clients could write a note directing money to be paid to another, the earliest form of cheque. A merchant would write an authority to his goldsmith to pay his tailor. The goldsmiths used cash and precious metals deposited to lend money to merchants, with the aim of receiving it back plus interest, following completion of a voyage. It gave rise to the phrase 'when my ship comes home'. By offering such credit facilities, the goldsmiths were operating like banks.

Banking outside London was almost nonexistent until the mid 18th century, but, by 1810, it had grown to be represented by 650 banks. By 1900, London had become the world's largest banking centre with about 250 private and joint stock banks. During the First World War, the banking business expanded in size and scope. Banks, however, were subsequently hit by poor inter-war trading conditions. During the Second World War, banks became subject to foreign exchange controls and lending priorities. In the 1950s, these were relaxed and banks expanded. In the 1970s, the government encouraged more active competition. From a comparatively few conglomerates, banks moved towards the broad provision of financial services that we have today. We have come a long way from the Victorian era when many small banks had provided limited facilities for a wealthy minority.

Today, investment banks cover not just investment banking (see Chapter 5) but also activities traditionally associated with commercial banking, including fund management, trade finance, leasing and factoring, venture capital, project finance, syndicated loans and foreign exchange. Convergence between the two types of banking has often been uneasy, and US politicians and financiers blamed the great crash of 1929 on the mix of commercial and investment banking.

To prevent a recurrence, the US Congress passed the Banking Act of 1933, known as the Glass-Steagall Act, which separated the two types of banking. Recent opinion has been that securities trading need not harm commercial banking and, in 1999, Congress passed the Financial Services Modernization Act, which eliminated the separation between the two types of bank.

On the cultural front, the entrepreneurial spirit of investment banking has sometimes been an uneasy bed fellow for the cautious commercial banking ethos. Investment bankers have been more likely to have a public school background, and commercial bankers a grammar school one, according to commentators, but the dividing line has now become much more blurred.

Commercial banks today

Commercial banks are mainly involved in deposit taking and lending. Deposits build up when people leave surplus money in saving accounts. When banks lend money to their clients, it comes from other banking clients. In effect, what goes into one person's account as a loan must come out of another's. The banking system is said to be like double-entry bookkeeping.

Banks pay a small rate of interest on cash deposited, and lend out much of it at a much higher rate, making a margin on the difference. In common alone with the government, they keep bank accounts with the Bank of England. A bank must retain a required level of liquidity, and it can borrow or lend money wholesale on the money markets (see Chapter 9), dealing with other banks or perhaps multinational companies. Every night, a bank may offer surplus funds for overnight loan, or it may borrow funds, perhaps because a large number of customers drew down significant sums that day.

The banks will lend to consumers, which is retail banking, or to businesses and governments, which is wholesale banking. Companies borrow more than retail customers and negotiate a better rate, which the bank endeavours to offer through its money market operations. On a bank's balance sheet, deposits are liabilities because the bank owes money to customers. Any sums that banks lend, both from deposits and from wholesale funds that they have borrowed, are assets because they ultimately belong to the bank.

Retail banking has developed dramatically over the past three decades. The Royal Bank of Scotland's acquisition of National Westminster, and Barclays' acquisition of the Woolwich, as well as the merger of Halifax and the Bank of Scotland have made the industry more concentrated, according to the British Bankers' Association. The system underwent a revolution from the 1990s, when traditional banks were forced to close branches. There was a trend towards centralisation as local industries collapsed, forcing workers to find jobs in the nearest town, where they would take their bank accounts. New cut-price providers of banking services, telephone-based and later internet-based, were springing up. The appeal of the new telephone-based banks is that they made personal banking possible from the office or home without the hassle of going into a branch.

In October 1989, First Direct, part of HSBC Bank, launched the first, fully fledged, 24-hour telephone banking operation. It has targeted individuals, across the socio-economic spectrum, who prefer not to use bank branches and like to be in charge of their finances, a spokesman says. The service has obvious appeal for night workers. Internet banking is the latest variation and an internet-based bank is not just open all hours but also saves money on overheads, which it may pass onto the customer in the form of higher interest rates on deposit accounts and cheaper lending. But a *virtual* bank still has some overheads, including security costs. It appeals to broadband users who are at home and comfortable with technology, according to First Direct.

Egg, launched in late 1998 by the Prudential, was the first entirely internet-based bank and, like others that have followed, has a slightly quirky image. The largest proportion of its customers is in the 25–45 age grouping whose average income is a fairly high £30,000 per annum. Older customers are less likely to use internet banks, although some *silver surfers* break the pattern, an Egg spokesman says.

In late 1998, Egg moved to capture market share by offering an internet account with a loss-making interest rate on retail deposits. It paid a hefty 8 per cent on all savings over £1, unlike deposit accounts in conventional banks which ratcheted up the interest rate payable in proportion to the amount deposited. Egg customers had easy access to their money and were not penalised for withdrawal. In the first six months, the bank gained 500,000 customers and £5 billion in deposits.

Egg's next major move was in mobile banking. In late 2005, Egg became a content provider to i-mode, an internet broadband service supplier to UK mobile users through O2. Users of i-mode may transfer money between themselves using their mobiles. If a young girl is standing outside the cinema in the High Street, she may phone her mother at home who may transmit her cash to pay for a ticket, the Egg spokesman says.

High street commercial banks today operate as mini-financial conglomerates. They can provide financial products, which may be *own brand*, or, if the bank operates on a multi-tied basis, from a number of providers (see Chapter 22). Banks sell savings products, and may own stockbrokers or have their own share dealing services. They will have linked up with insurance groups or set up insurance subsidiaries, and they sell insurance more easily than insurers sell banking products. They provide a foreign exchange service, including travellers' cheques.

Banks in the UK have a reputation for being more user-friendly and flexible than those in continental Europe. They pay interest on credit balances in some current accounts, and an overdraft is easy to arrange. At the end of 2004, 89 per cent of adults held a UK current account with a bank or building society, and about 80 per cent held a cheque book, according to the Association for Payment Clearing Services. Some retailers such as Tesco have joined forces with banks to offer *own brand* banking services, although without cheque book facilities.

Banks issue credit cards in a highly competitive market. Transactions are processed through Visa or MasterCard. Credit card issuers profit mainly from interest charged to users, but also from fees that retailers pay. They must take into account bad debts, card thefts and fraud. Borrowing on credit cards rose by 19 per cent in 2004, while the average credit outstanding per card account topped £1,000 for the first time, to stand at £1,065 at the end of 2004, according to the British Bankers' Association.

In 1999, Egg issued the Egg card, which paid zero per cent on balance transfers and new transfers for nine months, meaning that users of another credit card could transfer their balance to Egg and pay no interest on it for this period. It was the first offer of this kind, but there are now around 110 zero per cent credit cards on the market. Many cards offer up to 56 days' free credit but only if the outstanding balance is repaid in full by the due date. The precise period of free credit will depend on the point at which the transaction is made or appears on the account.

Banks offer a cash point card, which has a magnetic slip enabling owners to withdraw cash to a maximum sum from an automated teller machine, known as an ATM, in the high street. This card can be incorporated with a debit card, which is effectively an electronic cheque. Purchases made this way will be debited to the customer's account a couple of days after the transaction is made, in the same way that a traditional cheque would be. A credit card, on the other hand, will go across a separate account, with payments due monthly.

Building societies

Let us now take a look at building societies. They are lending and saving institutions and they compete with banks. There are 63 building societies across the UK, with assets of over £260 billion. As mutual organisations, they are collectively owned by their members, and 50 per cent of their lending has to be from retail deposits. Unlike banks, they are restricted from raising money on wholesale markets to lend on commercial products.

The societies often offer better value products than the banks, particularly in the core areas of savings accounts and retail mortgages, because unlike banks, they do not have to use around 35 per cent of their profits to pay dividends, according to the Building Societies Association. But bankers note that building societies may limit the availability of an offer to people living within a certain, relatively small, geographical area. Building societies have a total of 2,104 branches, but banks have more than 11,000 branches, according to the British Bankers' Association.

The Building Societies Act 1986 introduced demutualisation, which means to convert into an investor-owned company, and by the mid-1990s many societies had taken the plunge. Managers and directors favoured conversion into a bank to boost their own income, and *carpetbaggers* sought windfall profits by opening temporary savings accounts in the societies most likely to convert.

The downside was that borrowers from the newly formed banks could lose because the lending rates could rise. How far generally demutualisation replaced an out-of-date structure with a more efficient one is open to debate. It enabled the converted entities to tap into traditional banking markets, including commercial lending and money markets, and there is no restriction on how they could raise money or on products offered, which has provided opportunity to gain scale to compete with banks.

In practice, the game has not always proved so easy. In July 1989, Abbey National was the first building society to convert to plc status and to be floated on the London Stock Exchange. The risks of corporate banking became apparent in 2001, after which Abbey National announced two years of significant losses, £984 million in 2002 and £686 million in 2003. In this case, the bank remained structurally solid and it changed its business focus, shortening its name to Abbey. In November 2004, Abbey was acquired by Banco Santander Central Hispano, a Spanish financial group.

The Building Societies Act 1997 allowed traditional building societies, as distinct from the demutualised entities, to offer a wider range of banking products. Nationwide in particular has broadened its product range. But most societies have stayed with savings accounts and retail mortgages, offering the odd credit card or loan. Like banks, building societies may use the internet to offer savings account access to customers, or mortgage application access to independent financial advisers. Retail mortgage sales are sometimes carried out over the internet but most are managed through branches.

Building societies serve more than 15 million savers and over two and a half million borrowers. They account for 18 per cent of all outstanding residential mortgages and, on the savings side, hold 18.2 per cent of all personal deposits, but a much higher 36 per cent of cash individual savings accounts (ISAs) (see Chapter 22).

Now we have seen the basics of how banks and building societies work, let us focus on how the banking system provides finance.

Raising finance

General

Banks provide uncommitted finance only to businesses. In this case, the bank will provide finance facilities, but is not committed to allowing money to be drawn at a particular time. The process is an agreement in principle. It could involve any form of finance, including a loan, perhaps in the form of a term loan.

Committed finance applies to business *and* personal accounts. It is when a bank commits itself to providing finance through a formal agreement or structured fee payment. The bank might say: 'We'll lend you £10,000 for five years, at a given interest rate, with fixed fees payable, and an agreed procedure if you fall behind with payments'. A committed facility need not be a loan, but could be a guarantee or a letter of credit. For example, if a local authority gives a contract for work, it may require a guarantee from the contractor's bank that if things go wrong, it will get its money back.

The overdraft straddles uncommitted and committed facilities. It is used both for business and personal accounts. A bank can arrange an overdraft quickly and informally; it will agree a limit, and the customer will pay only for money borrowed. Daily interest on the overdrawn balance may be set at a margin over the base rate, or, typically for personal accounts, at a managed rate.

The syndicated loan

If a borrower wants more money than an individual bank will lend, a syndicated loan may be used to spread the loan across a number of banks. It will probably be for more than £50 million, and possibly for hundreds of millions of pounds. The bank awarded the client mandate may be either a commercial bank or an investment bank. If the borrower breaches its covenants under the loan agreement, the bank will be released from its commitment.

Project finance

A commercial bank may fund a large-scale infrastructure project through recourse lending. Investment banks may finance projects with non-recourse lending. A recourse loan means that the endorser or guarantor has a secondary liability in the case of a default by the borrower. Under a non-recourse finance arrangement, the lender does not seek repayment from the borrower personally, but is content with some other sources, for example the stream of income from the asset. In either case, the lender will require the project itself to repay the loan. It will assess the project's viability in terms of future cash flows, which may be guaranteed through a government contract to use the products or services generated by the project. The bank is likely to ensure it will be paid first by having a charge over escrow accounts into which income from the project must be paid.

Commercial banks provide some of the funding for projects in developing countries. Multilateral lending agencies – such as the European Bank for Reconstruction and Development – finance projects intended to benefit the infrastructure of less developed countries.

Asset finance

Clearing banks have broad businesses and investment banks more niche-oriented, but either can provide asset finance.

Asset finance has now overtaken bank loans as the main source of finance for capital purchases up to £100,000, according to the Finance & Leasing Association. The three main types are finance lease, operating lease and hire purchase. These arrangements can reduce pressure on the borrower's cash flow, enabling payments to be spaced out. Repayment terms can be customised.

Finance leasing is where the bank buys an asset and gives use of it to a company at an agreed rate over its whole economic life, with ownership usually remaining with the finance provider. The risks and rewards will have passed to the lessee. The lessee must treat this arrangement as an asset on its balance sheet, and it will be depreciated over its life. The bank can claim capital allowances on the assets it leases out, and will have a charge over them. For these reasons, it can offer the company a good rate of interest on the leased asset.

Over the life of the lease, the cost to the lessee is recognised in the profit and loss account as depreciation of the asset and a financing charge on the liability. The company must repay both the interest on the principal, which is the cost of the asset, and some of the principal itself. The repayments are known as the rental, which should cost the company less than borrowing to buy the asset directly.

At the end of the lease period, the asset's useful economic life is over. But the asset may still be useable, and the lessee may continue to lease the asset for a secondary term at a nominal rate. The company may as an agent for the bank sell the asset and, if so, would receive the proceeds in the form of a rental rebate, after the bank had taken a cut. If the company kept all the money, it would mean that there had not been a true lease, and HM Revenue and Customs could react by removing the bank's capital allowances.

Operating leases, unlike finance leases, are for only part of the economic life of an asset. They do not provide the benefits of ownership, given that the risks and rewards of ownership have not been passed to the lessee, and are not assets on the lessee's balance sheet. Instead, their lease rental payments are charged to the profit and loss account as an operating cost. Companies prefer to classify a lease as operating rather than finance lease, partly because none of the lease payments is classified as an interest charge.

Hire purchase involves finance for the whole economic life of an asset but ownership ends up with the client. The accounting treatment is similar to that of finance leasing.

Credit collection

Banks are involved in guaranteeing and collecting credit, as well as providing it. Let us see how they provide these services.

Trade finance

When a UK exporter of a product has found a buyer overseas, it commits itself to delivering the product and the importer commits itself to paying. The exporter shares its bank documents with the importer to confirm that the product has been put on transport for delivery and is of the specified quality, and the importer will either have funds in its account or will have made other financing arrangements.

The exporter will ask the importer to arrange a letter of credit (LOC) from the importer's bank. If the importer's bank agrees to issue the credit, it will send it to the exporter through the exporter's bank. The LOC will stipulate the documents required and any relevant timescales. At the time the goods are dispatched, the exporter will present the LOC to its bank together with the required documents. If all is in order, the exporter's bank will then pay the exporter under the terms of the LOC and claim reimbursement from the importer's bank.

Where a LOC is not involved, the collection of bills or documents works as follows. The exporter presents documents, usually with a bill of exchange, to its bank, with instructions to send these for payment to the importer's bank, of which the importer will have provided details.

The exporter's bank will proceed accordingly, presenting the documents for payment. On the importer's authorisation, the bank will send the money to the exporter's bank, which will then credit the exporter's account, less any charges.

Factoring and invoice discounting

Factoring and invoice leasing are where a business sells its invoices to the bank when they are issued. Invoice discounting is where the client maintains control of the sales ledger and factoring is where the bank takes over. In either case, the bank pays the business up to 80 per cent of the invoice value in cash immediately, and the rest, excluding charges, following a set period or once the debt has been collected.

The level of factoring and invoice discounting in the UK is around £11 billion at any given time. Banks are responsible for 75 per cent of the turnover and operate the business through a subsidiary, separate from their main activities. The industry grew 13 per cent in 2005, and recent legislation has helped to persuade banks to move funding from overdrafts to invoice finance, according to the Factors and Discounters Association.

Bad loans and capital adequacy

General

A bank may make a specific provision on its balance sheet against a bad or doubtful debt, for example where an identified customer is unable to meet an obligation to pay a specified loan. There may be a general provision. If, for example, a mine closes in a small town, people will lose jobs, and the local bank will know that some loans will have to be written off, but not which ones specifically. It will raise a general provision against, perhaps, 10 per cent of the money borrowed.

In 2004, major British banking groups wrote off £4.2 billion of their lending activity, up from £3.5 billion the previous year, according to the British Bankers' Association. The main component reflects bad debts of £2.9 billion in loans to individuals, but these reflect less than 0.5 per cent of the loan book.

If a syndicated loan to a country cannot be repaid on time, banks may restructure the borrowing to avoid the country being declared bankrupt, which could lead to an international crisis and harm the global economy. If a default gets too deep, banks may feel forced to bite the bullet. In May 1987, Citicorp declared a US$3 billion provision against loans to third world countries, which amounted to public acceptance of a loss. Other banks then announced provisions against similar losses.

Historically, banking crises have occurred when too many customers have withdrawn cash in a panic, causing an immediate liquidity crisis. This is known as a *run* on the bank. To ensure that they stay solvent at such difficult times, banks are required to have sufficient liquidity and capital to see them through. In the UK the FSA has set regulatory requirements in this area for banks based on best-practice recommendations of The Basel Committee for Banking Supervision (BCBS).

The Basel Committee

The BCBS was set up in 1975 as a standard-setting body within The Bank of International Settlements (BIS). The BIS is an organisation which fosters international monetary and financial cooperation, and serves as a bank for central banks, in the interest of monetary and financial stability. The Committee consists of regulators and central bank officials from 10 major global economies known as the G-10 (plus Spain and Luxembourg).

For capital adequacy purposes, the Basel Capital Accord, known so far as Basel I, recommended that regulators should require a bank to keep regulatory capital that is at least 8 per cent of its risk-weighted assets. The Accord has been amended a few times, including in 1996 to incorporate market risk. Basel I provides the standards applied by most regulators that supervise internationally active banks. All solvent banks hold more than the minimum capital, but the framework encourages better risk management.

The Basel Committee introduced Basel II in the first of three draft consultation papers in 1999, and the final version was published in June 2004. This was a new capital adequacy framework to replace Basel I, and the aim is that it will be implemented by the end of 2006. In the EU it has been made law by the Capital Requirements Directive known as CRD (see Chapter 18).

Basel II addresses some of the weaknesses of Basel I, such as the treatment of securitisation exposures and credit derivatives, and it rewards banks that use more sophisticated risk management techniques by requiring them to hold less regulatory capital. It retains the same capital-to-assets ratio. Credit risk is calculated differently, and operational risk, covering the risk of loss from the failure of internal systems, processes or staff, or from external events, is now taken into account.

Basel II is built on three pillars. Pillar 1 revises the 1988 Accord's guidelines by aligning the minimum capital requirements more closely to each bank's actual risk of economic loss. Pillar 2 requires a bank's management to consider all the risks it faces – not just credit, market and operational risks covered under Pillar 1 – and to assess whether it should hold additional capital over and above the Pillar 1 level. Regulators must then undertake a supervisory review of a bank's internal assessments of its overall risks to assure themselves that the bank is holding adequate capital against these risks. Pillar 3 relies on market discipline to motivate prudent risk management by enhancing the degree of disclosure that a bank must make in its annual report about its risk management practices.

A perceived benefit of Basel II is that those banks that manage risks better, and thus are required to hold less capital (subject to the 8 per cent minimum), will be able to price their products more keenly. But critics say that Basel II is too complicated and expensive to implement and monitor, and that the large banks may benefit more than the smaller ones, which do not use the highly advanced risk-management techniques. Another concern is that Basel II is being implemented differently across the rule books of individual countries, leading to issues about whether there is a level playing field.

4

Introduction to equities

Introduction

Much of this book is about institutional investors, which are responsible for the vast majority of investing by value. But in this chapter, we will assume the perspective of the private investor and will focus on equities.

We will look at the London Stock Exchange, how the stock market works, and how to read the financial press. We will explain indices, analysts' forecasts, and key financial ratios such as earnings per share and P/E ratio, as well as discounted cash flow. We will look at the types of stockbroker, and how nominee accounts work.

The London Stock Exchange

Equities are a type of security that represents ownership in a company. Equity is often used interchangeably with stock or share, which signifies the investor's share of ownership. You buy or sell a stock, which is commonly traded on the stock exchange.

If you buy shares in a large UK company, it will usually be trading on the London Stock Exchange (LSE), which started from 17th-century coffee houses in London. It is Europe's largest stock exchange, and is the best brand name among exchanges across the globe.

The LSE has two primary stock markets, the prestigious Main Market and, for smaller companies, the Alternative Investment Market (AIM). Companies are traded on these markets, both of which include an increasing number of foreign companies. In Chapter 5, we will see how the markets are used to raise capital for companies, either as an initial public offering of new shares, known as an IPO, or as issuance of further shares.

EBS is the world's leading provider of FX and precious metals transactional trading and data solutions to thousands of spot FX trading professionals across the globe.

The organisation facilitates global access and order in spot foreign exchange – one of the largest and most liquid markets in the world.

An average of USD 130 billion in spot foreign exchange, 700,000 oz in gold and 7 million oz in silver is traded every day on the EBS Spot Dealing System.

The continued increase in volume of deals transacted daily through EBS Spot creates unparalleled liquidity and market data, with access to a global community of traders – bringing together buyers and sellers, bids and offers.

Users of the EBS Spot system have access to 18 currencies, traded in 23 currency pairs. EBS is best know for providing the most attractive market for the most traded currency pairs – the US dollar (USD), Japanese yen (JPY) and euro (EUR) pairs – and for which EBS offers exceptional liquidity.

EBS is owned by 13 of the world's major banks and has its main offices in London, New York, New Jersey, Singapore, Tokyo and Hong Kong.

The EBS Spot dealing system was designed by FX traders, for FX traders and is consistently voted the most user-friendly and intuitive FX trading system by those who use the EBS Spot screen and ergonomically designed keypad.

EBS portfolio of FX solutions includes:
- EBS Spot (electronic FX spot broking)
- EBS Spot Ai (direct electronic access between the customer's trading system and the EBS Spot market)
- EBS Prime (access for the interbank and professional trading communities to the best EBS Spot prices from an EBS Prime bank)
- EBS Market Data
  - EBS Live (real-time streaming prices delivered with minimum latency direct from EBS to the customer's market data distribution platform)
  - EBS Ticker (third-party system distribution of EBS Spot prices)
  - EBS Rates (desktop view of EBS Spot prices, available exclusively through the BLOOMBERG PROFESSIONAL service)
  - EBS Data Mine (historical market data)
  - EBS Metals (electronic spot broking for the precious metals market)

More information about EBS is available at **www.ebs.com**

EBS®™ Spot

Facilitating an orderly market.

Are you part of it?

Increase your market advantage.
Get access to greater liquidity, the best prices,
global counterparties and an orderly market.

**Find out more about EBS Spot.
Go to www.ebs.com/spot**

FX SOLUTIONS

Once a company is quoted on the LSE or any other exchange across Europe, or elsewhere, you can normally buy and sell shares in it through your broker. In Chapter 13, we will look at the trading systems available to your broker. In the financial year to 31 March 2005, the LSE's broker services accounted for £100 million in revenues, which was 38 per cent of the £259 million total.

The LSE has a market supervision department that looks at all trades executed on the Exchange, on or off its books, and is responsible for running an orderly book. If the LSE suspects insider dealing, it will pass the case to the Financial Services Authority (FSA) to investigate. If a company breaches the Listing Rules, which cover listed companies, or if its financial position needs clarifying, the LSE has the power to suspend its listing, which means that most trading in its shares will stop.

Shares

Most stocks in London are traded on the LSE and can go up or down in value, which is reflected in a fluctuating share price. The selling price is below mid-price level, and the buying price is above it. Many companies quoted on exchanges pay a dividend, in the UK twice yearly, which represents a pay out from profits to shareholders. The share price is likely to rise a little as the so called Dividend Day approaches, and fall when the shares become categorised as ex-dividend. Dealings either on or after the ex-dividend date will exclude the dividend entitlement.

By owning a share, you are a part owner of the company, and may attend an annual general meeting (AGM). You also have voting rights. Equity investment in UK companies stands at about £18 trillion, which is almost £30,000 for every man, woman and child in this country, according to LSE chairman Chris Gibson-Smith in an October 2005 conference speech. If you are a private investor, you will often need to hold your shares for at least several months, and perhaps some years, to gain profit from your investment. Traders go in and out of stocks within a much briefer period and so base their investment decisions on more short-term factors.

Some private investors dabble on a one-off basis but for those with a more sophisticated approach, the conventional wisdom is to build a diversified portfolio, investing in a number of companies, each in a different sector, rather than only one. The sector spread reduces the risk because if the value of a share in one company falls, the share of another may outperform, balancing out the portfolio's overall performance.

On a broader scale, investments may be further diversified across assets and countries. Bonds are seen as safer assets than equities, and cash deposits are the safest asset class of all. Commodities and property may be included for even broader diversification. Western Europe is clearly a more stable geographical environment in which to invest than emerging markets such as South America and Russia, but has slower growth rate potential.

Investors take long and short positions in shares and other assets. A long position is where they own a share and expect to sell their position in the future at a profit. If they go short, they will sell a stock they do not own with the aim of buying it back at a lower price before settlement, so making a profit on the price difference. Today, the rolling settlement system makes it difficult for private investors to go short on shares. But they can take a short position using contracts for difference, covered warrants, or spread betting (see Chapter 7). In 2002, terrorist groups were suspected of having raised funds by taking short positions on various stocks before and after the 11 September 2001 terrorist attacks on New York, but it was never proven. In October 2002, the FSA issued a discussion paper on short selling. It considered it a legitimate activity but thought more transparency would be helpful.

If an investment bank has a net short position in a stock, it may borrow from a lender to deliver these securities on the agreed settlement date. From the buyer's perspective, there is no practical difference between borrowed and owned stock. If the bank has a net long position, it may lend the stock to borrowers for a fee. Stock lending figures, available from CREST and other sources, provide only a very loose indication of short selling levels as other factors must be considered as well. As a result of short trades, stock lending flourishes in bull markets, and improves market liquidity.

Let us now look at the most important data used for measuring the performance of the market and of individual shares.

Market indices

If you want to see how the broad market, or a part of it, is performing at any given time, you will look at market indices. Some of these are set out, with the last closing value and the day's rise or fall, in the business pages of *The Times* under the heading '*Major indices*'. The indices can serve as a benchmark against which to buy or sell individual shares or a portfolio.

The most widely quoted index is the FTSE 100, which covers the largest 100 stocks listed on the LSE by market capitalisation (share price multiplied by number of shares in issue). FTSE 100 companies each have a market cap that may be several billon pounds or more, with wide variations, and the index represents about 80 per cent of the UK market. FTSE 100 companies are referred to loosely as blue chips. The index is now more likely to include technology companies and it has some companies with assets in developing countries. The blue chips are more volatile than in the days before the internet company boom in 1999 and early 2000, but remain the least likely to go bust overnight, which gives them greater negotiating power in obtaining supplemental finance.

The FTSE 250 includes the next 250 stocks by market capitalisation behind the FTSE 100, and represents 17 per cent of the UK market. Companies on the FTSE 250 are large enough to survive hard times, but have more room for growth than the blue chips.

The FTSE 100 and the FTSE 250 together cover 97 per cent of the whole UK market. An even broader measure of the whole market is the FTSE All-Share Index, which represents the 900 largest shares on the LSE. The FTSE Ordinary Share Index includes 30 large companies and has an equal contribution from each of its constituent stocks, regardless of size.

Companies too small to be included in the FTSE 100 or the FTSE 250 (known together as the FTSE 350) may be in the Small Companies Index. Below this is the FTSE Fledgling Index, which consists of companies too small to be included in the All-Share Index. Although they have achieved a full listing on the LSE their market capitalisation can be as little as £700,000, but is usually at least a few million pounds. Smaller companies are quoted on the AIM, or, sometimes on Ofex, the off-exchange market run by PLUS Markets Group. Very young companies may be unquoted as they would more likely be seeking venture capital.

Institutional investors do not always give a lot of attention to small stocks because they are hard to trade in large quantities. The banks and stockbrokers research them less. But specialist funds focus on small stocks. This area is a favourite hunting ground for private investors, often guided by tip sheets (see Chapter 17). Stockbrokers note that small company stocks are volatile, have many more losers than winners and are not particularly liquid, which tends to cause problems in a market crash.

Bond prices have often moved in broadly opposite directions from share prices. Chapter 9 explains how government bonds work. There are two indices for government bonds. They are the FTSE Fixed Interest, which contains 25 UK index-linked government bonds, and the FTSE Government Securities, consisting of 111 UK government bonds, excluding index-linked bonds.

Stock valuation

Analysts' forecasts

The City is more influenced by analysts' forecasts for a company than by the latest figures, which are based on the past. The share price is always based on what the company is expected to do in one to two years' time, and this perception can change.

In the business pages of *Times Online*, you will find, where available, a consensus brokers' opinion. An easy-to-read chart shows how far along the scale from *strong buy* to *strong sell* a given stock is placed. If the opinion is exactly between the two, it will read a *hold*. More detailed brokers' forecasts are provided where available.

For more about how analysts work, see Chapter 17. Let us now take a brief look at how you may value stocks, borrowing from analysts' techniques.

Ratios

The financial ratios enable a quick assessment of a company against its own past or its peers'. To understand what the ratios mean, it is helpful to know how they are made up, but you do not need to calculate them yourself. In the business pages of *The Times* some of the key ratios and statistics are included under the two pages headed '*Equity prices*'. You will find here a list of companies quoted on the LSE under alphabetical sector headings representing broad categories of business. The first heading is '*Banking & finance*', and the last one is '*Utilities*'.

Against the names of companies, of which those in the FTSE 100 are in bold, the first column covers the high and low of the share price in the past 52 weeks; the bigger the difference, the more volatile are the shares. In Monday's edition a column for the company's market capitalisation (share price multiplied by number of shares in issue) is provided instead.

The next column has the company's name. It is followed by the share price, which is at yesterday's closing mid-price – halfway between the buying and selling price, based on the most competitive quote. To the right is a column headed by a plus and minus, showing any difference in pence between yesterday's and the previous day's close. On Mondays the share price change shown is weekly rather than daily.

Further to the right is the yield, which is the dividend, divided by the share price, multiplied by 100. The higher the yield is, the higher are the income payments to investors as a proportion of the current share price. Some sectors such as utilities are high yielding, but growth companies typically have a low yield.

Earnings per share is the ratio that City professionals follow most widely. It is made up of the listed company's profits after tax divided by the number of shares in issue. The City likes to see the company earnings per share steadily rising over the years. It is worth checking out the last five years of figures to see how far this has been achieved, taking into account that, despite recent standardisation of accounting practices across Europe, accountants have some discretion on how they allocate profits and will present the company in a favourable light. Obtain the earnings per share from a company search on the business pages of *Times Online* (www.timesonline.co.uk). You will find here also the prospective earnings per share from individual brokers, based on their own forecast figures.

Earnings per share divided by dividend per share will give you dividend cover, a figure which you will be able to calculate from data provided on individual companies in the business section of *Times Online*. Dividend cover says how easily a company can pay a dividend from profits. Of course it only applies to those stocks that pay dividends, which excludes some of the small growth stocks. A company in good financial health should be able to pay its dividend comfortably from current earnings. If not, it may have to use its reserves to keep up the payment. As a rule of thumb, when dividend cover is less than one, there may be cause for concern.

Let us return to *The Times* share price tables, where the last column is headed 'P/E'. This is the price/earnings ratio, which is widely used and shows how highly the market rates a company. The P/E ratio, as it is known, is the current share price, divided by the earnings per share in the most recent 12-month period. It moves in the opposite direction from the yield. If a stock has a P/E ratio higher than for its peers, the market rates it highly. If the P/E ratio is lower, the market is not attaching so much value to the stock's prospects, probably for a good reason. But, in the case of a less widely followed stock, the low P/E ratio suggests value has perhaps been overlooked. If a company has no earnings per share because it has not yet broken into profit, it will have no P/E ratio, and other valuation methods will have to be used.

The professionals use several ratios at once, and other valuation tools, to build a composite picture of how a stock is performing. For example a P/E ratio is more useful when considered in conjunction with profit growth. If a stock has a P/E ratio of 20 and is growing at 20 per cent a year, this may represent good value, but if the annual growth is only 5 per cent, it could look expensive. The PEG (price/earnings/growth ratio), which is the P/E ratio divided by earnings growth, covers both these factors, but you should also consider dividends, return on assets, level of borrowings, and a host of other factors.

For capital-intensive companies with large borrowings, such as in telecoms, a useful ratio is EBITDA, which is made up of earnings before interest, tax, depreciation and amortisation. In this type of company, EBITDA arguably presents a more realistic valuation than conventional earnings, which are calculated after interest and tax. On this basis, analysts may use the enterprise multiple, which is enterprise value, consisting of a company's market capitalisation plus debt, divided by EBITDA.

However, EBITDA is not recognised by accountants. Because it excludes tax, there is an obstacle in comparing stocks based on this valuation across international borders when the respective countries' tax regimes differ. Analysts had used EBITDA to value WorldCom, a US telecoms group which, in July 2002, made a Chapter 11 bankruptcy protection filing after it had revealed, a month earlier, a US $11 billion accounting fraud. Analysts then stopped using EBITDA as a stand-alone stock valuation tool.

The most widely used tool of analysts, and arguably one of the most dangerous in the wrong hands, is discounted cash flow.

Discounted cash flow analysis

Discounted cash flow (DCF) analysis translates future cash flow into a present value, and is widely used by analysts. It starts with the net operating cash flow (NOCF). You will find this by taking the company's earnings before interest and tax, deducting corporation tax paid and capital expenditure, adding depreciation and amortisation, which do not represent movements in cash, and adding or subtracting the change in working capital, including movements in goods or services, in debtors and creditors, and in cash or cash equivalents. This is the year's NOCF. It can be calculated for future years, and reduced in value to present-day terms by a discount rate.

Weighted-average cost of capital is often used as the discount rate. This is often abbreviated to WACC, and represents the cost of capital to the company. It is the average of the cost of equity and debt, weighted in proportion to the amounts of equity and debt capital deemed to be financing the business.

DCF has proved itself a flexible tool in the hands of analysts wishing to create valuations sometimes out of thin air but it has lost a lot of credibility since the market crash of March 2000.

The problem has been more how DCF is used than with the underlying concept. You only need to change one or two of the parameters, and you will get a different figure for DCF, and this leaves it open to manipulation. Professionals are wise to this, and to make an accurate forecasting scenario more likely, analysts may plot DCF models using different discount rates and different cash generation scenarios to present alternative valuations. The aim must be to present a prospective picture, including variables, and not to be too dogmatic although, at the same time, investors crave specific numbers.

Market influence

Biggest movers

The Times has a table headed '*The day's biggest movers*'. It shows the 16 companies whose share prices moved most yesterday. Against the company name is the share price, the change (plus or minus) from the previous day in pence, and news, which is not always the reason for the move. A big move is likely to be exaggerated because the market usually overreacts to news or speculation. But it could herald further share price movements.

Trading volume

Investor interest in a share is confirmed by rising trading volume, which is the number of shares traded, with buyers offsetting sellers. A picture tells you more than a thousand words and if you look up a quoted company through the business pages of *Times Online* and go to *Charts*, you will find charts of past performance with trading volume included, as is usual, at the bottom.

In the section '*Major indices*' in *The Times*, the daily number of bargains traded, which is different from the volume of shares traded, is reported. You will also find here the daily trading volume from SEAQ (Stock Exchange Automated Quotations), which is the LSE's market-making quotation system (see Chapter 13), and for the most liquid stocks on the AIM.

The LSE provides in the statistics section of its website (www.londonstock exchange.com) a monthly figure for the number of bargains in individual securities. Divide it by the number of trading days in the month for a daily average.

Company results

In *The Times*, company results are reported in the table headed '*Results in brief*'. Against the company's name and (in brackets) the sector, you will find the year or half year covered, for example *Yr to June 30*, or *HY to August 1*, the pre-tax profit or loss, and the dividend per share (if none, 0p) and payment dates.

The pre-tax profits and dividends for the same period last year are given in brackets. But the rise or fall over the past year is never the full story. A company may choose to cut expenditure now to increase profits now, at the expense of the long term. Or an expensive advertising campaign may reduce profits now, but raise them in future years. In either case, you need to take the long view.

Stockbrokers

Of an overall 650,000 clients, only 106,000 are execution only, 373,000 are clients of advisory and discretionary stockbrokers, and some others are with wealth managers, according to Compeer. Clearly, larger clients use advisory or discretionary services more often, and smaller clients make the most use of execution-only services. Let us look at the various types of broking service.

Execution only

The execution-only broker offers no advice to investors but simply executes their orders. By this limitation on its service, it reduces staff and other costs, and passes the savings on to the investor. Only 13 per cent of funds administered by execution-only brokers relate to portfolios valued in excess of £500,000, according to Compeer. Execution-only services are provided both online and by telephone, and charges are typically a fraction of those associated with using an advisory or discretionary broker.

Industry consolidation and the trend towards online services have contributed to a steady reduction in the average commission and fees per transaction from £45 in 1993 to £27 today, according to Compeer.

Advisory

Advisory stockbrokers advise clients on which stocks to buy or sell, and when. Some specialise in certain types of stock, and levels of expertise vary. In 2004, clients of stockbrokers conducting mainly advisory fund management paid average fees of 0.71 per cent of funds under management, according to Compeer.

The service provided by the advisory stockbroker is about getting the balance right between having the clients involved in decisions and protecting them from making mistakes. The broker can be handling a portfolio containing stocks he or she would not necessarily choose but that the client likes, perhaps because he or she inherited them or his or her uncle worked for a particular company. The broker has to deal with that and to try to encourage the client to make other investments that will show a good or better return. But there are no guarantees. It is a difficult balancing act and there can be faults on both sides.

Discretionary

Discretionary brokers take full charge of an investor's portfolio. They make buying and selling decisions on the investor's behalf for a fee. The charges overall are lower than on unit trusts. In 2004, clients of stockbrokers concentrating mainly on discretionary business paid charges averaging 0.76 per cent of funds under management and clients of wealth managers focusing on discretionary management paid 0.83 per cent, according to Compeer.

Following the March 2000 stock market decline, some discretionary fund managers produced unfortunate results. Sometimes, the client will personally have chosen a risky portfolio. One discretionary broker says: 'People say "I lost money, I did badly", but they forget they had instructed me to put them into specific equities and to run a high-risk portfolio'.

The key here is asset allocation according to the client's risk profile, and with a full understanding of what this entails. The broker may be at fault. Some discretionary brokers prefer to allocate too high a proportion of cash into risky assets such as equities because it pays them more. Some may overtrade portfolios. If the fund is making 40–50 trades a year, this is the level at which the broker often receives commission.

There are also many good discretionary brokers, but investors should make it clear that they are watching. They should ask plenty of questions about investment decisions, request frequent statements, and make sure that the general rule of 'run your profits and cut your losses' is reasonably adhered to, which, experience industry-wide shows, is easier said than done.

Nominee accounts

Nominee accounts are now the norm. Investors have their shares registered in the name of a nominee company but retain beneficial ownership. The account is run by their broker. Investors do not lose access to shareholder perks and voting rights, but it is up to the nominee company to provide them with the relevant information. Dividends are paid and regular account statements are provided.

Paper certificates are used now only to a limited extent. They account for about 3 million certificated transactions a year using the CREST settlement system (see Chapter 14), which represents about 5 per cent of its total.

Since February 2001, the industry standard for settlement of shares held in nominee accounts has been T + 3, meaning that both counterparties to a trade agree to *settle* a trade three business days after the trade date, although market makers, as opposed to the electronic order book, can offer some flexibility. For paper share certificates, it is T + 10.

5

Investment banking

Introduction

The investment banks raise money for companies and governments on the capital markets, and advise on mergers and acquisitions. These activities fall within investment banking, also known as corporate finance. We will use this chapter to focus on how venture capital and share issues work. We will briefly cover bond issues.

Capital raising

It is possible to raise cash, as we have seen in Chapter 3, through a syndicated loan. Another way is through equity or bond issuance. Bonds are debt securities. Equities (see Chapter 4) are a smaller market and, unlike bonds, represent ownership of the issuing entity.

The procedures for getting together a syndicate of banks, running a book and underwriting are broadly similar in equities and debt issuance, including bonds and syndicated loans. Banks are increasingly merging their equities and bonds origination activities.

Capital raising is part of a spectrum of activities within the investment banks. They also trade securities for themselves, as proprietary traders, and for clients. The traders work separately from the salespeople but liaison is easy. They will trade with other banks directly or through money brokers. The salespeople manage investor accounts.

You will find much relevant to proprietary trading elsewhere in this book. Let us here look at venture capital opportunities, and how flotations work.

Venture capital

Venture capital supports fledgling companies by providing seed capital and advising on business strategy. It is part of the UK private equity industry, which is the largest and most dynamic in Europe, accounting for 52 per cent of the European market, according to *The Economic Impact of Private Equity in the UK 2005*, a survey by the British Venture Capital Association.

Without backing from venture capitalists, many companies would never achieve the growth that makes a stock market flotation a realistic option. Many more companies seek such backing than there are venture capitalists. To attract finance, they will need a business model with potential for high growth and market leadership, driven by experienced management. The venture capitalist will take a high, perhaps 40 per cent, equity stake in selected companies. It aims to sell out once the company has achieved the exit strategy of either a stock market listing or a strategic sale as specified in its business plan, typically after five years, although business or economic conditions may cause delay.

Flotations

Choice of markets

When a company is ready to raise money through a share offering in the UK, there is a choice. A young company may float on the Ofex – the off-exchange market. A more ambitious choice is the Alternative Investment Market (AIM) or, most prestigious, a full listing on the LSE. Some companies go for a full listing immediately, others in stages, starting with an Ofex or AIM listing.

Ofex

Ofex is an independent, self-regulated UK market which enables investors to buy, sell or follow the prices of its small unlisted companies. The average market capitalisation of a company listed on this market is £10–20 million. The market is overseen by the Financial Services Authority (FSA). Ofex was once a trading facility rather than a market. A continual criticism was that its shares were not especially liquid, based on the previous system of a sole market maker, stock exchange member firm JP Jenkins.

In July 2004, a competing market-maker system was launched, and quoted prices have become more reliable. For up to one-third of Ofex companies, the spread subsequently narrowed by an average of 30 per cent. In October 2004, Ofex Holdings, the AIM-quoted company that owned Ofex, changed its name to PLUS Markets Group. The founding management left and the team was strengthened with executives from the LSE.

PLUS Markets Group now owns and operates Ofex. It put in a new set of rules in April 2005, which was designed to streamline the burden of red tape on smaller company management and to protect investors, and at the same time to ensure that regulatory costs were not too high. There are four competing market makers on this market. The name Ofex is likely to have changed in line with the PLUS Markets Group identity well before the end of 2006.

Companies may raise up to about £2 million through share offerings on Ofex. Alternatively, some raise no new cash but their shares are traded, perhaps to obtain a valuation for acquisition purposes, or to value employee share options. This *introduction* method of joining a market can enable a growing company to gain a period of experience and transparency on a public market, before embarking on future capital raising initiatives, if required.

For investors, Ofex remains a stock picker's market. The FSA considers it no more or no less risky than the AIM, by dint of the identical regulatory status. You may trade Ofex shares through your stockbroker like other UK markets, using the competing market-maker system. For Ofex stocks, capital gains tax taper relief and inheritance tax relief may apply. There is Venture Capital Trust and Enterprise Investment scheme eligibility, which provides tax breaks.

The AIM

The AIM was created by the LSE in 1995 to meet the needs of small growing companies. It is a high risk/high reward market. Since the AIM opened in 1999, more than 1,900 companies have been admitted and more than £17 billion has been raised collectively. As at March 2006, there were 1,188 domestic companies on AIM, and 220 international companies. Typically AIM companies have a market capitalisation of around £35–40 million, but the top 100 are capitalised at £100 million or more.

Disclosure is less rigorous on the AIM than for a full LSE listing. A start-up company can go to the AIM without three years of International Financial Reporting Standards (IFRS) accounts, but if it has a track record, it must show the accounts. If an AIM company wants to make an acquisition of less than 100 per cent of a company, it need not first obtain shareholder approval.

The AIM, like Ofex, is a non-regulated market, although it has exchange-regulated market status as *prescribed* within the UK regulatory regime. The regulatory framework of the AIM hinges on the Nominated adviser, or Nomad, which brings the company to the market, and is responsible for its behaviour afterwards. A company has a direct line to its Nomad, which is regulated by the LSE. There are 80 Nomads, and they tend to be protective of their reputations.

The Prospectus Directive

In July 2005, the Prospectus Directive was implemented. It is a single standard across Europe and applies as follows.

1. A company seeking admission to a full EU-regulated market, which excludes AIM and OFEX, must produce a full prospectus.

2. A company offering securities to the public must produce a full prospectus. Exemptions apply to issues: (a) directed at less than 100 persons, or (b) where less than €2.5 million is raised.

The AIM and the OFEX markets set their own disclosure rules.

In recent years, the LSE has been promoting the AIM to companies abroad as a secondary stock market listing in London while retaining their local market main listing. It has focused on, among other countries, Benelux, China, Australia, India, Russia and Kazakhstan.

By February 2006, the New York Stock Exchange was preparing for a merger with Archipelago Exchange, a fully electronic stock exchange, to create NYSE Arca, a small companies market that would compete in the same space as the AIM.

Full listing

To list on the LSE, unlike on the AIM, a company must have a three-year track record, and at least 25 per cent of its shares must be in public hands. Companies that launch international IPOs need high standards of transparency, and Western advisers. In the US, the corporate governance requirements of the Sarbanes-Oxley Act (see Chapter 19) has meant that many foreign companies have shunned the US and turned to the London market to list.

Preparing for the initial public offering

An initial public offering (IPO) is used particularly by large issuers. The raising of small amounts of capital, perhaps under £50 million, may instead take the form of a placing (covered later in this chapter) and through a broker rather than an investment bank. But there are many variations.

The 'beauty parade'

The IPO starts with the 'beauty parade'. One bank, or two jointly, if selected by the issuer, will land a lucrative job.

In choosing between bank candidates, the issuer will look for a track record in floating similar companies. There are other criteria. Software company Autonomy has appointed banks as book runners in its capital-raising initiatives based primarily on how well they understand the business, and partly on the bank's geographical distribution power, chairman Mike Lynch once told me.

A bank cannot become book runner if there is an unresolved conflict of interest, which could arise if it is launching the IPO of a rival company. It could also arise if another bank is selected as joint book runner; any historic conflicts will come under scrutiny in the selection process. As it turns out, most IPOs and secondary placings are handled by banks that have a corporate relationship with the issuing company, according to equity capital markets bankers.

The book runner takes lead responsibility for placing the newly floated shares with investors. In a sizeable deal, the book runner may organise backup from a syndicate of other banks. If it is at the top of the syndicate, it may have the status of global coordinator. Within the syndicate there are also key roles such as lead manager or manager.

A new method of selecting the book runner for an IPO, known as competitive IPOs, has arisen by which banks compete for a mandate based on how easily they can gain indicative support from investors for the proposed flotation. There is some regulatory concern that analysts may be under pressure to provide positive research about the issuer's investment products, thus compromising their independence without being properly declared.

Pre-marketing

In a pre-marketing phase, the book runner will meet with potential investors, and present the investment case for the company it is bringing to market. It will ascertain the price of the company's shares upon issuance and set parameters within which it believes the new issue should later be priced. The banks will often make this indicative price range public. Analysts away from the deal may say that the range is too high or too low against company fundamentals or peer ratings. The press may take a view, based on analysts' comments.

The book runner may occasionally move the indicative price range up or down. If so, it means that it had not properly anticipated demand. If the shift is downwards, which becomes more of a possibility in volatile markets, the risk is that the book runner may postpone the offering.

The book build

The book build is based on investor interest the banks have drummed up during the pre-marketing phase. The banks will build an order book through a road show, which, for large issues, travels across continental Europe and the US as well as the UK. Banks in the syndicate will organise group presentations and, for investment centres excluded from the visiting schedule, may use video-conferencing. The company's chief executive, finance director, and head of investor communications will address investors alongside the book runner's corporate financiers and analysts. One-to-one presentations will be organised by the banks with very large, *tier one* clients.

A traditional book build lasts two to three weeks, but can be longer in difficult market conditions. Most orders are confirmed two days or less before the book closes. The pressure is then on other investors to subscribe to the IPO. Once the IPO date has been declared, the entire process becomes highly susceptible to market news and conditions. The financial spread betting firms may run a bet on the future price of a popular pending new issue. They will have set what is known as the *grey market* price unscientifically but it may be quoted in the press and sway investors. It can become a self-fulfilling prophecy although usually only a few punters will have bet.

Pricing

The issuer and book runner will set the issue price ideally at the maximum level acceptable to institutional investors. If the deal is oversubscribed, the price may have been too low, but some oversubscription is likely in a successful IPO because, to ensure adequate share allocation, investors tend to request more shares than they want. This in itself helps to create demand, including in early secondary-market trading.

When pressed, major investment banks have admitted that the criterion for pricing the deal is not value but demand, which can partly be created. It is influenced not just by market conditions but also by perceptions of interest that the issuer, book runner, and PR initiatives have been able to whip up.

With retail investors involved, a book runner may price a new issue higher. This is not just because of the extra take-up and the publicity it generates, but also because when retail investors show interest in an IPO, the price will usually hold up better in early secondary market trading, which helps to safeguard the reputation of the book runner, particularly if it had overpriced the issue in the first place. Retail investors often hold new issues long after they ought to have sold, partly because they are inadequately advised. Therefore, the City has a vested interest in attracting retail investors to IPOs. In July 2000, Carphone Warehouse, the telephony products and services retailer, famously said that retail investors who agreed not to sell its shares for three months after the company's flotation would receive the full amount of shares applied for, and the rest only 60 per cent.

In the business pages of *The Times*, you will find a table headed *Recent issues*. It includes stocks recently issued on the stock market, including the AIM, with yesterday's closing price, and any rise or fall on the day.

Early secondary-market trading

In good market conditions, a deal will typically reach a small premium, perhaps 10–15 per cent, over the issue price in early secondary-market trading. This, coupled with oversubscription, creates further demand. If the free float is small, meaning that the shares are tightly held by company directors and few are available to the public, demand may quickly exceed supply and the share price may soar.

Institutional investors who bought shares during the IPO process may snatch a profit by selling the shares early in the first days or weeks of secondary-market trading. Such *flipping* is often the best way to make money quickly from new issues, which runs contrary to the buy-and-hold mantra often recommended to retail investors. The book runner may welcome a little flipping from favoured institutional investors because it needs liquidity to establish value in the shares and to meet the demands of buyers. After a few weeks the shares are likely to lose their initial momentum and, at least for a period, to slip below the offer price.

In poor market conditions, there are almost no new issues, and, where they have arisen, the newly issued shares may start trading at a discount to the issue price.

Specialist types of share issue

Accelerated book build

In an accelerated book build, the bank takes a selling company's shares in a listed company onto its books, and offers them to its investor clients. It will sell the shares over one day or, exceptionally, two or three days. This compares with several weeks for a conventional book build, and allows less time for market conditions to deteriorate. In market declines, such as from March 2000, institutional investors respond favourably to this form of capital raising.

Bought deal

The bought deal is where a bank buys securities itself from an issuer and resells them in the market. The bank will have assumed all the risk itself and so must have confidence in the deal. Issuers are often attracted to a bought deal because it gives instant liquidity.

Rights issues

If a UK company wants to raise more than 5 per cent of its existing market capitalisation, it must use a rights issue. The company will issue new shares to existing shareholders *pro rata* to their existing holdings. In a '1 for 5' rights issue, shareholders will have the right to buy one further new share for every five they hold. The process takes perhaps six to eight weeks, twice the length of a conventional share offering.

Through a rights issue, shareholders have an opportunity to acquire new shares without paying their stockbroker a commission. They do not have to buy and, to make it worthwhile, they need to be convinced that the company will use the cash properly. If the rights issue is to pay off debt, shareholders should assess the chances of success before they subscribe.

The issuing company will usually appoint an underwriter, usually a major bank, to the deal, which guarantees full subscription. If the issue fails, the underwriter will take up the rights. The riskier the deal, the larger is the underwriter's fee. Some rights issues are not fully underwritten, which can be a high-risk strategy for both the issuer and the underwriter.

Once the rights issue is underway, the share price can fluctuate, particularly in uncertain markets or if the issue is for a purpose that may not benefit shareholders, or is not underwritten. Hedge funds may trade the underlying shares, which can play havoc with the price.

The new shares in a rights issue will be priced lower than the market value of the existing shares. In difficult markets, the discount might be as high as 40–50 per cent, which is known as a deeply discounted rights issue and is more likely to attract subscription.

Following a rights issue, the overall share price will find a balance based *pro rata* to the price of the old shares and of the cheaper new shares, in proportion to the number of shares in issue of each. It is often slightly lower than before the rights offering. For capital gains tax assessment, the HM Revenue and Customs considers the new shares were acquired at the same time as the original ones.

Shareholders not interested in a rights issue may sell the rights to which they have not subscribed, known as *nil paid* rights, to other investors. After they have received the proceeds, and the share price has adjusted down as a result of the rights issue, they will be in a cash neutral position.

Unsubscribed rights are known as the rump. The book runner will later sell them to new investors in an accelerated book build (see above).

Placing

A placing is when the broker issues a company's shares privately to institutions, at least some of which are its own clients. Retail investors are not usually given the opportunity to buy.

Placing and open offer

A placing and open offer is when the placing (see above) takes place simultaneously with an open offer to existing shareholders. This dual approach is used to place shares in already quoted companies. The shares are placed provisionally with institutions but subject to claw back by shareholders that may exercise their right to take up shares under the open offer. Sometimes key shareholders will have undertaken to take up some shares.

A placing and open offer can be a quicker and more reliable way to raise cash than a rights issue, particularly in difficult markets. The amount raised must be below the size threshold at which a rights issue becomes compulsory (see above) and so a placing and open offer tends to be for small capital raisings, typically under £50 million.

Global depositary receipts

The LSE is competing internationally as the preferred market in which to raise capital. Global depositary receipts, known as GDRs, are bank certificates issued in more than one country for shares in a foreign company. When they are traded on the LSE, GDRs facilitate UK ownership of a foreign stock. Through GDRs, companies may raise capital in more than one market simultaneously.

Bond issues

In a low-interest rate environment, listed companies may find it cheaper to raise money through corporate bonds (see Chapter 10) than through equities. If a company issues bonds, it may have to pay a coupon of 6 per cent, but, if it issues equities, it may have to give shareholders a 10 per cent return. In the UK and some other developed economies, interest on bonds issued is tax deductible against the issuing company's profits. Based on a 30 per cent corporation tax, the true cost of servicing the bonds would be 6 per cent x 0.7 = 4.2 per cent.

Companies sometimes issue bonds and use the cash raised to buy back shares from investors. The downside of bond issuance is the risk of taking on too much debt in relation to equity, which is known as *high gearing* and gives the issuer a riskier profile with the credit rating agencies. Generally, banks have easier access to capital than companies and are more highly geared. Debt issuance is likely to be the second largest liability on a major bank's balance sheet, behind cash deposits.

The bond issuer cannot skip paying the coupon, as is possible with dividends on shares. It also must repay the principal on maturity, but can refinance by issuing new bonds.

Banks, like companies, invest cash in bonds, across the risk spectrum and in all major market currencies. Some bonds will also be included on the asset side of the balance sheet, where in terms of risk weighting under Basel II (see Chapter 3), they are more attractive than loans.

Issuers of bonds will usually offer a fixed rate of return, which is what investors prefer. But if, for instance, they offer bonds at an 11 per cent yield, and so will have to pay 14 per cent per annum inclusive of capital repayment, and then the bonds fall in value, investors will feel they have lost out. This is why investors use the swaps market, which enables them to swap fixed for floating rates. The majority of the swaps market consists of interest rate swaps (see Chapters 6 and 9).

Mergers and acquisitions

Companies may use the capital markets to raise cash to finance an acquisition. Mergers and acquisitions (M&A) is the area where investment banks are often compared and judged. They will advise a company planning a takeover or that is a likely bid target. The company itself usually appoints an investment bank as an adviser, choosing the one with the best ideas. In the UK, unlike in some other parts of Europe, a bank can act as adviser only for one of the two sides because of the potential conflict of interests. The fee for M&A advice is up to 2 per cent of the deal's value, diminishing as the deal becomes bigger. But the bank is only paid if the bid proceeds. The bidder may withdraw, perhaps after it has concluded a due-diligence inspection or a rival bidder has muscled in.

Most M&A deals are small and are agreed between the parties. If a bank is advising a company making an acquisition, it may also raise capital for it, which is more lucrative. If a bank is acting for a target company, it may fend off the bidder with the intervention of a *white knight*, a congenial rival bidder. It may block a deal with a *white squire,* a significant minority shareholder. The bid target may make a counter bid for the bidder.

If a takeover is to go ahead, the predator must obtain more than 50 per cent of the target company's voting shares. Once its stake has reached 30 per cent, it must make a formal offer to all shareholders. If some shareholders decline to take up an offer, a buyer can acquire their shares compulsorily if holders of 90 per cent of the voting shares have accepted. The acquirer pays for a target company's shares either with cash, its own shares, or a combination of the two.

The Takeover Panel, an independent UK regulatory body without statutory powers but widely respected in the City, has at the time of writing proposed to abolish the Substantial Acquisition Rules (SARs) which restrict the speed at which an investor or potential acquirer can build a stake in a company of between 15 and 30 per cent. The SARs rules had been introduced in 1980 after some raids on UK-listed companies led to concerns about shareholder protection.

The Panel said the SARs rules were no longer needed because of recent improvements on the rules on disclosure of shareholders. But some felt that abolishing the rules could lead to more dawn raids, which is when a predator makes a sudden, unexpected purchase of a large number of shares in the target company at the market opening as a way to build a stake before making a formal bid.

6

Introduction to derivatives

Introduction

In this chapter we will define derivatives, and see how they work. We will examine the distinctions between on-exchange and over-the-counter (OTC) markets, and the various products, as well as settlement and clearing, and issues related to hedging and speculation. In later chapters, we will focus on related areas.

Cash and derivatives

In the cash markets, trades represent an actual underlying investment, for example Microsoft stock, or British Airways bonds, or 100,000 barrels of oil. In the cash market, there is always a delivery aspect, a payment of cash for some class of assets. With derivatives, the transaction depends on the value of the underlying asset. It is a financial or paper transaction that can turn into a deliverable. Recently, the demand for derivatives has been increasing far more than for cash products.

There are two types of trading, on-exchange and OTC. Each type can represent trades in the underlying instrument such as shares or bonds, or their derivatives, which are based on the underlying instrument.

Derivatives include four basic transactions: spot, forward, option and swap. More complex terminology may be used, depending on which of the asset classes are involved. They are credit fixed income, financials, interest rate market, equity and commodities.

Let us take a more detailed look. Credit fixed income includes credit derivatives, bonds, commercial paper and loans; financials include foreign exchange and forwards; interest rate markets include interest rate swaps and options, and deposits, as well as forward rate agreements and overnight index swaps. The derivatives and cash instruments in these asset classes are traded in the money markets (see Chapter 9).

Of the rest, equity covers the stock market; commodities include soft commodities such as food, feedstuffs and beverages, including grains, pork bellies, shrimp, wines, wheat and corn, as well as industrial raw materials such as oil, gas, electricity, nuclear fuel and metals.

Within all these asset classes, you will find products traded on exchange and OTC. Some products are cash and others are derivatives. In the following four subsections we will focus on the four main derivative transactions, any of which may be used for taking a position or hedging.

Four types of derivative transaction

Spot

When a derivative is spot, you know the price now, and you buy and take delivery. The transaction timescale is typically short. It is expressed as T + 1 or T + 2, which is the trade date plus the number of days until settlement. For example, trades in foreign exchange (covered in Chapter 12) are T + 1: you trade today and transfer the money and receive your purchase the next business day.

Forward

On a forward transaction, the price at which you will trade is set in the future. If you trade a forward on an exchange, it is called a future. If you trade a forward on the OTC market, it is called a forward.

For futures, there could, for example, be a March delivery, which stipulates delivery of 1,000 lots of an underlying commodity on 23 March. As a trader, you will either reverse out of the future before that date, or there will be delivery of the underlying instrument. On the forward market, you will choose the day of delivery.

A brief case study best illustrates how the different trading methods work. You may know that you will need to exchange one billion dollars on 23 March because, on 24 March, you are required to pay for a factory. If you buy through the on-exchange traded market and delivery is on 23 March, this fits exactly with your requirement. But if the exchange contract expires on March 15, you will receive the money earlier than you need, or if it expires on April 15, you will receive it later. Either would be an imperfect hedge.

On the OTC market, you can avoid this because the contracts can be tailor-made. You may buy a three-month forward on 23 December and receive payment on 23 March. If, alternatively, you ask the bank on 6 January for a forward to 23 March, you can get it, but this is a *broken date* because it is not over a standard period and it will cost more due to the decreased liquidity and the need to find a counterparty.

Option

An option is a right. It is not an obligation, which distinguishes it from a forward or a swap (see below). If you have an option to buy euros at £1.50 in three months, and the price rallies to £1.55, you will be pleased to exercise at £1.50 and make 5p profit less expenses per option held.

The risk with OTC trades is that if the entity that wrote the option is no longer viable, you cannot exercise it, and no clearing house will take on the responsibility of completing the transaction. The message is that, if no clearing house is involved, you will need to look at credit risk much more carefully.

For OTC options and similar, banks will have a team of specialists assessing the creditworthiness of counterparties and clients. For a detailed explanation of how options work, see Chapter 7.

Swap

The swaps market has developed from nothing in 1982 to a level that dwarfs the bonds and equities markets together. The notional global outstanding volume of interest rate swaps and options and cross-currency swaps was US $183.6 trillion during the first six months of 2005, and the amount of credit default swaps was US $12.43 trillion, according to a 2005 mid-year market survey by the International Swaps and Derivatives Association. Equity swaps, forwards and OTC options amounted to US $4.83 trillion.

To see how swaps work, let us imagine that company A and company B each needs a loan of £100 million. Company A can only get a variable rate loan (also known as floating rate) from its bank. It wants a fixed rate loan because it believes that rates will rise, and fears that the variable rate could be too expensive. Company B, however, can only get a fixed rate loan of 4 per cent (based on an agreed compromise between a 3.99 per cent bid from one bank and a 4.01 per cent offer from another). It wants a variable rate because it thinks that rates will decline, in which case the loan interest would become cheaper, and the company would keep more of its profits.

An interest rate swap gives each company the chance to achieve strategically what it wants. Company A will swap its variable-rate loan with the fixed rate loan of company B. There are charges, but both company A and company B benefit.

From a company perspective, swaps can save money. If you are a mid-sized company and you embark on a 10-year investment project in Japan, let us assume that you need to borrow yen, the local currency, at a fixed rate to cover the cost of the project. Let us say that nobody in Japan has heard of you, and so you can have a 10-year loan at a high fixed rate but at a lower floating rate. You may take a floating rate loan and instruct your bank to arrange a 10-year swap, which gives you fixed interest cash flows. The overall cost will be lower than for a ten-year fixed rate loan.

Sometimes, companies can negotiate 10-year fixed rate loans at a very low fixed rate, but actually require floating-rate money to meet short-term commitments. A company may borrow the money by issuing a low fixed rate 10-year bond (see Chapters 5 and 10) and swap it for a floating rate.

Banks trade swaps with each other, typically acting for clients, which are increasingly hedge funds. In about 50 per cent of cases, the banks will use a broker. Contractual terms have given rise to problems in the past as it was easy to cancel the contract if conditions were not met. The International Swap Dealers Association has since introduced full *two way* agreements by which, if there is a default, swap counterparties will net swap agreements.

On-exchange versus OTC derivatives

An exchange-traded contract has the advantage of being standardised, which makes it much cheaper and means that you can move a large deal quickly, with very little price impact. There is no counterparty risk when you are dealing with the exchange. An OTC contract, unlike its exchange-traded counterpart, is negotiated between both parties to the contract. It is more flexible than the contract traded on exchange, but is less transparent and harder to value.

The main use of exchange-traded derivatives for professionals is for hedging, according to market sources. For example, a bank that buys a government bond may automatically hedge it in the futures market. Products tend to start on the OTC market, and it is only after several years of established maturity that they are mimicked in the on-exchange markets, where a lot of liquidity in one place is needed.

In broad terms, the market for OTC derivatives is about four times the size of that for exchange-traded derivatives, and is a market only for professional investors. Banks prefer to use a market where they do not compete with the man in the street and, when trading on their own book, will use the OTC market more often.

The OTC derivatives market has seen enormous growth. In the UK, average daily turnover in OTC currency and interest rate derivatives was US $643 billion in April 2004, up from US $275 billion in April 2001, according to a survey by the Bank for International Settlements. The UK's share of the global OTC derivatives market rose from 36 per cent to nearly 43 per cent over the period, which makes it the global market leader. Trading of international derivatives has become more concentrated in the UK and the US. The 10 largest UK institutions accounted for 80 per cent of total reported turnover in April 2004, up from 74 per cent in 2001. Institutions most active in interest rate derivatives markets were not necessarily active in currency derivatives.

Interest rate derivatives (see Chapter 9) and credit derivatives (see Chapter 10) are the largest categories of OTC derivatives, but there are many others. The demand for any one type of OTC derivative may fluctuate. In 2000, the energy derivatives market crashed, partly because of supply and demand dynamics, and partly because of market manipulation by, among others, US energy company Enron, although the proportions of each remain open to debate. The credit derivatives market is booming and is heralded as the equivalent in size to an early stage interest rate market, but time will tell whether it develops on a similar scale.

The growth that some OTC derivatives markets can achieve is demonstrated in the niche area of freight derivatives. Shipping represents 10 per cent of City activity and the notional value of trading in forward freight agreements rose from US $2.5 billion in 2001 to US $30 billion in 2005, according to industry estimates. This market is based on the freight costs of transporting cargo by sea, which the United Nations estimated in 2003 at US $380 billion. Ship owners and charterers use freight derivatives to hedge against market volatility and some large investment banks now take a position. The Baltic Exchange provides benchmark price data.

The banks are constantly inventing new OTC derivatives products, the latest of which is property derivatives. This is the largest remaining physical market that has not had associated derivatives. In the year to September 2005, interdealer broker ICAP saw 15 per cent of its revenues derived from early life cycle property derivatives.

If a group hopes to open an operation in Hong Kong with 3,000 people in a year's time and property prices are rising, the group may be well advised to buy now. But this would require the work of finding and leasing a building and if it later decided not to make the move, it would need to resell it. The bank would find it easier and more flexible to buy a property index option.

Settlement and clearing

There are two ways of proceeding to clear and settle derivatives: central counterparty clearing and bilateral settlement. If a clearing house is involved, as when dealing through an exchange, it can only clear trades either entered into by or given up to its clearing members. So, a broker, if itself not a clearing member, would have to give up the trades to a clearing member to enable the delivery of central counterparty clearing services. Clearing members, generally banks, must place collateral with the central counterparty, in each case perhaps tens of millions of pounds, to protect against default by any other clearing members. They receive some interest on the money, but are not able to have full use of it.

On-exchange futures and options trades are cleared through a central counterparty, which takes on the risks associated with the trade. Trader A has no time to assess whether trader B is an acceptable credit risk. The central counterparty eliminates not only the credit risk but the delivery risk as well. In an OTC environment, there is no central counterparty, so traders A and B must assess their counterparty's credit and delivery risks. If they are satisfied, the deal is bilaterally settled; if not, the deal does not get done. Traders are not happy with this arrangement and increasingly OTC environments are seeking the introduction of a central counterparty.

If an acceptable OTC counterparty is found and the trade is bilaterally settled, the buyer and seller are anonymous until the broker has put them together. The deal is the responsibility of the two counterparties, and the broker simply matches them. The broker identifies them post-trade, which may not be a disadvantage. Bilateral settlement is used for interest rate and credit derivatives, currency options and most spot and forward transactions. In some of these markets, the potential loss is so great, and movements are so volatile, that no entity is willing to be the central counterparty. In foreign exchange futures and options, there has not been enough demand for central counterparty services, according to clearing sources.

Hedging and speculation

Warren Buffett, regarded by his admirers as the world's most successful investor, has famously described derivatives as weapons of mass destruction. A few large scandals have left the public with much the same impression and some companies flaunt the fact they do not use derivatives. The professionals are unimpressed. Without derivatives, companies are not using a cheap and effective way of hedging their position. Hedging has the effect of insurance. It is at the other end of the pole from speculation, for which the very same types of derivative may be used. If a company takes a 4 per cent variable loan, it should hedge itself against the risk that the rate could soar to 12 per cent, failing which it is vulnerable to the full hit.

A company's treasurer will assess the cost of using forwards or options, and will deal directly with a bank to arrange an appropriate derivatives strategy. For example, in the third quarter of 2005, after Hurricane Katrina, the price of fuel was soaring, but discount airline easyJet was not hit badly because it hedges with options against short term fluctuations in the fuel price. EasyJet also hedges against movements in the dollar, a currency in which aeroplanes, spare parts and fuel are denominated. Hedging costs little compared with easyJet's £1.5 billion in sales and it has saved more than £10 million in profits according to company figures.

Some of the big corporate scandals in 2005, including Enron, WorldCom, Ahold and Parmalat, made no ripple in the market because the financial risk was hedged with derivatives, according to City brokers. When a company invests in derivatives, it is across a number of them, which reduces the risk of systemic failure. The economic rationale behind the earliest futures was to hedge against price risk. Speculators have always taken second place, but they are the key liquidity providers. They make hedging possible and sometimes advisable.

The problem with derivatives is not in the product itself, but in how it is sold or managed. An overzealous derivatives salesman could go to an unaware company treasurer and say: 'Swap your fixed rate for a variable rate loan. Nothing will happen to rates. It's free money'. If rates then go from 4 to 12 per cent, the company would have problems.

Swaps have not always been used responsibly. In the 1980s, the London Borough of Hammersmith and Fulham used interest rate swaps to bet on interest rates, and sold *swaptions*, which are options to enter a swap at a fixed rate, and it lost money. Some banks took court action over contracts with the authority, but ultimately lost after the House of Lords ruled that the municipal treasuries were acting beyond their power if they entered swap agreements.

If a company is to trade in derivatives, it must understand their value. Software data will calculate the *value at risk*, known as VAR, which is how much the company is willing to lose at any time. The VAR changes daily. Banks have thousands of loans on their books, both receiving and giving. They need good systems and procedures to determine VAR, and this is an underlying complexity.

Another risk is pure fraud. It happens but is infinitesimal compared with the amount of trading. For details of how Nick Leeson destroyed Barings Bank by playing the derivatives market, see Chapter 18.

The Financial Services Authority performs a useful function in authorising individuals in client-facing roles and monitoring the procedures and risk controls of entities. It aims to reduce systemic risk. Banks are now more sensitive to internal risk and have tighter procedures, including *know your client*. But there are always rogue traders, or treasurers of companies who do not behave responsibly.

7

Derivatives for retail investors

Introduction

Retail investors use derivatives for speculating and hedging in the same way as professionals, but are more confined to exchange-traded products. They trade in much smaller sums and have a narrower range at their disposal. We have seen in Chapter 6 how derivatives work. In this chapter, we will focus on those relevant for retail investors, which are options, futures, warrants, contracts for difference and spread betting.

Options

We have already noted that options may be over-the-counter (OTC) or exchange-traded products. For retail investors, a traded option on exchange has some appeal. It enables you to bet on the movement of individual shares, or of indices, currencies, commodities or interest rates, or may be used for hedging. Through an option, you have the right to buy or sell a security at a pre-determined price, the exercise price, within a specified period.

The option is geared, which means that the underlying share or other asset is under control for the comparatively small upfront cost of the premium, which is the market price of the option. The premium is a small percentage of the option's size. For every buyer of an option, there is a seller, also known as a writer.

An option buyer on completion will pay an initial margin, which goes to the writer of the option. Initial margin is calculated to cover the worst loss in a day that could arise. The option buyer must regularly top up the initial margin to any extent that his or her position has declined in value to an uncovered level.

If the investor does not exercise the option, the premium that he or she has paid will be lost to the writer. But if it is exercised, the writer must provide the underlying financial instrument at the exercise price. One side will gain and the other will lose, but neither has the odds intrinsically in its favour.

You can buy a *call* option, which gives you the right, but not the obligation, to buy the underlying security at the exercise price. If the asset price is more than the exercise price of the option, the difference represents the option's value, and the option is *in the money*. If the asset price is less, the call option is *out of the money*. If you buy an option deep *out of the money* and the underlying price moves a lot, the premium could move in absolute terms much less, but in percentage terms more proportionately.

As the buyer of a *call* option, you will make money if the price of the underlying share moves up so that it becomes higher than the exercise price plus the premium that you have paid. In this case, you could sell the option and realise the profit on the options trade, but it is usually simpler to trade it as a profit.

You can buy a *put* option, which gives you the right, but not the obligation, to sell a security at the exercise price. If the exercise price is higher than the underlying security's current market price, the option is *in the money*. If it is lower, the option is *out of the money*. You will make a profit if the option price falls to below the level of the exercise price plus the premium that you have paid.

The extent to which the underlying stock's value surpasses the option's exercise price is known as intrinsic value. An option only has intrinsic value when it is *in the money*. The time value of an option is its total value less intrinsic value. The more time an option has until it expires, the higher this figure is likely to be, as the price of the underlying stock has more chance of changing in the option buyer's favour.

The premium consists of both intrinsic and time value, both of which can change constantly. These are factors used in the Black-Scholes model, which was developed in 1973 and is widely used in financial markets for valuing options. Other factors used in the model are volatility, the underlying stock price, and the risk-free rate of return. But Black-Scholes makes key assumptions which are not always tenable, including a constant risk-free interest rate, continuous trading, and no transaction costs.

Equity options tend to come in the standard contract size of 1,000 shares. To find the cost of an option contract, multiply the option price by 1,000. If a call option is priced at 70p, it will cost £700 per contract. The contract size may vary if the underlying company is involved in a capital restructuring such as a rights issue.

the**share**centre:

we're out to make buying shares as easy as buying anything else

If shares and other stock market investments take your fancy, then so will The Share Centre. We aim to make buying and selling shares as easy as buying a tin of beans. Of course, investing in shares isn't right for everyone – share prices, their value and the income from them can go down as well as up and you may not get back what you originally invested; but our free *guide to investing* can help you decide if they're right for you. And when they are, we'll make the whole business simple and inexpensive – by providing you with all the tools you need, including free expert help. So what are you waiting for? Visit us at www.share.com, or call us now.

● **www.share.com**
● **0870 400 0253**

The options on Euronext.liffe, the London-based exchange, have expiry dates grouped three, six or nine months ahead. A first group of companies has the expiry dates of January, April, July and October; a second group has February, May, August and November; and a third group expires in March, June, September and December. In any given month, options for only a third of the relevant companies will expire. When, for instance, a contract expires in March, a new one is created for expiry in June.

Options on stock market indices, known as index options, are essentially contracts for difference. They are riskier than equity options as they often trade for larger amounts, perhaps several thousand pounds per contract against several hundred pounds. They are also more volatile.

The interest rate option enables traders to speculate on or hedge against interest rate risk. The price level of a contract is derived by subtracting the interest rate from 100. An interest rate of five per cent means that the contract is $100 - 5 = 95$ per cent. Settlement is on a value per fraction of a percentage change in interest rates. Because of the price structuring, the higher the interest rate rises, the further the contract price declines, and the reverse.

Futures

Futures are a binding agreement to buy or sell a given quantity of an asset at today's price by a specified future date. The market has become increasingly open to private investors and it has made available some small-sized contracts and packaged futures products.

The futures market started in the US in the early- to mid-19th century, when mid-West farmers sold their future crops at a fixed price in Chicago. By this early form of commodity futures, the farmers had a guaranteed sale and a certain profit. The traders who bought from the farmers were speculators who hoped that the crops would be worth more on the sell date than they had paid.

Today, futures could be on commodities such as cocoa or coffee or, since the 1970s, financial futures, which are available in a form especially accessible to private investors. The trader who goes long or short on a contract will put up an initial margin rather than the entire value of the contract. This margin takes the form of a deposit, usually about 10 per cent of the contract size, on which the broker can draw should the trader incur losses.

Any profits will be added to the balance on the margin account, but the trader must top it up if funds are reduced too far. The trader can place a stop loss to sell an off-setting contract at a price that has fallen to a specified level or, should the market have fallen too rapidly to enable this, at the best price available.

In theory, a trader can run a futures contract to expiry, but in practice, will usually trade it. If you have bought a contract, you will sell it, or if you have sold, you will buy.

The trader buys a commodity future committing to buy a commodity at the given price, and if its value rises well above it, the trader may close the position with the opposite contract. By such trading before expiry, the trader avoids physical delivery of the commodity such as cocoa, and may sell short.

Financial futures are based on a financial instrument such as a bond, share, index, interest rate or currency, and the agreement is to exchange a cash sum reflecting the difference between the initial price of the underlying asset and its price on settlement. Interest rate futures enable buyers to hedge against adverse movements in interest rates by buying a future to offset it. Contracts on indices or on interest rates cannot go to delivery, and any buyer or seller who doesn't close the position is closed out by the clearing house. Most major bond futures contracts can go to delivery.

In the 2005 calendar year, Euronext.liffe traded 605 million options and futures contracts, up 7 per cent on the same period the previous year, with figures rebased for fair comparison. Of these, 250 million were equity based, and 347 million were interest rate products. Only 8.4 million were soft commodity products (see Chapter 11), which is a small proportion of the whole, and there were under 0.5 million of other products.

Warrants

Covered warrants are an exchange-traded packaged derivative mainly for retail investors, which have been popular for some years in continental Europe. The London Stock Exchange (LSE) introduced them in late 2002 in an early move to obtain a significant presence in derivatives after its failed attempt the previous year to buy the London International Financial Futures Exchange (LIFFE). So far, covered warrants in the FTSE 100 index have proved the most popular in a market which has been slow to take off.

The covered warrant is a security and, not like an option, a contract. As with options, traders in covered warrants pay a small premium, which is how much you pay for the right to buy or sell the underlying asset, and the warrants are split into calls and puts. As time passes, the covered warrant becomes less valuable, which is reflected in a declining premium. Every covered warrant is normally traded before its maturity date and is *covered* because the issuer covers its position by simultaneously buying the underlying stock or financial instrument in the market.

Covered warrants are expensive compared with some equivalent derivative products and cannot be shorted, but the spread (the difference between the buying and selling price) is often narrow, and the packaging is user-friendly. The LSE says: 'In theory, private investors could go straight to the banks and get a similar product created for them over the counter. In reality, they would not have the knowledge to get the product specified for them, and the banks wouldn't issue anything at such small values.'

Unlike in *contracts for difference* or spread betting (both covered later in this chapter), the trader cannot lose more than 100 per cent of his or her money, and at the end of the term, covered warrants that are *in the money* are automatically closed out on the investor's behalf. No stamp duty is payable on purchase, and owners will receive no dividend from the underlying share. Capital gains tax is payable.

Some warrants are traded on the Central Warrants Trading Service (CWTS) platform, which is part of SETS, the LSE's electronic order book, and the product may generally be traded via Retail Service Providers. For more on trading systems, see Chapter 13.

The covered warrant should not be confused with the conventional warrant, a product that may be used to buy a specified number of *new* shares in a company at a specified exercise price at a given time, or within a given period. Companies like to issue conventional warrants because they do not need to include them on the balance sheet. They are not part of a company's share capital and so have no voting rights. Sometimes the warrants are packaged as a sweetener to accompany a bond issue. They tend to rise and fall in value with the underlying shares, sometimes exaggerating the movement. Capital gains tax is payable on profits.

Contracts for difference

The contract for difference (CFD) is a contract between two parties to exchange the difference between the opening and closing price of a contract, as at the contract's close, multiplied by the specified number of shares. If you want to be exposed not to the shares in an underlying company but to the price movement, you can buy a CFD. If the share price goes up, you will make money on the difference. CFDs are available on most UK and US stocks, as well as in European markets, although the range offered by brokers can vary.

Historically, only institutions used CFDs but, in recent years, private investors have become significantly more involved. The institutions that trade the CFD most are the hedge funds, and it allows them to take a position in equities without revealing their identities. The private investors who trade CFDs directly tend to be sophisticated. They can trade CFDs through spread-betting firms (see below), which operate as market makers. Alternatively, like institutions, they may use brokers, where the deal will be cheaper but the minimum size larger.

If you buy a CFD, you will not own the underlying share, but you will be entitled to dividend payments and, depending on your broker, will have full access to corporate actions, including rights issues, takeover activity and similar events. There are CFDs based on indices, currencies and commodities. The CFD is highly geared, and you will trade it on margin, which is typically 10 per cent, but may be higher for CFDs on stocks outside the FTSE 100. It works on a sliding scale; the smaller the stock size, the greater the initial margin required.

You will pay no stamp duty on CFD purchases. You are liable for capital gains tax on profits beyond your annual exemption level (£8,500 in 2006–07), but you may offset losses against future liabilities. The CFD is a short-term investment and after you have held it for about 60 days, the amount that you will have saved by not having paid out on stamp duty will be cancelled by your interest payments. It is not economical to continue holding the CFD unless it is significantly increasing in value.

Spread betting

Financial spread betting is an over-the-counter market, but is also something of a hybrid in that some bookmakers operate what is effectively their own exchange. Traders may place a bet with a financial bookmaker on the direction of a share price, index, interest rates or other variable. The bookies are major users of CFDs, which they use to hedge bets into which they have entered with private investors.

Financial bets give private investors access to derivatives because the bet is usually on futures or options, which anticipate the underlying financial instrument. The bookmaker quotes a two-way price, and a bet is placed on margin. It is a way for private investors to take a short position, something impractical for them in the stock market because of the way the rolling settlement system works. If you are taking a financial bet, a stop loss will typically be available, but the underlying financial instrument's price may move too fast for you to apply it in time. The more attractive alternative is a *guaranteed* stop loss (not usually available on options), which the bookmaker will apply automatically at a set level.

Before traders make a profit, the price movement must cover the spread, which is the main source of the firm's profit. There is no stamp duty on purchases and profits are free of capital gains tax, but these perks do not stop most spread bets from losing money. Spread betting attracts a large number of

Only **one** spread betting company ticks **all** the boxes

- ✓ Stock Index Futures from 4 point spread
- ✓ Daily Markets from 2 points
- ✓ Trade Small Cap Shares from £6million market cap
- ✓ Tax-free trading*
- ✓ Advanced on-line trading platform
- ✓ Extensive risk management tools
- ✓ Interest paid on unencumbered funds**
- ✓ Credit facilities available
- ✓ Part of a FTSE 100 company

Man Spread Trading

Dealing in Excellence

To find out more or to open an account and start trading instantly, speak to an account manager on

020 7144 4080

or go to

www.manspreadtrading.com

gamblers, and some sophisticated traders, as well as the naive. More than a few attend courses and seminars in spread betting. They can be expensive, and not all the trainers have good credentials.

The spread-betting industry boasts plenty of City professionals among its private clients, but it has a not very transparent, sometimes uncompetitive pricing structure and is a marketplace mainly for amateurs. US futures trader Jake Bernstein has said spread-betting firms, user-friendly as they are, are the modern equivalent of the bucket shops of the early 1900s and make money in the manner of casinos. The Financial Services Authority has shown its teeth in regulating the industry, particularly on financial promotions.

You don't need a suit to deal in the city.

Our Share Dealing Service has a range of accounts which allow you to trade from the comfort of your own home or office via the internet, by phone or even by post.

Nominee trading
- Hold shares in electronic form for quick and simple trading
- Option to trade in international stocks
- PEP or ISA wrapper available for tax-efficient investments, where regulations allow
- Commission rates from only £9.95

Certificate trading
- Hold shares in paper form
- Make quick payments by debit card
- Choose between telephone trading, or selling by post
- Open your account now by phone

You can also track your portfolio online with up-to-date pricing and share movements. Call today or visit us online to find out more.

Talk to the experts

Norwich and Peterborough
BUILDING SOCIETY

0151 242 3571
8am to 4.30pm Monday to Friday
www.npbs.co.uk

8

Wholesale market participants

Overview

Wholesale markets cover short-term interest rate instruments, credit, foreign exchange and commodities, in both cash markets and derivatives. This is separate from equities trading. In this chapter, we will check out the role of market participants, which are banks, investors and interdealer brokers.

Banks

In City jargon, banks are on the *sell* side, which means that they sell to funds, investors and other customers, who are on the *buy* side. The banks employ traders in derivatives, money market instruments, foreign exchange, bonds and equities.

The traders complete transactions with traders in other banks, sometimes for their own bank, which is proprietary trading, and sometimes for a client, in which case they will sometimes use an interdealer broker (see below). Traders will specialise in a particular area. For example, traders will work on the short-term interest rates (STIR) desk, where they will trade repos, cash, certificates of deposit, forward rate agreements, and very short-term interest rate swaps. The products are all driven by interest rates and the dealers will try to arbitrage between them.

The banks described as first-tier, which denotes a large size, are the main participants. The second-tier banks are not so large. Third-tier banks offer banking facilities to corporate customers but are in their turn customers of the larger banks. *Hanky Panky* Bank in Lithuania may have a client that knows local fish farming and wants to hedge its business with derivatives. The bank will not have a foreign currency book so will offset the risk by working through a bigger bank.

The banks will have their own strengths and weaknesses, often for historical or geographical reasons. For example, Royal Bank of Scotland is strong in the freight derivatives market because it has a long track record in providing services to the shipping industry.

Investors

Investors who buy products are the *buy* side. They could be companies, investment funds, pension funds, hedge funds or insurance companies (see Chapter 15).

Interdealer brokers

Banks do not always use brokers, particularly in liquid markets. On swaps, banks deal directly with each other for about half the time but for the rest use a broker as middleman, according to market sources.

The interdealer brokers will serve mainly first-tier, sometimes also second-tier banks. They will trade in a number of products, including derivatives, money market instruments, bonds and foreign exchange. They used to be known as money brokers based on their involvement in the money markets. The interdealer brokers do not lend or borrow, or take a principal position. They charge a small commission and arrange the deal, much like estate agents.

At large firms, the individual brokers are organised so that distinct groups cover specific areas of the market. One desk is for credit derivatives, and another for interest rate derivatives. The desks are situated next to each other in an open-plan style. It enables brokers sitting at one desk to communicate with those sitting at another, which is useful because, for example, bond trades may affect credit derivatives trades. At ICAP, there is a desk for foreign currency and OTC foreign currency options, and products are separated into currency clusters, so, for example, a dollar-based cluster will include desks for repos and other products in dollars.

The brokers will shout across at each other across desks, which, coupled with sound from telephone speakers, creates a buzz on the trading floor. It is useful for one desk to know what trades are being done on another because they may have a knock-on effect.

Markets are becoming more electronic, which means that trading is faster and more automated and picks up opportunities that may otherwise have been missed because of the complex mathematical calculations dealers would have had to make under time pressure. The less liquid the market, the more likely it is that a voice broker will be used. For example, repos are traded electronically because they are a highly liquid market, but OTC options are less liquid, tailor-made products and do not lend themselves to this method.

In cases where full electronic trading is inappropriate, the traders in the banks will call brokers to complete a deal at a price. The broker will chase round other traders finding a price that will match it. If the bid-offer spread on a derivative product is 50–60, it means that traders will buy at 50 and sell at 60 in the market. The broker will seek agreement to a compromise price of 55 so that the deal can take place. The broker is paid on commission for deals, the amount reflecting how easily and quickly deals go through, which can vary enormously.

If traders use a broker, they can buy or sell anonymously, according to brokers. It can be useful if the seller does not want the buyer to know the price of a previous deal, or whether one was done at all. If it was known such a deal was done cheaply, it would set a precedent.

In general, electronic broking serves to differentiate between brokers. The larger firms have risen to the challenge but electronic broking has driven some of the smaller firms out of business. Trading in OTC credit and interest rate derivatives is just starting to go electronic. About 10–15 hedge funds and arbitrage houses do programmed trading. The programs are written on the basis of theoretical models of how markets should work, but the trading is entirely electronic.

In the chapters that follow, we will look at interest rate products, credit products, foreign exchange and commodities. Banks will trade these from one floor, although separately.

9

Interest rate products

Introduction

In this chapter, we will focus on money markets, which include short-term (up to two years) interest rate products, traded in both cash and derivatives markets. We will see how banks buy treasury bills and borrow cash from the Bank of England, as well as lend to each other overnight. We will focus on debt securities, including certificates of deposit, commercial paper, bills of exchange and floating rate notes. We will look at the repo market and government bonds, as well as interest rate derivatives such as forward rate agreements.

Money markets

Banks use the money markets for earning maximum interest on short-term money held, and also for raising money to keep requisite funds in accounts with the Bank of England. The large companies use the money markets to manage idle cash balances and use the bond markets for the longer term goals of raising cash or financing investments. The credit-rating agencies – most notably Moody's Investor Services, Standard & Poor's and Fitch Ratings – assess the creditworthiness of some of the money market issuers. Others are not credit rated.

Banks invest in treasury bills, which are short-term interest rate instruments issued by the government, and will need cash to pay for them. They will need to borrow cash if deposit holders are withdrawing more than they are keeping in their accounts. The Bank of England provides an estimate of the money shortage in the market, and publishes revised figures, up to four times in any day. It will lend money at the rate set at its last Monetary Policy Committee (MPC) monthly meeting, as discussed in Chapter 2.

On a hypothetical day, there could be £120 billion in the money markets, and a shortage of £1.55 billion, and banks may borrow from the Bank of England at 4.5 per cent. The Bank of England will have obtained the cash to make loans from government issuance of treasury bills. The banks in their turn will take the loans in order to pay for the treasury bills they have bought from the issue, and so the entire process is circular. Later the Bank will allow the banks to deposit money with it at 4.25 per cent.

Sometimes, banks do not need to borrow from the Bank of England because they will have been able to raise the loan more cheaply. But there is a finite amount of cash available elsewhere for lending.

Interbank market

One of the roles of money markets is to enable the government to change the balance of money that it holds in relation to private companies. If the government issues financial instruments such as treasury bills to private companies, they pay for these in cash that they withdrew from the banking system. But if it issues the bills to banks, they pay for it in cash that stays in the banking system, which means that the broad money supply is unaffected.

Banks use the money markets to lend each other secured and unsecured money spanning a period from overnight to several months, enabling them to re-access funds quickly to meet any cash demands from depositors. Banks with a cash surplus assist those with a deficit, and those without access to retail deposits may borrow in the wholesale market to fund loans. Once trading in a money market instrument is completed, the banks of the two parties arrange an instant transfer electronically through the Clearing House Automated Payment System (CHAPS).

The average offer rate at which banks will lend to each other overnight is the London Interbank Offered Rate (LIBOR). Each bank may offer a different rate and it is applicable only when the borrowing institution is in good financial health, failing which a loan, if it proceeds, will be on less favourable terms. The bid rate, at which banks will pay interest on cash deposited, is the London Interbank Bid Rate, known as LIBID. The difference between the bid and offer, which is the spread, will be small. LIMEAN (pronounced 'lie-mean') is midway between the bid and offer rates.

Some banks and wholesale counterparties use the money markets only to generate income from money on deposit or from cash flow. But many will use the markets for arbitrage, which is to take advantage of price anomalies arising from the same instrument traded in different markets. The instruments they use range from cash instruments to OTC derivatives such as swaps and options, in various currencies.

This is the interbank market at work. Brokers can play a part in resolving disputes, which is one reason why parties use them. There are risks. Secondary banks used this market to lend to property companies in the early 1970s, which led to the Secondary Banking Crisis of 1973–75, when base rates rose sharply.

Debt securities

Cash instruments

Borrowers can issue debt securities, including commercial paper, floating and fixed rate notes and certificates of deposit, through the money markets. Some securities are issued at par, which is face value. They include certificates of deposit, money market deposits, and interbank deposits of at least £500,000. Other securities are issued at a discount to face value. They include treasury bills, bills of exchange, local authority bills and commercial paper.

Let us first look at some debt securities issued by governments, public sector bodies and banks. The Debt Management Office (www.dmo.gov.uk) sells three- and six-month treasury bills on the government's behalf every Friday in a tender offer to banks. The T-bill, as it is known, is issued in sterling at a discount to face value, and the face value is later repaid in full, which means that the holder will have gained an equivalent to interest.

The T-bill is traded less than it was. Developed countries such as the UK and US are able to borrow for longer periods. This is cheaper based on the inverted yield curve that reflects a decline in bond yields as the maturity extends into the future. Issuance is consequently more likely in bonds. The euro bill is similar to the T-bill but is issued in euros. The Bank of England issues €900 million a month in three- and six- month euro bills, which helps it to fund euro liabilities.

The certificate of deposit (CD) is a liquid money market instrument distinguished by its maturity date and its fixed interest rate. It has the advantage of high liquidity in that it can be sold on before maturity if the lender needs money back earlier, but one broker has spoken for many when he described it as a bit 'yesterday's game'. A bank or building society issues the CD, which certifies that the CD holder has deposited the money with it. The issue is typically for at least £50,000 with a five-year maturity, and need not be repaid until maturity. But it has the advantage that it can be sold on if the lender needs money back earlier. If the CD is traded, market conditions will influence its value and investors may receive more or less than the amount originally invested.

The local authority bill is a discounted short-term loan. Local government bodies issue such bills in the money markets as a non-tradable instrument, with a maturity of up to six months. The market for these instruments is far weaker in the UK than in the US.

Let us now look at some debt instruments issued by companies. Commercial paper is a short-term loan issued at a discount to face value, representing a promise to repay money borrowed at the face value. The discounted amount over the period will be the equivalent to interest paid. Commercial paper is unsecured, and the minimum denomination is £100,000. On issuance, the loan has a life of up to one year, but it can be rolled over. It is a bearer note, which means that ownership is transferred only in paper form, and whoever physically holds the note on maturity receives the money.

The bill of exchange is a promise to pay for goods sold in a specific transaction. A bill is drawn up by a company that is owed money and is presented to the debtor company. The company receiving the bill signs it to acknowledge its debt, for which a payment deadline may have been specified. The company that drew the bill may hold it for eventual payment, or could sell it to a third party that would collect the debt. A bank, known as an accepting house, may have put its name on the bill of exchange, so accepting responsibility for paying the bill on maturity. Bills of exchange were originally bought by the now extinct discount houses. This form of debt security is not as widely used as it was.

The UK Debt Management Office (DMO), an executive agency of HM Treasury, or companies, may issue a floating rate note, a debt security that pays interest regularly in the form of a floating rate coupon, as an alternative to bonds. The note has a typical maturity of five years and the coupons are reset typically every three or six months, in accordance with LIBOR or another standard money market rate. If a bank lends at floating rates, it is useful to have borrowed likewise, so the cost of borrowing rises or falls in proportion to interest received from lending. There may also be a fixed rate note, which is a debt security paying interest regularly through a fixed rate coupon. The rate is higher than on a floating rate note of the same maturity.

These financial instruments have in common that they pay a return expressed as an annual interest rate or an equivalent as a discount to maturity value. Supply and demand drive interest rates. If there are ten borrowers and one lender, the rate will rise. The higher the counterparty risk, the higher the interest rates; the risk of the instrument is less important. It is corporate cash flows that determine how much use is made of the money markets, and when. If a local authority lender borrows on the 15th of the month and pays salaries on the 26th, it will lend the cash on the money markets between these dates.

Repos

The popularity of repurchase agreements, known as repos, reflects the over-whelming shift in the money markets from unsecured towards secured lending, where bigger sums may be borrowed. The trend is driven by the 1990s banking crisis in Japan, and recent banking problems in Germany, according to brokers. The repo market arises in money markets when the bank borrows money from the Bank of England and provides collateral, usually in the form of government bonds. The banks are sitting on large portfolios of mainly government bonds, which they need to hold for reserves, and which have low yields, but high collateral value.

The Bank of England will take the UK government bond, or any other type of eligible security, from the bank and will lend money against it as part of its open market operations (see Chapter 2). It will return it to its owner at a future date at a specified higher price. The collateral is almost never called on, but it provides the Bank of England with the security it needs, and it is typically 2 or 3 per cent more than the loan. For £100 loaned, the collateral may be £103, and the £3 difference is the *haircut*. The Bank of England cannot recall a default on repos.

A debate rumbles on about how far central banks in selecting bonds as collateral in the repo market should differentiate between risk profiles. Bonds issued by the Italian government currently have a lower credit rating, as set by the large credit rating agencies, than those issued by the German government. This implies that Italy has a higher chance of defaulting on debt than in Germany. But the European Central Bank accepts the bonds of both countries equally as collateral, which some feel should not be the case. The repo method is used outside central banks in stock borrowing and lending.

Through open market operations in sterling money markets, the Bank of England determines and implements repo rate changes. This is how the Bank can influence short-term interest rates, and it provides liquidity to the banking system. The Bank of England has introduced a reform initiative, phased in by June 2006, which encourages bigger deposits in accounts with the Bank from more market participants with the aim of improving liquidity management and, by implication, the system's financial stability.

The reform programme was designed, among other things, to improve the Bank of England's reserves and provide a deeper, more widespread level of protection if a systemic banking failure should arise, according to brokers.

In the old world, the settlement banks may have had to scrabble around to find money to keep their Bank of England account balance positive daily or face overdraft charges. They held as little as possible in end-of-day balances because the Bank paid no interest. The banking system targeted aggregate balances of only £45 million compared with average daily flows in the CHAPS system of more than £150 billion.

The crux of the reform was a new voluntary reserves system. Settlement banks are paid interest at the MPC's repo rate on their accounts with the Bank of England and need to maintain only an average rather than an end-of-day specified positive balance over a maintenance period lasting from one MPC meeting to the next. Individual banks will choose the level of balances targeted. These favourable terms may encourage others to become settlement banks, and will significantly increase the amount of money held on deposit with the Bank of England.

It is a way of taking money out of the market, and so repairing the high volatility of overnight rates on UK money markets, which it is felt may have impeded the development of the overnight interest rate swap in sterling relative to the euro, and has definitely left the Bank of England in less control of short-term interest rates than it would like. Some foreign banks, securities houses, corporate treasurers and money markets previously told the Bank that such characteristics deterred their own full participation. The reform will have greatly increased the Bank's reserves and should persuade more banks to open accounts.

Interest rate derivatives

Interest rate derivatives, most popularly using the euro, are the main instrument in the OTC derivatives market, accounting for around half the volume of its turnover in April 2004, according to a survey by the Bank for International Settlements (BIS). These derivatives enable companies that have made large borrowings to protect themselves against adverse interest rate movements, and are a major part of the money markets.

Interest rate FRAs (forward rate agreements) in April 2004 had the largest turnover among UK interest rate derivatives across the UK, above interest rate swaps, according to the BIS. But industry sources suggest that the market is starting to mature.

In Chapter 6, we saw an example of an interest rate swap in which company A borrows at a variable rate, company B borrows at a fixed rate, and the two swap the interest rate flows. Behind repo transactions, the second most prominent type of trade is the overnight index swap, where fixed rates are swapped for floating rates, with the floating rate set according to the Sterling Overnight Index Average (SONIA), or the Euro Overnight Index Average (EURONIA). The indices track actual market overnight funding rates, and are provided by the Wholesale Markets Brokers' Association (WMBA). They are a

Triparty services for securities collateral.

High on value, low on cost.
Two good reasons to

smile

Enjoy the benefits of a single collateral management platform for equities and fixed income. Consolidate your financing activity with Europe's leading triparty agent. Find out how we can bring added value to your securities business, contact Olivier Grimonpont +32 2 224 1133.

weighted average of unsecured overnight cash transactions brokered in London by WMBA member firms between midnight and 4.15 pm in a minimum £25 million deal size.

The FRA came to the market in the 1980s and is a contract between counterparties to pay or receive the difference between a floating reference rate and the fixed FRA rate agreed in advance. It is for a single forward period only, while the swap is an agreement for many forward periods. A number of FRAs are the equivalent to a swap.

The FRA is sold with a bid-offer spread and some banks will buy FRAs at one rate and sell them at another. Banks tend to prefer the FRA, which is OTC traded, to the future, which is exchange traded, according to interdealer brokers. The FRA is a medium with which banks are familiar, is easy to trade through the brokers, and is flexible in terms of the delivery date.

Banks with a low credit rating find FRAs expensive and instead look to cover interest rate exposures through futures, where the same institutional pricing is available to all the banks. The futures market tends to be aligned with the cash market through arbitrage. For more on futures, see Chapter 7.

The interest rate forward has been used less than the FRA because it is based on real money, which means that it has been recorded on the balance sheet. This type of contract, sometimes called a *forward for an exchange*, is when two counterparties agree to borrow or lend a fixed cash sum at an agreed rate for a specified period starting on a future date. Swaps and FRAs, when used for hedging, have been off the balance sheet, allowing a deferred profit or loss. International Financial Reporting Standards (IFRS) and UK GAAP are introducing a new requirement that all derivatives are accounted for at fair value on the balance sheet.

The interest rate option enables traders to speculate on or hedge against interest rate risk. The price level of such a contract on Euronext.liffe, the international exchange, is derived by subtracting the interest rate from 100. An interest rate of 5 per cent means that the contract is 100 - 5 = 95 per cent. Settlement is on a value per fraction of a percentage change in interest rates. Interest rate derivatives are priced in alignment with bonds, where the only way to boost the yield is to reduce the price.

Government bonds

Bonds are medium- to long-term debt vehicles. If the debt has a short duration it will be a note. When a debt security has a maturity of a year or less, it is a money market instrument such as a bill, or commercial paper. The global bond market has outstanding issues of US $35 trillion, almost twice those of the stock market at US $20 trillion, and is linked to the swaps market.

Of bonds issued, half are government bonds, on which we will focus here; the others are corporate bonds, which are covered in Chapter 10. A minority of bond issuers are supranational issuers (ie bigger than some governments) such as the World Bank, and US agencies which use the money raised to finance the housing market.

Bonds as an asset class are more stable than equities, although show much lower long-term gains. Pension funds (see Chapter 15) are the largest traditional investors because bonds help to match their liabilities more precisely than equities or other instruments. Annuity rates (see Chapter 22) are linked to bond returns. Mutual funds, central banks, and high net-worth individuals favour bonds.

UK government bonds, known as gilt-edged securities or gilts, are considered as risk-free as you can get. The government has never defaulted on its debt obligations. The DMO issues gilts so that the government can fund its annual net cash requirements and make gilt redemptions (the amount paid back to investors when gilts mature). Let me give you an idea of the amounts involved. In the 2005 Budget, the Central Government's net cash requirement for 2005–06 was forecast to be £40.2 billion, and gilt redemptions were £14.6 billion. Planned gilt sales would reach £51.1 billion.

Gilts are classified according to when they mature. Gilts maturing in 1–7 years are classed as short term; if they mature in 7–15 years, they are medium term; if they mature in more than 15 years, they are long term. There are about 50 gilts currently in issue, of two main types: conventional and index-linked. Conventional types, which account for approximately 75 per cent of the gilt portfolio, are fixed coupon, which means that they pay a fixed amount of annual interest. There are three older double dated conventional gilts, which means that the government may repay the principal at any time between the two maturity dates given; they account for only 0.5 per cent of gilts in issue.

About 25 per cent of UK gilts are index linked, which means that they are guaranteed to keep pace with inflation. The principal amount is increased if the Retail Prices Index (RPI), a measure of inflation, should rise, and the interest rate would rise accordingly because it is applied to the principal. On the gilt's maturity, the principal is repaid at the increased amount. Holders of conventional fixed-coupon gilts require a higher yield than holders of index-linked gilts to compensate for the greater risk.

About 1 per cent of gilts are undated, which means that redemption is at the government's discretion. Because these are the oldest gilts in issue they have low-rate coupons. The government has little incentive to redeem such borrowing while it is cheap, and investors can retrieve their capital only by selling to other investors.

Coupons and yields

Government and other bonds pay interest through a coupon, the annual rate of interest on the bond, and it is stated as a percentage of the nominal value. If a bond offers a 3 per cent coupon, it will pay £3 a year in interest for every £100 of nominal value. For UK bonds, it will be in two instalments. The coupon will have been decided by the level of interest rates in the market at the time of the bond issue.

On redemption of a bond, the bond issuer repays the principal sum at nominal value or par, which, in the case of UK government bonds, is £100. In practice, the bond will have started its trading life at par, or close to it (allowing for fluctuation of value in a one-week period before starting to trade). The market price may deviate from nominal value at any time in the bond's life.

The dividend yield that one receives from buying a bond on the secondary market can vary from the coupon because it consists of the return expressed as a percentage of the bond's price, which can fluctuate from the nominal value. The yield can be expressed in different ways.

The current yield is the annual interest of a bond, divided by the current bond price. It is also known as the running yield, flat yield, simple yield or annual yield. The higher the bond price rises, the lower the current yield will be, and, conversely, the lower the price falls, the higher the yield. The gross redemption yield, also known as yield to maturity, is widely used to compare the returns on bonds. It is the current yield plus any notional capital gain or loss at redemption. If an investor pays £85 for a stock that is repaid at £100 in 15 years, there will be a gain of £15 over the 15-year period, amounting to £1 a year. It is slightly more complicated than this as, in calculating the redemption yield, future interest and redemption revenue are discounted to today's value.

In the period between interest payments, interest accrues on a daily basis. A buyer of bonds pays not just for the financial instrument but also for any income accrued since the last interest payment. This is cum (with) dividend. If he or she buys it ex dividend, it is the seller who will have retained the right to the pending interest payment.

Gilt prices may be quoted either clean, where accrued interest will need to be added to the bargain because it has been excluded, or dirty, where an interest adjustment is made to the clean price. The bond issue may be timed so that capital repayment will coincide with anticipated income from specified projects. An exception is the undated bond, which is not redeemed.

Gilts are repaid at their nominal value and so the price moves towards this level as the redemption date approaches. This is the *pull to redemption* or *pull to par*. As a broad generalisation, as interest rates go down, bonds rise in value, and when interest rates are up, the price of bonds falls. But the closer bonds are to maturity, the less influence this will have in comparison with the pull to par.

Long-term bonds, particularly if undated, will be more exposed to interest rates because redemption is further off. If you think interest rates will go down, you should buy long-term bonds. The yields are generally higher to compensate for the greater risk, although this has not been true in the gilts market for several years. The gilt curve is currently inverted, ie yields on the longest dated gilts are lower than, for example, medium gilts. This reflects the weight of demand, particularly from pension funds, for long-dated gilts.

The mid part of the curve has traditionally risen in a hump. Fewer people save for 10–12 years because the consumer is uncomfortable tying up his or her money that long, but companies want to borrow for that period and so the yield has risen. The hump has now become historical because emerging economies have channelled substantial savings for that time period.

Duration shows how risky a bond is by measuring its price sensitivity to interest rate changes. It is the weighted average period until maturity of a security's cash flows. The longer the duration of a bond, the more volatile it is likely to be. To calculate duration, find the present value of annual cash flows (coupon payments) on the bond. Add the figures to the bond's principal, and divide the result by the bond's price.

A bond may often be callable, which is where the issuer, usually a company, may redeem it before maturity. If interest rates should decline, the issuer is likely to call the bond and reissue it at a lower rate of interest. The investor would then be left with money to reinvest in a world where interest rates are low. To compensate for this *reinvestment* risk, the bond will often pay a high coupon.

10

Credit products

Introduction

In this chapter, we will cover credit products, as distinct from the interest rate products covered in Chapter 9. We will focus on corporate bonds, international debt securities, junk bonds, asset-backed securities, zero-coupon bonds and equity convertibles. We will take a look at the fast-growing phenomenon of credit derivatives, and how the back office has struggled to keep up.

Bonds

Corporate bonds

Corporate bonds work in a similar way to government bonds, covered in the last chapter, But they have a risk of default and so pay slightly higher interest. For example, the yield might be 60 bps above that of gilts (bps are pronounced '*beeps*' and are basis points, each of which is a hundredth of a per cent).

Large companies issue corporate bonds as a way to raise cash without using up conventional credit sources. Small or medium-sized companies do not find it economically viable. Corporate fixed interest bonds can be secured on specified assets, which is reassuring to investors as an insurance against insolvency. They can also be unsecured, which is most usual for international bonds (see below), in which case they have higher yields to compensate for the greater risk. Restrictive covenants may be in place to set a borrowing limit.

Investors in corporate bonds face price risk, linked to interest rates, as applies to government bonds, and credit risk, which is the likelihood that the bond issue will fail to pay interest or repay the principal. The credit rating agencies try to measure this risk, which depends on the underlying company's financial status. The higher the credit rating, the less interest the issuer will have to pay, a principle of credit which applies also to short-term financial instruments. Highly rated bonds are unlikely to default, although the agencies do not always agree on their ratings. There is also liquidity risk on corporate bonds, and it is measured by the size of the bond's spread (difference between bid and ask price).

International debt securities

London has a large market in international debt securities, which are Euro-bonds. The Eurobond is a tradable bond with a maturity of at least two years, denominated in the currency neither of the issuer nor of the country where it was issued. The Eurobond market started in 1963 when the President John F Kennedy imposed a compulsory interest equalisation tax on interest that Americans took from stocks and bonds that foreign entities had issued. It led to a move of dollar-denominated debt business from the US to Europe. In 1974, the US requirement for this tax was abolished, but by then Eurobond business had already been established in London.

Large companies as well as banks, governments and financial agencies issue Eurobonds to borrow cheaply in a foreign market. They will need good credit ratings because this type of bond is unsecured. Some issues are more liquid than others. Eurobonds pay interest gross, which gives time for the gross interest to be invested before tax is paid. Eurobonds are listed on an exchange, which distinguishes them from loans.

The larger Eurobond issues are global, to high net-worth individuals as well as institutions. Investment banking methods are used to sell Eurobonds, rather than the commercial bank methods used to sell syndicated loans. A lead bank will run a syndicate of banks to underwrite the issue. A group of selling banks that need not be underwriters will retail the bonds to investors.

In practice, Eurobond issuers raise cash in the fastest and cheapest way, selecting floating or fixed rate, and currency accordingly. Taking the advice of investment banks, they will exchange the money flows for those that they really want through the swaps market. More than two-thirds of Eurobond issues are swapped, according to industry surveys.

Eurobonds tend to be held in book entry form by the international central security depositories, Euroclear Bank and Clearstream Banking Luxembourg; ownership records vary according to whether the Eurobonds were issued in registered or bearer form.

Junk bonds

The rating agencies classify some bonds as sub-investment grade or high-yield bonds, less flatteringly known as junk bonds. The bonds pay a high yield to compensate lenders for the credit risk of the issuer, just as banks lend on credit cards at a rate reflecting default experience. The bond is likely to have fallen to junk status due to deterioration in the issuer's financial performance. In May 2005, Standard & Poor's Corp, the leading US credit rating agency, downgraded General Motors Corp and Ford Motor Co, the car manufacturers, to junk bond status, which made it harder for the companies to borrow money.

Junk bonds have been used to finance takeovers, and have a poor reputation. They are not acceptable as collateral for repo trades. Pension and insurance groups may hold only a limited number of these bonds in their funds. But pooled investment schemes may spread the risk, and will potentially gain from the high yield. Junk bonds from two companies with the same yield may perform differently.

Asset-backed securities

These are bonds in the form of securities backed by ring-fenced assets, excluding property. The cash flows could be in finance or mortgage payments, for instance, and if they stop, investors will have assumed the risk. Asset-backed securities are often issued in tranches. The market is growing at about 70 per cent a year, according to City sources.

Zero-coupon bonds

Zero-coupon bonds do not pay interest in their life. Investors buy them at a deep discount from par value, which they receive in full when the bond reaches maturity. In this case, the bonds give investors predictability, but the price swings easily with interest rate changes and the market is fairly illiquid. If investors should sell before maturity, they might not make a profit. Gains are subject to capital gains tax.

Equity convertibles

Equity convertibles are bonds with an embedded stock option. The holder may convert the bond into a given number of shares in the underlying company. If the company does well, its shares will rise in value but its bonds will not do much, and the holder will want to convert. If the company does badly, the holder will prefer to stay in the bonds and, if it goes bust, bondholders are repaid before shareholders.

The issuer will offer a lower level of interest than on a conventional bond because of the conversion option. The option could be one of various kinds, including a US option, which you can exercise whenever you want, or a European option which you can exercise on maturity.

The exchangeable bond is where the holder has the right to convert a bond issued by one company into the shares of another.

Credit derivatives

The market

A credit derivative is where you pay a premium for protection against a counterparty default. It is an off-balance-sheet arrangement that permits one party to transfer a credit risk in an asset it may or may not own to a guarantor, without selling the reference asset. The asset could be a portfolio of assets, and so you can have a portfolio credit derivative, as well as a credit derivative.

The market for credit derivatives started to grow in the late 1990s and it is now doubling in size every year. Its range of users has expanded from bank lenders hedging their risk to include fund managers and insurance companies. Hedge funds have contributed to the industry's growth by their arbitrage activity.

Globally, the notional amount of credit derivatives outstanding rose from an estimated US $919 billion at the end of 2001 to US $3.5 trillion at the end of 2003, according to the British Bankers' Association (BBA) in its *Credit Derivatives Report 2003/2004*. London saw its market share decline from 49 per cent to 45 per cent but remained the dominant centre, well ahead of Asia and the rest of Europe and slightly above New York. In 2003, 64 per cent of credit derivatives were written on corporate assets. Only 11 per cent were written against sovereign (government) assets, down from 54 per cent in 1996.

Credit default swap

The single-name credit default swap (CDS) was the first credit derivative. In 2003, it accounted for 51 per cent of credit derivatives' market share, up from 45 per cent in 2001, which made it the most popular credit derivative, according to the BBA report. Traders used a voice broker to trade the CDS until mid-2004, and then, with the advent of credit default indices, the market went electronic, which improved its efficiency.

Banks are the largest users of the CDS, and use it to hedge their loan book. Hedge funds use it to short the market and in arbitrage. Investors in corporate bonds, including fund managers and insurance companies, can buy a CDS as an insurance against a default by the bond issuer. They will pay quarterly premiums to the bank selling protection. If there is a default, the buyer will give his or her bonds to the seller of protection and will receive their full value.

If an investor holds bonds issued by 50 different companies, the bank selling protection puts them into a basket, which it will protect more cheaply than the names individually. Protection against default by the first name in the basket is more expensive than against subsequent names. Greater correlation between bonds in the basket will increase the price of protection because the defaults are likely to be more and protection at every tranche level would be quite expensive. This would arise on a basket of, for example, 20 German banks.

However, if the basket has different industries and countries, the correlation will be lower, which will be reflected in a lower cost. The quality of names in the basket is another influence on the price of protection. The basket of bonds may be standardised, allowing *index* trading.

Back office issues

Some back offices struggle to keep up with product innovation in credit derivatives. A problem arises when contracts are non-standardised, or when the standards used by two parties differ. There is negotiation on which party's contract will take the lead during a lock-in period, which takes resources from other contracts, and has at the time of writing led to a bottleneck. Banks and hedge funds are in some cases each doing eight to ten transactions a day by email and paperwork.

The perceived way to resolve this is through the greater use of electronic trading platforms. Within the next two years, equity and commodity derivatives and interest rate swaps are the most likely over-the-counter (OTC) products to migrate to electronic platforms, according to industry views expressed in the PricewaterhouseCoopers/Futures and Options Association (FOA) 2005 survey. The technology providers have not yet quite come up with a solution for fast enough processing, according to Robert Benedetto, manager, financial services practice at consultant BearingPoint. In his view, the credit derivatives industry should learn from foreign exchange, a market that is similarly unregulated but where digitalisation and T + 1 settlement have made for high efficiency.

Hedge funds (see Chapter 16) are investing more in the front office, which brings in the money, than in back office technology, according to Benedetto. It is arguably in their interest to avoid progress in clearing up the backlog of credit derivatives settlements because they benefit from the arbitrage opportunities thrown up by the present inefficient market.

BearingPoint has noted in a February 2006 report *Alleviating the Credit Derivatives Crisis* that most statistics on the global credit derivatives market are developed through extensive use of participant surveys and estimates, not standardised data sources, and that data is lacking from large hedge funds. The report concludes that such poor disclosure increases the potential for inaccurate calculation of systemic risk in the market, creating a significant hurdle for market regulators in risk monitoring. The systemic risk is based on potential corporate debt default, which is the triggering event in many CDS contracts.

The Financial Services Authority has said it is working with the New York Federal Reserve Bank (known as the Fed) in monitoring credit derivatives. In February 2005, it wrote to chief executive officers of financial institutions active in the credit derivatives market and warned them about the backlog of unsigned confirmations, with some transactions remaining unconfirmed for months. In September of the same year, the Fed warned banks to get their back offices working properly.

11

Commodities

Introduction

In this chapter, we will look at how metals are traded. We will focus on gold, which is the dominant metal, and then turn to the London Metal Exchange (LME), which is where other metals are traded. We will look at oil and gas, energy markets and soft commodities, including sugar, cocoa and wheat.

Overview

The commodities market is at an earlier stage of evolution than the financial derivatives market. Industry wisdom has it that the financial derivatives market is 15–20 times the value of the underlying cash market in terms of value of trading, but in the commodity markets there is a reversal and the physical market is 15–20 times more than the derivatives. Over time, commodities are expected to catch up.

The main participants in commodity markets came from the energy industry until energy company Enron filed for bankruptcy in December 2001, and financial institutions started to become involved, providing deeper liquidity.

Energy

Energy is the largest market in commodity derivatives, and it covers electricity and gas contracts in the over-the-counter (OTC) derivatives market. The energy market has grown in recent years, partly due to the deregulation of electricity generation in the US and Europe, and an increasing range of energy-related financial instrument trades, according to International Financial Services, London. Notional turnover in London related to UK gas and electricity contracts was US $60 billion in the second half of 2003 and US $70 billion in the first half of 2004. Investment banks and hedge funds are now active in the market, as well as oil and gas producers and consumers.

The oil contracts traded on ICE Futures, Europe's energy futures and options exchange, are on gas, oil and Brent crude, as well as, from February 2006, West Texas Intermediate crude. ICE Futures was previously known as The International Petroleum Exchange (IPE) but its owner, Atlanta-based Intercontinental Exchange, decided that its subsidiaries and units would operate under the ICE name from 26 October 2005.

In April 2005 the IPE ended face-to-face, or open outcry, trading in favour of electronic screens and, in reflection of this change, reported record volumes in total energy futures and options at 4.15 million contracts in August 2005, and 4.18 million in September. It trades many more contracts than Nymex Europe, a rival exchange run by the New York Mercantile Exchange, which started a London open outcry operation in September 2005.

APX Power UK is a recognised investment exchange in London where power and gas contracts are traded. It is owned by APX Group, a provider of power and gas exchanges, operating markets in the Netherlands and Belgium, as well as the UK.

Metals

Gold

Gold is a basic store of value against inflation, depreciating currencies, revolution and war. It is an easily mobilised and virtually indestructible stock, and, if the price rises sharply, there is often a resale, which is why gold is historically less volatile than most commodity prices. Gold differs from other metals in that it does not have industrial uses but is mainly bought for jewellery.

London has had a market in gold for centuries. From 1717, it was on a *de facto* gold standard, and from 1816, on a legal gold standard. From 1934, the US adopted a gold exchange standard, requiring it to buy gold at US $35 an ounce. In recent times, the gold price has been less restricted.

In the 1960s, a consortium of central banks was dealing in gold through London in not always successful attempts to curb speculative price movements. In 1968, central banks replaced such intervention with a dual system of central bank dealing to maintain the US price, and free market dealing. In 1971, the US devalued the dollar and ceased its link with gold.

The majority of global gold trading is through OTC transactions, which are flexible and subject to the agreement struck between the counterparties, although there are also standardised exchange-traded futures and options, including through London terminals of the COMEX division of the New York Mercantile Exchange.

London is the main centre for the 24-hour a day OTC market, and the lowest transaction size is typically 1,000 ounces. Most OTC trades are cleared through London, and most major bullion dealers round the world are members or associate members of the London Bullion Market Association. Trading is done by telephone and electronically. The market is most liquid in the London afternoon, which is when it is morning in New York and both markets are open.

The reference price for the day's trading is a *fix*, which is done twice a day during London trading hours. There is a bidding process in which the gold price adjusts until orders are all matched and the price is *fixed*. From 5 May 2004, gold-price fixing ceased to take place at NM Rothschild and instead started to be conducted daily by telephone at 10.30 am and 3.00 pm, London time. There are five gold-price fixing members: the Bank of Novia Scotia-Scotia Mocatta; Barclays Bank; Deutsche Bank; HSBC Bank USA; and Société Générale. The chairmanship of the gold fixing rotates annually among its members.

The basis of settlement is delivery of a standard London Good Delivery Bar. The clearing process is a system of paper transfers, avoiding the security risk and cost of physical movement.

The gold price quoted in the international market is the spot price – for delivery during the two days after the transaction date – in US dollars per troy ounce. If the dollar moves, gold tends to move. *The Times* publishes price data for gold and other precious metals. In a table, the bullion price is shown at open, and at close, with the high on the day. Under the heading 'Data day', a two-month graph of the gold price, and of North Sea oil, is shown.

Other forms of transaction, notably forwards, futures and options, will be settled against a date further in the future than the spot settlement date. The forward or futures price is a function of the underlying spot price and the prevailing interest rate in the money markets plus insurance and storage.

Because London has a large amount of above-ground gold stock, forward prices will usually rise as the contract maturity increases. The forward premium will usually be quoted as a percentage of the underlying price. When there is a premium over the nearby price it is called a contango. Gold is nearly always in a contango because of the ready availability of above-ground stocks, which can be borrowed at low interest rates. If a price for delivery in the future is lower than for delivery nearer the time, it is a backwardation, which could happen during a price squeeze but is extremely rare.

Exchange-traded funds (ETFs), which we discuss in Chapter 16, are an efficient way of buying gold. It measures up well against buying bullion, which incurs cost of storage and VAT and is the prerogative of some City banks. In an ETF, you will buy units in a fund collateralised against a gold holding sitting in a City vault. In the past three years, ETFs have created an unprecedented UK interest in speculating on gold. They are derivatives listed on the London Stock Exchange, denominated in dollars, and tradable like any shares.

Other metals

Other metals are traded on the LME. It is where around 95 per cent of all futures traded non-ferrous metals in the world are traded. The LME provides futures and options contracts for metals, and futures contracts for plastics, which enable industry to hedge against movements in the price of raw material.

Of the six metals traded, the largest contracts are for aluminium and copper, and the others are zinc, tin, lead, nickel, plus two aluminium alloy contracts. There is also a metals index future. Futures contracts can be traded any day from cash (two days forward) to three months ahead; they can then be traded weekly, followed by monthly.

Since May 2005, two plastics contracts have been traded on the LME: polypropylene and linear low-density polyethylene. Both are monthly contracts, and in the early months, trading volumes were light, as expected. The LME will launch additional plastics contracts if these are successful and it also plans to test the market for launching steel futures. In November 2005, it was tendering for a price compiler as partner in establishing steel reference prices.

The LME provides three core services: hedging, pricing and physical delivery. The hedging activity of industry runs parallel to the buying and selling of physical raw materials. For example, a car manufacturer may use futures contracts to lock in the price it will pay for metal as a buyer. Once the futures position is financially closed out, the hedge will offset any adverse changes in his or her physical purchases or sales.

The LME says its contracts are highly liquid, and some can be traded out as far as 63 months. They are usually settled financially but, if required, they are all backed by ultimate delivery of the underlying metal or plastic. To facilitate this, the LME has more than 400 approved warehouses where metals and plastics may be delivered.

Trading on the LME is through open outcry, telephone-based or electronic systems. Only the 11 ring-dealing members (category 1) are able to trade by open outcry on the *ring*, a market that is open from 11.45 am to 5.00 pm. Category 2 members typically include large financial institutions such as ABN AMRO, HSBC and UBS. They can trade by telephone, which is a 24-hour a day market, or electronically via LME Select, which is open from 7.00 am to 7.00 pm.

A metals company wanting to hedge would select a member firm depending on the level of trading and access to the market it requires and based on its business model and internal processes. The open outcry process sets the official physical prices in metals and plastics for the day.

Stock levels at the LME are indicative of global industry supply and demand, which obviously can fluctuate. A labour strike at a new mine can impair supply of a given metal and so make it more expensive to buy. Metal prices ultimately permeate through all aspects of daily life from cars to the packaging of supermarket products.

The LME has seen trading volumes rise to 72 million lots in 2004, up from around 50 million lots in 1994. Trading is conducted in lots rather than tonnes. For example, each lot of aluminium, copper, lead and zinc is 25 tonnes, but nickel is traded in 6-tonne lots. Contracts are priced and traded in dollars, but can be cleared in sterling, euros or yen.

Occasionally a mess has arisen on the metal markets. Historically, it has tended to be for long-only positions. In the copper market, Sumitomo Corporation, a Japanese firm, reported a US$2.6 billion loss in 1996, because of the activities of a former copper trader, Yasuo Hamanaka. Subsequently, the LME brought in new regulations. When traders held more than 50 per cent of metal futures for the next day, they would have to lend back to the market at a set price. This was aimed at long positions.

Soft commodities

General

Manufacturers use soft commodity futures to ensure that farmers deliver raw material such as sugar or wheat at a fixed price when required. The farmers use futures too. The trader buys a future committing to buy a commodity at the given price, and if its value rises well above it, will almost certainly close the position with the opposite contract, which is committed to selling the commodity. By such trading before expiry, the trader avoids physical delivery of commodities such as cocoa, and may sell short.

The prices for some commodity futures are included in tables under '*Commodities*', a section in *The Times* published Tuesday to Friday. If the contract is not closed out, there will be delivery of the underlying physical, and the future prices are ultimately aligned to those in the underlying industry. But the *basis differential* – the difference between the futures price and the underlying commodity – will fluctuate during the contract's life.

Delivery months are quarterly. The futures price on the earliest of these months, called the front month contract, is closest to the spot price. It will be slightly more, however, to include interest, dealing charges, and, where relevant, the cost of storing the underlying commodity. If the gap between the futures price on the front month contract and the spot price became too wide, traders' arbitrage would reduce it.

Cocoa, Robusta coffee and white sugar futures are traded on Euronext. liffe, the international derivatives business of Euronext run out of London. They set global price benchmarks for the underlying physical markets and are actively traded by managed funds, institutional and short-term investors. These markets are much smaller than crude oil. These products are also traded on the Coffee, Sugar and Cocoa Exchange (CSCE) in New York in contracts strongly correlated to those on Euronext.liffe, and there are arbitrage opportunities.

12

Foreign exchange

Introduction

London has the largest foreign exchange market in the world. In this chapter, we will look at its history, the main drivers, and its participants, including dealers, brokers and investors. We will examine main currency combinations and transaction types, as well as settlement and clearing. We will profile a currencies analyst.

Global overview

Foreign exchange is an international market where currencies are traded quickly and exchange rates fluctuate rapidly. It is unregulated and it has no physical location, but business is conducted from financial market centres. Foreign exchange has a knock-on effect on other markets, including equities and bonds. A trader buying into a currency will often invest the amount in high-interest paying liquid securities.

The market is driven mainly by speculative flows, followed by trading from governments, central banks and companies. Foreign exchange, like derivatives, is used for hedging (see Chapter 6).

In the City

Foreign exchange is the most liquid of the financial markets in the City, and the largest. In 1979, exchange controls were abolished, which made it easier for companies to export money. By this stage, there were a lot of dealers working in banks, and the infrastructure was in place to do foreign exchange trading. The market in London expanded.

London accounts for the highest trade volumes in traditional foreign exchange markets, about a third of the total, partly because it has easy access to Europe and it can talk to the other major centres at different times of the 24-hour clock. London's biggest global competitors are New York, with around a fifth of trade volumes, and Tokyo. Behind these are the smaller centres of Frankfurt, Paris, Zurich, Hong Kong, Singapore and Toronto.

In the UK, average daily turnover was US $753 billion during April 2004, 49 per cent up on three years earlier, according to a recent survey by the Bank for International Settlements (BIS). Based on data excluding Malta and Cyprus, the UK accounted for 64 per cent of foreign exchange turnover in the EU in 2004, followed by Germany with 10 per cent of turnover.

In London, the 10 institutions with the highest level of turnover have a 61 per cent market share, and the top 20 institutions have an 80 per cent market share, according to the BIS. Four of the largest participants at the time of writing are UBS, Deutsche Bank, Citibank and JP Morgan. Other significant players are Goldman Sachs, Morgan Stanley and Credit Suisse.

The Bank of England oversees, but does not regulate, the foreign exchange market. It may intervene in it, either openly or through an intermediary, when the government or a financial authority wishes to influence exchange rates.

The participants

Dealers

Dealers operate in this business in much the same way as they do for money markets, OTC derivatives and bonds. They are traders in large commercial banks, which run day and night shifts. They buy and sell currency for clients and they take speculative positions for themselves. A dealer of one bank will deal directly with those in the trading room of another. They make money from the spread, which is the difference between the buy and sell price.

Brokers

Dealers may use direct dealing, which is when they deal without a broker, but this is a little out of fashion. As in the money markets, they may use a voice broker, who operates as a go-between for dealers, or electronic trading, which since 1992 has started to compete with the voice brokers, particularly in smaller transactions. In April 2004, 55 per cent of foreign exchange business was conducted through electronic platforms, consisting of 76 per cent of spot business and 46 per cent of forwards and swaps, according to the BIS. Most electronic spot trades were executed via automated order-matching systems.

The two major brokers in electronic trading are UBS and Reuters Dealing.

Electronic trading has increased the efficiency and transparency of the market, reducing arbitrage. But this trend has led to a situation where supply and demand no longer entirely dictate exchange rates, according to analysts. There is a new *liquidity mirage* by which some large banks promise at any time to trade a given amount of currency at a given price. The banks cannot get out of the deals, and it could put them in the position of holding what they cannot sell.

Investors

Investment funds do most of the foreign exchange business, and they invest real money. The fund manager may manage foreign exchange risk through a currency overlay programme, which hedges, or seeks to generate return for assuming extra risk, known as Alpha. If a company knows that it will receive a large US treasury coupon in November and takes the view that the dollar will go lower before then, it will sell it straightaway or take a short position using the options market.

On anecdotal evidence, the hedge funds do up to half of all foreign exchange trading. They can drive a currency further up or down than it would otherwise go, and it sometimes sends the foreign exchange market into chaos. On 22 September 1992, George Soros initiated his most famous transaction. His hedge fund vehicle, the Quantum Fund, took a US $10 billion short position in sterling on a bet that it was overvalued. The British Government raised interest rates to prop the currency but Soros only increased his position. The Bank of England eventually withdrew the pound from the European Exchange Rate Mechanism, and sterling plummeted in value. Soros made an estimated US $1 billion from his bet.

The central banks play a huge role as customers in the foreign exchange market, trading their reserves in a process known as *reserves adjustment*. They regularly adjust their massive dollar reserves, and so become significant buyers and sellers of sterling, the yen and euro, as well as dollars. They can trade anonymously through the BIS, which is a bank for central banks.

Sometimes, central banks work together internationally to keep exchange rates at an agreed level, as, for example, under the Louvre Accord in 1987. But this practice is less common nowadays. If a government practices intervention without cutting interest rates in support, it is *sterilised*, and is less likely to move markets effectively.

Companies are quite heavily involved in foreign exchange, although their participation has dwindled compared with the capital flows of speculators. A commercial risk arises if, for example, a UK firm is selling into another country and sterling becomes stronger, which makes its goods more expensive. The firm can hedge against the risk of currency fluctuations and it can speculate. In the 1980s, Japanese companies were involved in a scandal where they traded more in currencies than was justified by their business. Disgraced US energy company Enron had also done a lot of foreign exchange business.

Currency combinations

Traders focus on the exchange rate, which is how much a foreign currency costs outside its country of origin. The dollar is the global reserve currency. There are clear reasons. The US has the biggest and most liquid bond markets, and commodities are priced in dollars. In April 2004, some 90 per cent of all trades in April 2004 had one side denominated in dollars, according to the BIS. But many believe that, in 10 years' time, the dollar will no longer have this status.

At the time of writing, China, Japan, and some other Asian countries have an exchange rate that is formally or otherwise fixed against the US dollar, which gives them a trading advantage over countries with floating rates such as the UK. The Asian central banks have been buying US treasury bonds on the open market as a way to keep the dollar lower. It gives these countries an artificially generated advantage in international trading over countries with floating rates such as the United States.

The situation is sometimes offered as an explanation for the low yields of US bonds. The US has a deficit as high as about 6 per cent of gross domestic product in its current account, which is the balance of the country's gains or losses from buying and selling physical goods and services overseas. This deficit is matched by the supply from developing economies, much of which is generated by the central banks in Asian countries, and is unsustainable on historic precedent.

Normally, a large current account deficit would take the dollar into a sharp decline, with the result that US exports would become cheaper and rise, and US imports would become more expensive and decline, but in this case it has not happened, which some attribute partly to the central bank intervention and currency fixing in Asian countries.

Others believe that if China and others moved to a floating exchange rate, it would not greatly affect the dollar or bond yields because it is savings and not central bank intervention that is the main driver of change. One European investment bank takes the view that US bond yields are low because there is a new low-volatility era for inflation.

The euro, introduced at the start of 1999, initially in non-physical form, has enabled member countries to trade with each other directly without the need to exchange their currencies. London was able to increase its share of foreign exchange markets because transactions in sterling no longer had to compete with those in a variety of European currencies.

Currency traders see the euro as second in importance to the dollar, followed perhaps by the Swiss franc, sterling and the yen, and then the Australian dollar. Next in priority are currencies such as the New Zealand dollar and the Norwegian kroner, followed by emerging markets, and the less popular currencies such as in Arab countries.

Currencies may be expressed against other currencies. They may also be expressed against the dollar, but sterling is the exception and it is normal to talk of dollars to the pound. If liquidity is lacking, one currency will be changed not into another directly, but first into dollars, which are then changed into the required currency. The most traded currency combination is the US dollar/euro, according to the BIS.

An analyst's perspective

Chris Furness, head of currency strategy at 4CAST, a market analysis company, has information feeding into him from three sources: fundamental, technical and market analysis. Fundamental analysis covers how exchange rates reflect interest rates, inflation, speculative capital flows and economic factors.

Figures from the US are the most important, followed by those from the euro zone, including from individual countries within it, according to Furness. Japanese and Swiss currency data are sometimes important because of interest rate moves within those countries, which affect interest rate differentials.

The most important figure about 20 years ago was the US money supply, but it is now the monthly non-farm payroll numbers, which show US employment, according to Furness. Price data is currently significant and he also looks at the US trade figures. If there is a record trade deficit, the dollar will come under pressure, and if it falls, other currencies will rise, with bigger reactions seen when expectations are exceeded in either direction.

Inflation expectations influence interest rate expectations rather than the other way round. 'If there is talk of raising US interest rates, the minutes of a previous Federal Reserve Bank meeting could become important', Furness says. He believes that technical analysis can become a self-fulfilling prophecy in foreign exchange because of huge numbers of users in the market place. In his view, it has become indispensable in timing transactions.

Market analysis covers activity in each market, and indicates where the liquidity is. In early 2006, for example, there was major dollar repatriation related to a tax window by the US Government allowing US companies to repatriate profits made abroad at a very low tax rate. Furness says: 'This is partly why the dollar started to lose ground. When there is movement in one direction, the hedge funds and momentum players get involved, and the movement becomes exaggerated.'

Purchasing power parity (PPP) says that exchange rates will converge to a level at which purchasing power is the same internationally, so counter-ing inflation. It is the oldest theory of how exchange rates are formed, but, according to Furness, it rarely works in the short term. Economists say that an imbalance between exchange rates and inflation is driven by speculative capital flows seeking to make money from currency differentials and can last a while, but PPP works better over the long term. Governments take PPP seriously in the quest to keep their currencies stable.

Transaction types

When a company trades overseas, it must agree with its trading partner not only which currency should be used, but also whether delivery should be immediate or subsequent. To suit delivery needs, the currency transaction may be spot, or use derivatives such as forwards and options. Let us take a closer look at the choices.

Spot market

The spot transaction is the most common type of currency transaction. Two currencies are exchanged at once, using an exchange rate agreed on the day. Dealers quote a different rate for buying the currency than for selling it, and the difference is the spread. The transaction normally takes two working days for cash settlement.

Derivatives

There are a variety of currency derivatives, and they are traded on the over-the-counter (OTC) market. We will look at some below.

Forwards

Forward contracts in currencies provide for the sale of a stated amount of currency at a specified exchange rate and on a specified future date or within a given time period. If you will need dollars in six months, you can buy now in the forward market.

Let us consider a UK exporter to the US who does not know in which direction the exchange rate between the two countries' currencies will move over the next three months, or how far. To avoid the currency exposure, the exporter can, after completing its business transaction, sell his or her dollars forward and, after three months, receive a fixed sterling price for them.

The bank's role will be to take the dollars from the exporter at the three-month forward rate. Because it is due to repay these dollars after three months, the price that it charges now, the spot rate, will have to cover its own risk. General interest rate parity means that the difference between the spot rate and the forward rate equals the interest rate differential between the two countries over the period. The bank will usually cover its risk by a foreign exchange swap.

Of the US$753 billion daily turnover in the London market during April 2004, US$531 billion was in the forward market, compared with US$222 billion in the spot market, according to the BIS. The forward market figure includes forward foreign exchange agreement transactions, non-deliverable forwards and forward contracts for difference.

Options

Besides straightforward, known as *vanilla*, options, there are exotic options. They may be used, among other things, to trade the volatility of volatility. Among the exotica are barrier options, where banks *knock* deals in and out at various levels to make them more marketable to clients.

Let us take a hypothetical example. If there were €1.20 to the US dollar, and a client of a bank was to buy the right to buy euros at €1.25 to the dollar in six months' time, the cost could be 2 per cent of an underlying €1 billion, which the client could say was too expensive. The bank may instead sell a

€1.25 call option for three months, but to make it cheap, knock it out at €1.28, which would mean that the client would lose everything if the currency reached this level. Let us say that the client only made real money at €1.25. The return would increase up to €1.28, at which point the client would lose all to the bank.

Barrier options eventually started being traded in their own right, and volatility often overcame movements in the underlying currency, although there was a ripple effect on that currency. Channel trading demonstrates how, for example, the euro/US dollar variations, influenced by options trading, move within a narrow range, then jump out of it into another. Instead of a zig zag on the graph, there is a zig, a straight line, and then a zag. Each of the barrier trade positions will be hedged or dealt against by both sides of the transaction, which multiplies the turnover of the options markets.

Swaps

In a currency swap, a company may raise an amount in the currency which it can borrow most cheaply, and swaps the proceeds with the equivalent amount in a target currency. Behind interest rate swaps, this is the most common type of swap.

Settlement and clearing

On settling a large foreign exchange trade in London, the two parties make or take one net payment on a currency deal for a given settlement date. There is a theoretical risk of default, which is higher when the trade is between different time zones such as London and Tokyo. This is the Herstatt risk, named after a German bank that failed in 1974 with more than US$620 million of uncompleted trades outstanding. But the larger traders may be required to put up margin for trades, adding to it daily if their open position becomes riskier.

Banks provide clearing services. Clearing is through Nostro accounts. A trader's euro Nostro account will probably be with one bank and its US dollar Nostro account with another. In every Nostro account, traders can borrow against an open position but may not take an overdraft.

13

London Stock Exchange trading systems

Introduction

There are three tiers in the equity capital market infrastructure today: trading, clearing and settlement. They are integrated, but each performs a different function. In this chapter we will look at the main systems for trading, electronically and through the quote-driven market maker system. In Chapter 14 we will consider clearing and settlement.

Trading systems

The London Stock Exchange (LSE) controls two centralised equities trading systems. First, there is the traditional market maker system, which now focuses on smaller stocks, and is mainly provided for by Stock Exchange Automated Quotation Systems (SEAQ). Second, there is the electronic order book, which focuses more on larger stocks and is based around Stock Exchange Electronic Trading Service (SETS). The trend, led by the LSE, is to provide the option of using the order book in addition to the market maker system.

Market makers

Market makers provide liquidity and price formation in those shares in which they choose to make a market. They are wholesalers of shares and they may specialise. The market maker commits itself to providing a price and to dealing in a minimum size, known as normal market size or NMS, throughout the trading day. It has a responsibility towards the client companies in whose shares it makes a market, but also to brokers and share dealers. The firm makes

You'll Like the View

Client Servicing

Operational Compliance

Security & Audit

Performance Measurement

Marketing

Reporting

Get the ultimate view of your operations from prospecting to reporting

**Introducing Advent's integrated portfolio and client management solution—
Advent Portfolio Exchange®**

Leveraging more than 20 years of proven innovation, Advent Portfolio Exchange® is a next generation portfolio management system that completely integrates portfolio accounting, reporting and client relationship management. Using a fully relational database and sophisticated security and audit features, Advent Portfolio Exchange® can handle both your front and back office operations, all in a single solution. And that's a view you can appreciate every day.

Advent Portfolio Exchange.®
Ultimate Vision, from prospecting to reporting.

Learn More:
www.adventemea.com/vision
+44 020 7631 9240

Advent Software: Helping Investment Managers Improve Operations For Over Twenty Years

Since 1983, Advent Software has been providing reliable, trusted solutions to investment management organisations of all types and sizes throughout the U.S., Europe, the Middle East and Africa. Asset managers, hedge funds, fund administrators, prime brokers, wealth managers and private banks in 55 countries use Advent's industry-leading solutions on 60,000 desktops to manage US$8 trillion. Advent solutions improve operational reconciliation, help reduce risk and errors, and enhance client service, freeing investment managers to focus on what they do best. As the world's financial markets continuously demand greater speed, accuracy and efficiency, Advent delivers mission-critical solutions, helping our clients gain a competitive edge in a complex industry.

Advent in EMEA: Fluent in the Language of Investment Management

Widely acknowledged as the investment technology leader in the U.S., Advent is growing rapidly in Europe, the Middle East and Africa, with a network of offices representing expertise in seven countries: the U.K., Sweden, Denmark, Norway, the Netherlands, Switzerland and United Arab Emirates. With 15 different languages spoken collectively among our team, Advent is equipped to deliver support in your local language.

Most critically, however, we speak the language of investment management. We are a technology company that has focused exclusively on this industry throughout our history. Many of our staff come from the investment management industry with a firsthand understanding of the issues you face. A stringent validation process guides our product development process. We work closely and continually with clients to fully understand their business operations and challenges. The knowledge gained helps ensure that the technology we develop meets the needs of firms like yours.

The Investment Technology Leader

Since its inception, Advent has set and continually raised the standard in investment technology. Today, Advent technology forms the operational backbone for over 4,000 client companies worldwide, including:
- More than 1,800 asset management firms
- More than 400 hedge fund managers
- 8 of the top 10 global prime brokers
- 8 of the top 10 fund administrators, servicing over half of the world's hedge funds

Over 700 investment managers worldwide use our trade order management system, the most widely used in the industry.

London • Zurich • Stockholm • Oslo • Copenhagen • Athens • Dubai • USA
www.adventemea.com • info@adventemea.com

its money on the spread, which is the difference between the bid and offer price. *Bid* is the price at which customers can sell, and *offer* at which they can buy. A bid-offer spread of 8–10 means that one can sell to the market maker at 8p or buy at 10p.

Large market makers such as Winterflood Securities are liquidity providers, and are highly willing and able to commit capital. Most market makers are part of an integrated house, which is a different business model; the banks may view market making as part of a corporate relationship, and make a market in the shares of a company only because it is a corporate client. Such banks are responsible for very little dealing activity and the market dubs them *fair weather* market makers.

SEAQ is the quote-driven market for small- to mid-cap stocks, including on the Alternative Investment Market (AIM), see Chapter 5. It has not changed much since it started in 1985. Before SETS was introduced in 1997, all UK stocks used SEAQ. On the SEAQ screen, a yellow strip shows the most competitive bid and offer price for a given stock. Above it are details such as the previous day's closing quote and trading volume, and the NMS. On the lower part of the screen, *level 2* information lists every market maker in the stock, with its buying and selling price, which investors may find useful to compare with the current spread.

Procedure

Competing market makers display continuous buying and selling prices on SEAQ terminals globally. They set their own prices based on their anonymous proprietary position and their knowledge of order flow as well as supply and demand. If the market maker is approached by a broker acting in a proprietary capacity, it is not obliged to deal, but, if it does, its price will be firm subject to the minimum quote size.

If the broker is large or has a strong relationship with the firm, it may be able to negotiate a price better than the spread on SEAQ. But most brokers must accept this spread as given. Market makers claim they can offer brokers flexibility and immediacy of trading, and avoidance of the greater costs associated with order book trading, but critics say the system does not promote a level playing field and has high barriers to entry.

The broker must reveal to the market maker the whole size of any order for which he or she is seeking to transact only a part. If there were 10 market makers offering one NMS each at best price, a broker wishing to conduct business of 10 x NMS should reveal the full extent of his or her business to one market maker, who will price the business taking account of the size. The market maker need only quote for one stock per telephone call, and if it is quoting the stock elsewhere or has not yet changed its price following an execution in it, it may declare '*Dealer in front*' and not provide a quote. Market makers have occasionally misused this process.

M trades

If one market maker has dealt with another anonymously, or privately through interdealer brokers (IDBs), the screen price is altered. Trades between market makers are marked up as *M* and are published instantly. Such trades are rare because it means that market makers are *crossing* each other's trades, and the seller is offering shares at the buyer's price. The *M* trades indicate likely volatility; some traders will have waited for these trades and will try to deal at the screen price before it changes.

Market makers may use IDBs to balance the books. If one bought a lot of shares, it may unload some, perhaps through an IDB, onto other market makers. Market makers now prefer to use the order book for this purpose because it is more liquid, including for smaller stocks, according to the LSE. But this is less so for smaller stocks, where order book liquidity sometimes dries up, market making sources say.

Broker crosses

Broker crosses are where the buyer and the seller trade at a keener price than the spread. Institutional investors do it to avoid market impact. Many trades take place at mid-price, which is halfway between the current bid and offer price. About 200 institutions, broker dealers and hedge funds use Portfolio System for Institutional Trading (POSIT) for this purpose. The LSE once operated a similar order-driven mechanism for SEAQ stocks, but no longer; it claims the appetite has dwindled as the LSE has introduced order book trading for more securities.

Order book

SETS

SETS is used for trading UK FTSE Euro top 300 securities, which include all the securities in the UK's FTSE 100 index, and the most liquid in the FTSE 250 (for an explanation of indices, see Chapter 4). The system matches buy orders with sell orders automatically and, as commentators have put it, like a game of snap.

Market makers are not used on the order book, but they provide a service in order book securities for their customers through retail service providers (see below).

SETSmm

In December 2003, the LSE introduced SETSmm, which provides an order book trading facility for FTSE 250 stocks not already traded on SETS, some dual-listed Irish securities and now the companies included in the FTSE Small Cap Index and AIM 50. SETSmm combines order book trading with the liquidity backing of market makers, an approach designed to suit those stocks that could not go onto SETS because they were not always liquid enough to get a good pricing mechanism on a pure order-driven system.

Users of SETSmm enter orders on the book and trade with other users as well as market makers. Every stock has a notional minimum of at least one market maker but in practice at least two, and mostly five or more. The market makers provide two-way prices in a size of at least 25 per cent of the stock's NMS.

We will look again at SETS and SETSmm later in the chapter.

SEATS Plus

SEATS Plus (Stock Exchange Alternative Trading Service) combines an order book with market maker competing quotes, but unlike on SETSmm, there is no interaction between the two. The system is used for some stocks on the AIM as well as for those on the official list with only one market maker.

Retail service providers

The Retail Service Provider (RSP) network was developed by Merrill Lynch and other financial institutions. The RSP is the interface between retail brokers and the equity markets. Because its operation can be opaque, the RSP is sometimes described as a black box. The RSPs and market makers are mutually supportive.

Through RSPs, retail brokers execute small orders fast. The broker may keep his or her client holding on the telephone while the broker gets the price from the RSP, and if it is satisfactory, the broker can execute the trade immediately. But if the client wants to trade on the order book, the broker will place it and say: 'I'll call you back when it's hit'. Brokers use RSPs for the vast majority of the 10 million plus retail trades a year, according to market sources.

When asked by a customer for a price, the stockbroker will relay the request electronically to the RSP, which will send back the best price it will have determined, with reference to SETS, SETSmm, SEAQ and the PLUS Service, a recently established market making service (see below). The RSP is itself a market maker in some stocks to a size limit, beyond which it will refer the trade to its own market makers, which provide a service in both quote-driven and order book securities. Brokers choose how many RSPs they poll; it could be three or it could be a dozen.

Brokers may use different ways to allocate the prices quoted by RSPs, and not all are equally to the trader's advantage. A large internet broker is likely to have an RSP relationship with at least five or six market makers, and it will contact all of these for quotes, the most competitive of which it will relay to the client. The price achieved on dealing may be better than quoted. Other brokers rotate RSPs in turn on the basis of one per deal, communicating the price received to the customer. If you are a private investor, ask your broker how it deals with RSPs because this will affect the price quoted, the LSE suggests.

Regular traders on SETS and SETSmm prefer DMA (direct market access) to the RSP route. Like the brokers themselves, they make an entry directly onto the order book. It is the only way to place a limit order that is visible in the market. The LSE takes the view that the price improvement so obtained offsets by a significant margin the extra cost involved, although some day traders are not convinced.

Hubs such as the LSE's RSP Gateway, Proquote, and Royal Blue provide a central facility for routing quote and execution messages between private client providers and RSPs. In reaction to competitive pressure, they have reduced entry costs for RSPs and brokers alike.

Order book developments

Let us now take a more detailed look at the order book. The orders entered on SETS compete directly with each other. All market participants are given access to the same information and opportunity, which is unlike through the traditional market maker system. Spreads have narrowed, transaction costs have been reduced, and trading volumes have risen.

Traders using SEAQ have access through level 2 data to market maker prices but cannot use these to help their own trades because they cannot display their own orders to the market and influence prices, according to Stuart Paul-Clark, head of product management at the LSE. The SETS order book allows this display, he says.

If liquidity is defined as ease and efficiency of trading, SETS has improved it, according to Paul-Clark. 'You can press a button and trade a hundred stocks instantly at the lowest-ever cost.'

Investors in a SETS stock have discretion to place any trade *off the book*, a facility used mainly for large institutional trades, and RSP business. 'People break up their large trades and place them on the order book to get better prices. It has helped the trading volumes on SETS go up', says Paul-Clark.

To trade on SETS, a screen is required. The LSE publishes display guidelines and makes available *exchange blessed* data. The software providers offer their own screen formats, attempting to customise them with superior features. As on the SEAQ screen, there are two levels of information: level 1 provides the basics, including the best bid and offer, and level 2 offers more detail.

On SEAQ there are only a few market makers in a stock and level 1 can give enough information, according to Paul-Clark. But on SETS there are many orders, which means that level 2 information is useful to see the depth of liquidity, he says. 'It gives details of pending buy side orders and gives a better feel for how the stock is doing.'

Prices on the order book are more transparent than on SEAQ because they are based on orders direct from the market and not the market maker's decision, according to Paul-Clark. Dealers can conduct large trades for clients on SETS which influence share prices immediately, although they are not published until completion. This very transparency means SETS is not immune from manipulative tactics. Some traders have placed orders with the sole aim of influencing the share price and so paving the way for a larger trade on better terms. Trades may be reversed at the last minute. The order book enables traders to point a machine at the market for arbitrage or to feed in large orders piecemeal to reduce market impact.

Traders may put their money where the high volume seems directed only to discover that they had followed a red herring. It is reminiscent of Flipper, the legendary trader in the Schatz, a two-year government bond future, who placed large bogus buy orders which attracted copycat buying before he unexpectedly turned seller.

In November 2003, the LSE introduced iceberg functionality onto the SETS and SETSmm. The facility enables order book participants to enter a large limit order on the book and reveal only part of it at any time. Once this *peak* is fully executed, a new one will automatically replace it on the order book. This process of placing the large order in tranches will continue until the order has been exercised fully or a remaining amount has expired or been cancelled.

The procedure eliminates intervening orders with an impact on the price, a feature of tranche trading outside the iceberg system. If you placed a tranche of a large order on the book without using the iceberg facility, another large order could take it out, taking the price of the underlying stock to a new level, and another trader's business could be put through at a price inferior to that at which your trade took place. By the time you added your next tranche to the order book at the original price, the market would have experienced two price movements. The first would have been from the level at which your first order was hit to the new price that the trade generated. The second would have been a shift from this level back to your original price as you replenished your order. But with an iceberg order, the price would not have moved at all.

The iceberg functionality is discreet and trades are not stamped *iceberg* but they appear on the screen as an ordinary limit order. 'If the iceberg trade is in an actively traded stock like Vodafone you're unlikely to spot it, but in a less liquid stock, it might be noticeable', Paul-Clark says.

In a Worked Principal Agreement (WPA) a market maker takes a position in a SETS or SETSmm stock of a minimum size (8 x NMS on SETS, 4 x NMS on SETSmm) and is given time to trade it as principal to obtain better execution, with publication delayed until the end of the day; if the order is given after 3.00 pm, the next day is considered to have started. The WPA on SEAQ stocks is subject to a separate charging mechanism.

Publication is delayed on some block trades, which are large trades completed in a single unit, usually of 10,000 shares or more. In this case, the trade size must be at least 75 x NMS, or 50 x NMS in AIM stocks.

Auctions

The LSE organises auctions for SETS stocks, which has been extended to include SETSmm. They are open to anybody who trades the order book. 'Some might use the auctions to balance their books, and others to fulfil a trade that they want to execute', Paul-Clark says.

Every trading day, a pre-market auction takes place for each stock between 7.50 and 8.00 am (London time) which sets the opening price for the day, and there is a post-market auction between 16.30 and 16.35 pm, which sets the closing price. If there is sufficient volatility during the day in a particular stock, it can go into auction midday to establish a mid-price. 'If news of a hurricane hitting an oil refinery is out, market activity could move share prices a few percentage points and it could trigger an auction', Paul-Clark says.

In the auction, market participants can enter limit buy and sell orders, and the LSE automatically calculates and displays the real-time *uncrossing* price, at which the maximum volume can be executed provided a stock is crossed (ie a buy order is equal to or higher than a sell order).

The trend

The LSE has been moving stocks from the 20-year-old SEAQ market-making system to the two-year-old SETSmm order book, partly to meet demand from hedge funds that do electronic programmed trading to exploit arbitrage opportunities. The spreads on SETSmm are tighter and traders need not accept the prices on offer.

But SETSmm, like SETS, conducts trades at a quarter of the NMS, which is a limitation. Settlement is T + 3, which does not work for trades involving old-fashioned paper share certificates. Market makers can trade at NMS or higher, and can be more flexible about when settlement is required, which allows paper share certificates (see Chapter 4) to be used. Market makers can also trade with greater immediacy than the order-book system.

Angela Knight, chief executive at the Association of Private Client Investment Managers and Stockbrokers (APCIMS), has said that SETSmm has a high cost for retail investors because of the multi fills and slow execution time. She says that most of the turnover on SETSmm takes place off the order book and that, although top line spreads are narrower than on the market maker system, the spread has not improved after it has been adjusted to meet liquidity demands.

Robbie Burns, share trader and author of *The Naked Trader*, puts it like this: 'SETSmm can have very narrow spreads but not necessarily for long. The spreads can suddenly widen and you have to really be on your toes.' The LSE says that volatility affects less liquid stocks but is much lower for larger stocks. It says that investors should be spread-aware and increasingly are, and if the spread has gapped out, investors should either wait for it to narrow again or use a DMA product to put in electronic limit orders and narrow the spread themselves.

In an attempt to introduce greater clarity, the LSE and APCIMS jointly commissioned an independent review of SETSmm from the prestigious ISMA centre at Reading University, which was completed in February 2005. The review considered stocks traded on SETSmm in October 2004 and also in October 2003, a month before SETSmm was established. It found that the *headline* touch, the best bid-offer spread, was sharply reduced and that transaction costs were significantly reduced for all but the largest transaction sizes, where trades tended to be priced more individually. The review noted that order book transactions in all sizes had lower costs than the comparable sized trades done away from the order book. But the report acknowledged problems that order book trading posed for many market participants.

In Burns's view, market makers should be required to ensure a maximum basic spread of perhaps five points, to reduce volatility. The LSE says it continually reviews obligations and privileges of market makers, including the requirement to make continuous prices, and it has incentive schemes to encourage them to make tighter spreads on larger-sized orders.

Market maker developments

In December 2005, PLUS Markets Group, the holding company that owns the Ofex small companies market, set up in December 2005 the PLUS Service. It says it was reacting to the erosion of the SEAQ market maker system coupled with the movement of more stocks onto SETSmm.

The PLUS Service provides market makers and retail brokers with a quote-driven system through which shares may be traded independently of the LSE order book. The focus is on small to medium-sized companies. PLUS Markets takes the view that institutional investors and hedge funds may benefit from the drive towards electronic trading, but private client investment managers and brokers have suffered from its *one size fits all* approach.

The PLUS service is based on firm two-way prices quoted by competing market makers. During the trading day, trades are reported to PLUS by market makers. These are transmitted immediately to the market via the PLUS market data feed, providing full post-trade transparency. The system has no trade reporting fees, although these would be very small and not necessarily passed on by the broker to the end-investor. The investor will still be paying broking charges, and a potentially higher spread than through the LSE order book. There is a data charge for seeing prices that are going through PLUS, which investors will need to pay to see where they stand in comparison with others.

The future

The LSE order book trading system will inevitably become more powerful. The RSP has been forced to reduce the sizes in which it is prepared to trade, is making fewer price improvements, and is unlikely to remain in its present form. The market maker will play a continued role in UK markets because of its flexibility, speed of execution, and price stability, but will focus mainly on small stocks where order book trading liquidity can be a problem.

A Complete Front to Back Solution

Linedata Services Asset Management provides a comprehensive range of global front-to back-office solutions for leading buy-side institutions. Available as a comprehensive suite or individually, to integrate with in-house or third-party systems, our best-of-breed products include:

Trading/Portfolio Modelling
- LongView Trading: The leading, global Trade Order Management System which enables the efficient implementation of an investment strategy.

Compliance
- Linedata Compliance: Providing centralised and in-depth monitoring of pre- and post-trade compliance.

Fund Accounting
- Icon: The leading back office investment management, fund administration, valuation and reporting solution for all types of funds and all types of institution.

Transfer Agency
- Icon Retail & MSHARE: These adaptable, scalable systems fully cater for the demands of both retail and institutional fund providers of all sizes.

Hedge Fund Services
- Beauchamp: A front to back solution, from electronic trading to real-time P&L, portfolio reporting and ledger accounting, for the hedge fund industry.

• 800+ Customers • 1,100+ Sites • 30+ Countries •

Flexible Deployment Options
At Linedata Services, we pride ourselves on offering the most comprehensive solutions to our customers, both in terms of functionality, services and delivery options. The products can be deployed as fully In-House, Facilities Managed and ASP (Application Service Provider) solutions, allowing you to select the option that best suits your business today, and then reselect if your business needs change in the future.

LINEDATA SERVICES
Global leader in financial IT services

Linedata Services (UK) Ltd I Bishopsgate Court I 4-12 Norton Folgate I London I E1 6DB I United Kingdom
Tel. +44 (0)20 7360 1927 I Fax. +44 (0)20 7360 1972 I Email. info@ldsam.comv I Web. www.ldsam.com

14

Post-trade services

Introduction

In this chapter, we will focus on post-trade services in the equity and government bond markets, the main aspects of which are clearing and settlement. Clearing defines the settlement obligations of the parties to the securities transaction and assigns accountability. Settlement is when investors pay for the securities bought and are paid for securities sold.

Let us see how these services are performed and what happens afterwards, including the role of the custodian and registrar.

Clearing

Clearing is the link between trading and settlement. LCH.Clearnet Limited is the UK's central counterparty. It started in 1888 as the London Clearing House (LCH) with the task of clearing soft commodity transactions. In February 2003, LCH merged with Clearnet SA which, since 1990, had been the central counterparty service provider of Euronext, a multi-market stock exchange. LCH.Clearnet Limited is now the sister company of Paris-based LCH.Clearnet SA, and is the only legal central counterparty operating in the UK. The two companies are owned by LCH.Clearnet Group Limited, a holding company that resulted from the merger.

In its role as central counterparty, LCH.Clearnet Limited becomes the buyer to every seller, and the seller to every buyer for eligible London Stock Exchange (LSE) trades, and gives traders pre- and post-trade anonymity. Once the trade has been made, LCH.Clearnet Limited assumes any monetary and delivery risk and so acts as guarantor to the transaction. It collects a margin from the trading parties to make the transactions secure and has so far not had to tap its further resources of a members' default fund, valued now at £582 million, and a £200 million insurance policy.

Purging the paper

One shudders to think of the amount of paper that our securities and funds markets churn out daily: stock certificates, trade confirmations, renunciation forms, dividend cheques and more. This heavy reliance on paper in securities-transaction processing is an unnecessary source of high cost and risk that you, the end investor, ultimately must bear.

Just suppose for a moment that your next dividend cheque went missing in the post. Our postal system is not infallible; there is a real risk that the cheque never arrives. Nor would you appreciate a typing error that resulted in the incorrect dividend amount on your cheque, especially if it was less than your entitlement. These inconveniences are what we term operational risk.

Riskier still if there are stock or currency options attached to a distribution entitlement. The manual process of sending instructions to inform issuers of your elections for scrip, dividend reinvestment plans and currency alternatives remains a costly and laborious affair. A paper-based instruction from you to your bank and then on to the issuer, or its paying agent, could be open to misinterpretation and human error several times over.

These types of costly mistakes do happen because our industry has not yet fully embraced the electronic age. Despite moves over the last ten years to dematerialise as much paper as possible, more effort is required. Only by continuing to remove paper, will we have the means to stem the haemorrhage of avoidable delays and financial loss.

A history of removing paper

At CRESTCo, we have been firmly committed to the removal of paper from securities-market processing for over a decade. A case in point from 2001 was the decision by

Dr Tim May, CEO, CRESTCo
and Executive Director,
Euroclear SA/NV

British Telecom to undertake a £5.9 billion rights issue through CREST. The receiving agent used CREST to distribute the nil-paid rights in electronic form to the accounts of CREST members, who in turn could take up the rights on a Delivery-Versus-Payment basis. Over half a million pieces of paper were replaced by 30,000 electronic messages, saving the securities market tens of millions of pounds in processing costs, not to mention drastically mitigating risk.

More recently in 2003, we worked with the Bank of England to migrate all paper-based money-market instruments, such as Certificates of Deposit and Treasury Bills, from the now-defunct Central Moneymarkets Office to CREST. We delivered a cost saving to the market of about 85% by replacing the distribution and handling of physical paper with secure electronic book entries in CREST. Furthermore, under the new regime, new money-market issues can be created and distributed to investors in a matter of minutes as there is no printing to do. The move heralded a welcome reduction in risk, and equally important, brought with it greater liquidity and substantial savings for issuers and investors alike.

Automation paying dividends

Even the tax authorities are ceasing to use paper in some of their processing. In 2005, the Inland Revenue revised UK tax legislation, empowering issuers listed on the London Stock Exchange to distribute tax vouchers to securities holders electronically instead of in physical paper form. Thus, in a single swoop, issuers and their agents can now transmit both the dividend payment and the tax voucher via electronic means. Furthermore, this watershed development also enables you, or your bank, as a CRESTCo member, to receive cash or securities distributions entirely in electronic form.

We believe that CRESTCo is the first Central Securities Depository (CSD) in Europe to automate tax vouchers, and are encouraged to see that a growing number of investors and issuers are already benefiting from it. Not only does it reduce the manual administrative effort to issue and post cheques and vouchers, it eliminates the risk inherent in paper-based payments. We are highly optimistic that this electronic dividend-payment and tax- voucher service will be offered by many, if not all, of the companies in which you may want to invest within the FTSE 350.

Every vote counts

Corporate governance and shareholder protection have also been improved by the tangible removal of paper. As a shareholder, even if you only hold a minimal number of shares, it is your right to be informed of the company's performance and future plans. Likewise, you have the right to have your voice heard on matters covered at an annual general meeting or other company meetings.

However, when shares are held in physical form, companies must work through a chain of intermediaries to dispatch important informational materials to you by post, often including issues for which they are soliciting your vote of approval or disapproval. In too many instances, these materials arrive too late or with not enough time for you to form a considered opinion, complete the voting card and return it to the issuer's agent in time for it to be counted. And, sometimes, physical voting cards never make it to their intended destination.

CRESTCo's electronic proxy-voting service provides a highly efficient means for holders of dematerialised shares to vote their shares in a straight-through and timely manner. There is no paper involved. Company meeting announcements, the appointment of, and giving instructions to, a proxy, and the results of company meetings are provided electronically in formatted messages.

Moreover, there is a clear, time-stamped audit trail from the registered holder to the issuer's agent. This allows issuers and their agents to verify if a voting instruction was received and when. This is very useful as it is sometimes the only evidence available to determine if the votes were received before the relevant cut-off time.

Like other corporate-action initiatives within CREST, electronic proxy voting is now very much considered an industry standard. All FTSE 100 issuers are now using this service or have undertaken to do so. Volumes have also been healthy – in 2005, voting instructions received through CREST were 350% higher than in 2004, and almost 500 meetings were announced, double that of 2004.

In 2002, CRESTCo became part of the Euroclear group. Euroclear Bank, a Belgium-based company that has for years operated successfully in the settlement of Eurobonds and other fixed-income securities, has combined with the CSDs of Belgium, France, the Netherlands as well as the CRESTCo-serviced markets of Ireland and the UK. With this in mind, we are looking to extend electronic proxy voting beyond Ireland and the UK, specifically across all of the other Euroclear markets. Each of the CSDs in these local markets will explore the best way to use this technology. Furthermore, the European Commission's recent proposal for a new directive on shareholder rights, which aims particularly at the electronic facilitation of voting rights, is adding to this momentum. We may soon see the end of paper-based voting instructions.

Shaping a paperless pan-European market

As Europe strives to be more internationally competitive, its capital markets can no longer afford to sustain the costly and risky use of paper to process transactions. This is becoming increasingly evident as more clients look beyond their domestic market for investment possibilities. Cross-border securities transaction processing needs to be rationalised if we are to foster true European prosperity and sustainable growth.

Is this a Utopian dream? I think not. Today's investors are progressively freeing themselves from their paper shackles by insisting on greater market-practice standardisation, further consolidation of processing platforms and the universal usage of tried-and-trusted electronic message standards to communicate between the various market participants.

While CRESTCo is actively helping the UK and Irish capital markets to revolutionise transaction processing, as a user-owned organisation, we prioritise our service enhancements according to market demand. CRESTCo has assisted Ireland's drive towards dematerialisation by providing input to a consultation document which was published in 2005. Additionally, for the UK, CRESTCo has joined issuers, registrars and various trade associations as part of a dematerialisation reference group led by the Institute of Chartered Secretaries and Administrators (ICSA). This group is exploring the feasibility and market appetite of removing all paper-based share certificates. Furthermore, the group recently released a consultation paper that will form the basis of how best to proceed, should the market and the UK authorities want to do away with physical share certificates entirely. In parallel, a new Companies Bill, which contains new provisions to facilitate mandatory dematerialisation in the future, is progressing through Parliament.

The momentum is strong to modernise our industry and dispense with paper-based transactions. In addition to the work that we are doing on physical share certificates, we are also focusing on the dematerialisation of other instruments, such as gilts, OEICs and unit trusts. However, whatever we do, we do for the greater good of those active in both the UK and Irish securities markets. And we are responding to a groundswell of opinion from clients to remove as much paper as possible from the securities processing chain. By harnessing existing technology, we are making the management of clients' securities transactions easier, less stressful and safer. At the same time we are consigning superfluous paper to where it belongs – the dustbin.

LCH.Clearnet Limited plays a second role in clearing transactions, which it explains as establishing who owes what to whom. As a spokesman puts it: 'everyone owes us and we owe them'.

LCH.Clearnet Limited has a third role of facilitating netting, although it has outsourced the netting process itself to CREST, the UK settlement system. Instead of processing individually every transaction in the same security with a given broker due for settlement at the same time, it nets these amounts, leaving one payment due to or from the broker per security. 'This is where we really add value. Because we see both sides of the transaction, we can determine how much is owed to, and by, any given broker', the spokesman says.

Across Europe, LCH.Clearnet now clears some 70 per cent of trades executed on stock exchanges, 50 per cent of exchange traded futures and options contracts, 95 per cent of cleared fixed income trades and, globally, 100 per cent of cleared interbank interest swaps. In 2004, it was the central counterparty to over 1 billion contracts with a combined notional value of 350 trillion euros.

Settlement

Settlement is the point in a transaction when the buyer and seller exchange securities for cash. Until August 1996, the LSE did its own equities settlement, but not very efficiently. The 1986 market deregulation, known as *Big Bang*, brought much higher trading volumes through the late 1980s, which put extra pressure on the LSE's Talisman settlement system, and the LSE decided to replace it with Taurus.

The Taurus system was designed to bring about compulsory dematerialisation of all UK corporate securities. Critics said it tried to satisfy too many conflicting market interests. On the advice of two management consultants, the LSE abandoned Taurus in March 1993 and decommissioned Talisman in April 1997. At the LSE's request, the Bank of England established a securities settlement task force chaired by its director, Pen Kent, which recommended a phased introduction of more cost-effective settlement for UK equities, including the introduction of rolling settlement. CREST was proposed as a new settlement system for UK equities and bonds.

CRESTCo Ltd, the UK's only central securities depository (CSD), was capitalised in October 1994 and owns the CREST system. CREST settles money market instruments, bonds and equities, but not futures or other derivatives trades, which are settled between counterparties directly. By August 1996, CREST had settled its first transaction. At the time, all trades settled on a gross basis, that is, transaction by transaction.

In July 2002, CRESTCo, LCH and the LSE launched an optional netting service for LSE SETS (Stock Exchange Electronic Trading Service) trades.

Under the netting process, all the buy and sell trades in the same security from one firm are added or subtracted from its account and a single netted transaction is settled. Netting reduces the number of trades that settle by as much as 98 per cent. Investors are not required to use netting but most prefer it. The service is currently only available for UK equity trades on the LSE's SETS platform and SEAQ (Stock Exchange Automated Quotation Systems) Crosses for which LCH.Clearnet is central counterparty. CREST charges for settlement on a gross basis, which is for every bargain settled. Its charges have been criticised, but have come down and are well below the equivalent levels in much of continental Europe.

The LSE has outsourced to CREST the gross trade reporting to the relevant authorities, including the Financial Services Authority (FSA). On this basis, CREST needs to receive gross settlement trading information and so its netting role makes sense. Once CREST has netted trades, they are sent to LCH. Clearnet Limited as central counterparty. If the trade is from outside the UK, it is sent directly to LCH.Clearnet Limited, which does the netting. UK post-trade plumbing is idiosyncratic, but it undoubtedly works efficiently and cheaply.

The real-time process

Settlement takes place through CREST on Settlement Day, no matter how long the agreed settlement period, ie the time between the trade date and settlement date. Settlement is a real-time electronic process conducted on a delivery versus payment basis, which entails simultaneous and irrevocable transfer of cash and securities. Full legal title of the securities is transferred at the point of settlement.

Settlement in CREST is in *central bank money*. Cash movements are ultimately reflected in accounts held at the Bank of England, which are facilitated by appointed commercial banks serving as CREST *settlement* banks. Each settlement bank maintains a pool of cash resources with the Bank, part of which is reserved strictly for CREST-related payments.

CRESTCo clients each have an account with a settlement bank of their choice. Each settlement bank transfers cash payments on behalf of CRESTCo clients to and from the other settlement banks during each day. These cash transfers are made using CHAPS (Clearing House Automated Payments System) for payments in euros and the Bank of England's RTGS (Real Time Gross Settlement) system for sterling.

At the end of each settlement cycle, CREST will notify the Bank of England's RTGS system of the inter-bank payments that took place. RTGS will release earmarked funds that were not used and will allow the settlement banks to rebalance their liquidity before they restart the process.

Crest's settlement rate is around 98–99 per cent by value, but 90 per cent by volume, with failure usually arising because a broker has not received stock from its client. CREST can amend the consideration of a transaction within agreed parameters to achieve a matched trade. CREST has also established a *settlement discipline* regime consisting of matching and settlement standards, and if a broker breaches these standards, CREST may impose a fine or take other disciplinary action.

Safekeeping and custody

CRESTCo does not provide safekeeping facilities, but it offers corporate action and other custody-related services.

Some foreign banks and insurance companies deal with CREST through a local or global custodian. The role of the custodian is to safeguard the financial assets of its customers, process trades and corporate actions such as dividends and interest collections, rights offerings, scrip issues and takeovers. A custodian typically offers value-added services such as performance measurement, securities lending desks, fund administration, tax services and a range of banking services.

Registrar services

After settlement, CRESTCo notifies the registrar appointed by the security's issuer of the change in the security's ownership. Examples of UK registrars are Lloyds TSB Registrars, Computershare and Capita Registrars. The balance of assets held in CREST must be reconciled with the register four times a year.

Cross-border activity

Competing services

Investors usually choose to settle multi-market, cross-border trades in domestic securities through an agent bank selling cross-border settlement services, such as Citibank or BNP Paribas, or an international CSD (central securities depository), known as an ICSD, such as Euroclear Bank. The ICSD has a higher cost base than the CSD like CRESTCo, due to the multi-market complexities of its service offering.

The Fair & Clear Group represents four agent banks/local custodians, including BNP Paribas and Citigroup, which claim 80–90 per cent of cross-border equities settlement volumes in Europe. These banks help broker-dealers and other financial institutions access multiple markets for trading, clearing and settlement purposes. They offer a wide range of value-added services such as portfolio valuation and fund administration services.

Europe's two ICSDs are Euroclear Bank, which is wholly user owned, and Clearstream Banking Luxembourg, wholly owned by Deutsche Börse. They both provide settlement and custody for domestic and international securities and are interconnected by an electronic *bridge*, enabling a customer of one to settle with a customer of the other.

The agent banks may use CSDs and ICSDs to settle trades for their clients, or instead, complete the settlement of client trades on their own books. They are competing with these entities in providing commodity-like settlement and custody businesses. Each type of entity has a vested interest in how the settlement infrastructure evolves in Europe.

Fair & Clear has complained about the banking status of Euroclear Bank and Clearstream Banking Luxembourg, and of some local CSDs. The banking status is single purpose and enables the CSDs and ICSDs to offer credit and securities borrowing services to their customers to help them avoid failed transactions. CRESTCo does not have a banking status.

The Fair & Clear case is that the income earned from banking services helps the ICSDs and CSDs to compete with the agent banks for settlement business, and it does not allow a level playing field. The agent bank concerns are mainly directed against the sizeable Euroclear Bank, which was originally the owner of several national CSDs.

The Euroclear Board responded to Fair & Clear's allegations by restructuring the company in January 2005 so that Euroclear Bank was no longer the owner of the CSDs and Euroclear Bank's business was clearly separated from the businesses of CRESTCo and the other CSDs in the Euroclear group.

Among the 24 users on the Euroclear Board are two Fair & Clear members. Euroclear Bank supplies services to agent banks and buys services from them, which has given rise to a perceived conflict of interests.

Takeover talks

Clearing and settlement issues have influenced takeover talks and speculation surrounding the LSE over the last few years. In early January 2005, Deutsche Börse, the German exchange, followed up an expression of interest in the LSE with an indicative 530p-a-share bid, which was rejected on the claim that it undervalued the business. It was not the first time that then Börse chief executive Werner Seifert had shown an interest in the LSE. In May 2000, he had wanted to merge with the LSE to create a pan-European bourse, iX, but the plans were shelved.

Within days of Deutsche Börse's indicative bid, Euronext, a pan-European exchange, had declared its interest. In February 2002, Euronext had beaten off the LSE in acquiring the London-based derivatives exchange LIFFE.

Deutsche Börse said that if it combined forces with the LSE, the tariff structure for UK electronic order book trading would be cut by 10 per cent, with prices capped at that level for at least five years, and that it hoped for further decreases later. The Börse would allow LCH.Clearnet to work out a year's notice of its existing clearing services to the LSE provided that it implemented a *material* price reduction. If the condition was not met, the Börse would replace LCH.Clearnet's facilities with those of its Eurex Clearing subsidiary, at a 50 per cent lower price. The Börse would agree a long-term arrangement with CRESTCo for the settlement of LSE trades.

Critics found Deutsche Börse monopolistic in its business structure, and were uncertain about would happen after LCH.Clearnet's one-year contract expired. Some market participants expressed concern that the Börse would eventually force settlement of LSE trades through its own settlement subsidiary Clearstream. Euroclear, CRESTCo's owner, said that Deutsche Börse should sell both Eurex Clearing and Clearstream, if it was to take over the LSE.

Deutsche Börse said that Euroclear's own banking and settlement businesses should be separated, echoing the Fair & Clear Group's allegations of this nature made before Euroclear's restructuring. There was some irony in Deutsche Börse's accusation as Fair & Clear had directed the same allegations at Clearstream Banking Luxembourg and Frankfurt, which are wholly owned by the Börse.

Some shareholders of Deutsche Börse said its proposed 530p bid price exceeded the potential benefits of acquiring the LSE and that it should seek shareholder approval before going ahead. Under pressure from these investors, which were hedge funds, it was agreed that Rolf Breuer, chairman, and Werner Seifert, chief executive of Deutsche Börse, would step down.

The UK Competition Commission launched a seven-month investigation into the two bid indications. On 1 November 2005 it announced that either exchange could bid for the LSE provided that, if successful, it took specified steps to ensure the independence of the clearing service provider used. In December, Australia's Macquarie Bank put in a bid for the LSE at 580p per share.

In early November 2005, the LSE said that once the offer period was over, it would return £250 million of capital to shareholders and start an ongoing share buyback programme, which the City saw as a classic bid defence. At the time of writing, the LSE remains independent.

A European central counterparty

There is a clear need for a pan-European central counterparty, which would, among other things, reduce transaction costs and capital employed by users, according to a December 2005 report by Bourse Consult. Interviewees favoured consolidation between LCH.Clearnet and Eurex Clearing. But they were concerned that LCH.Clearnet might not be able to drive forward the consolidation process and that Deutsche Börse would not be willing to give up the significant profits it was making from Eurex Clearing. LCH.Clearnet said it did not see how there could be true consolidation within Europe's central counterparty infrastructure without bringing together LCH.Clearnet and Eurex Clearing. Interviewees in the report thought consolidation of settlement into regional groupings was as much as could be achieved.

In its business plan, Euroclear aims to dispense with the concept of cross-border settlement, so a CRESTCo member will be able to settle a trade with, for example, a Euroclear France member as if in the same domestic market, at domestic settlement prices. Interviewees in the Bourse Consult report supported the project, but were apprehensive about whether it could be completed by 2011, as planned. In the US, consolidation of clearing and settlement took 20 years, and that was in a single country, with a single currency and a single regulatory framework, the report noted.

Giovannini and Directive talks

The European Commission has appointed the Giovannini Group, a team of market experts led by Alberto Giovannini, chief executive of Unifortune Asset Management, to focus on market practice, legal and regulatory inconsistencies within clearing and settlement in Europe. The group has identified 15 barriers preventing efficient clearing and settlement arrangements in the EU.

Some progress has been made on agreeing standards to address these barriers. The European Central Securities Depositories Association, of which CRESTCo is a member, has developed standards enabling intraday settlement finality in all links between settlement systems in the EU, harmonisation of operating hours and settlement deadlines, and corporate-action harmonisation. SWIFT (Society for Worldwide Interbank Financial Telecommunication) has developed a common communication protocol for EU clearing and settlement, which addresses another barrier. But all new standards will be effective only if they are adopted across the EU.

At the time of writing, the European Commission is considering a Directive on Clearing and Settlement. Critics have said a Directive could have unwanted provisions, progress to date could be hampered, the consolidation and harmonisation processes could become more expensive, and that the regulatory authorities already have the power to address the main issues, according to the Bourse Consult report. But some acknowledge a Directive could instil greater transparency and force the government to take action to remove nine of the Giovannini barriers assigned to the public policymakers, the report said.

LCH.Clearnet believes that legislation will be needed to make a single European capital market a reality. The European Parliament's own report said that a rigorous Regulatory Impact Assessment, to be delivered in the first half of 2006, was needed before legislation was decided. The debate continues.

15

Investors

Introduction

In this chapter, we will take an overview of the types of investor operating in the City. We will look first at retail investors, including the size and market share of this group. We will turn then to institutional investors, including fund managers, insurance companies and pension funds; we will see how they allocate assets and what trading power they have.

Retail investors

The retail investor market in the UK is large, and many smaller stockbrokers specialise in serving their needs. Securities worth around £250 billion were held at 31 December 2004 for private clients of UK firms, either by the UK firms or the clients themselves, up from £233 billion at the end of 2003, according to the Compeer Private Stockbroking and Wealth Management Survey 2004. High net-worth individuals make up a growing minority. In 2004, US $30.8 trillion was managed globally on behalf of 8.3 million high net-worth individuals with over US $1 million in assets, and the UK has a 5 per cent market share, according to the *World Wealth Report 2005*, published by Merrill Lynch Capgemini.

By the number of trades, private clients have a significant share of the market. Let us look at the figures for agency bargains, which are where a client buys or sells a stock through an agent, with a principal, usually a market maker, as the counterparty. In 2004, 40.8 million agency bargains were traded on the London Stock Exchange (LSE) on all markets, according to Compeer. Private clients, trading through members of the LSE, accounted for 10.5 million agency bargains, 26 per cent of the total, and institutions for the remaining 74 per cent. In terms of sums invested, private clients have only a small percentage of the total, although they also put cash into pooled investment schemes (see Chapter 16), which is used to invest across asset classes, including the stock market.

Some retail investors buy shares and hold for the medium to the long term, while others trade over a short period. Traders can make money from stock markets when there is volatility. They can take short positions, benefiting from pricing downturns, as well as long positions to benefit from upturns. But in bear markets, they often make the mistake of hanging on to loss-making positions too long and, as in the market decline that started in March 2000, can lose a fortune this way.

Various gurus encourage retail investors and traders to make their own investment decisions. There are heaps of advice available from newspapers and magazines, and financial websites and their message boards, some of which is poor or biased, and some more valuable. Some private investors have followed their own investment strategy and profited from it. But most do not have the same information resources as professionals, and they may have limited understanding of company accounts or how markets work. The Financial Services Authority (FSA) constantly recommends that financial advice should be sought.

An investment club can be an enjoyable and interesting hobby, combining the chance to get together with friends and colleagues for learning about and investing in the stock market. It enables a group of like-minded individuals to meet on a regular basis, and everyone contributes an agreed regular sum, perhaps £30 a month, to an investment fund. This will finance the club's purchase of shares in companies researched and recommended by club members. Because investors have pooled their contribution, the club has bigger buying power; a broker will be more interested in a trade with £5,000 than one with £500.

Institutional investors

Institutional investors buy shares and bonds, as well as property, commodities, derivatives and currencies, spreading their risk across the asset classes to diversify their risk. They invest in private equity funds, which investment banks may run specifically to take public companies private, and in mergers and acquisition deals.

Institutional investors may be fund managers, insurance companies or pension funds, and we shall now take a closer look.

Fund managers

The fund manager runs retail funds such as investment trusts or investment funds. It may be an independent investment firm, such as Fidelity, or part of a bank or an insurance company. Insurance companies and pension funds use external fund managers to manage wholesale money because it enables them to diversify their risk, and to have managers specialising in particular markets.

Contrary to popular belief, conventional fund managers have far more trading power than the hedge funds (see Chapter 16). They can move prices by their buy and sell decisions, and by accepting or rejecting a bid for a company in which they hold shares, they may determine its success.

Fund managers, unlike some institutional investors, cannot invest in anything they like but are subject to rules on such matters as asset allocation and eligible assets. Some funds invest in large blue chips, others in small companies, some in the UK and others abroad. These boundaries are known as the fund manager's universe. Some fund managers are top-down, which means that they start with the global macro-economic view and, within this framework, select individual stocks. Other managers are bottom-up, which means that they focus initially on the stocks, and only then on the broader picture.

An independent trustee monitors the fund's compliance with its investment objectives, and managers have their own monitoring procedures and controls. The balance between equities, which are high risk, bonds, which are lower risk, and other assets should fit the risk profile of the investor, and a small amount will be kept in cash to cover any redemptions. About 37 per cent of assets managed in the UK are invested in bonds, and 46 per cent in equities, according to the May 2005 Asset Management Survey by the Investment Management Association (IMA).

Under new regulations from the UCITS III Directive (Undertakings for Collective Investments in Transferable Securities), an institutional fund manager will be able to use derivatives as an active investment vehicle, rather than only, as before, to hedge positions. Funds must meet UCITS III standards by February 2007. This means that funds may start competing with hedge funds in derivatives trading. Fund managers lack the operational processes to support OTC derivatives, and so may, as speculators, confine themselves to the exchange-traded products that some already use for hedging.

Other

Insurance companies invest premiums received from the insured to increase their reserves. Pension funds invest regular pension contributions from individuals and employers into funds.

The pension fund aims to make a high long-term return both to meet liabilities in the form of payouts to those receiving their pension and, if possible, to maintain a surplus in the fund. An actuary will advise the fund.

Structurally, the pension fund is a trust for pensioners, known as members, and the trustees that run the fund have a fiduciary duty to them. The trustee may set balanced funds targets over a benchmark index, or not to underperform the average, and may give higher targets to specialist funds.

Large pension schemes are self-administered, and the largest are often linked to former state-owned enterprises that were privatised such as British Rail. Smaller pension funds are managed by fund managers.

In the 1990s, pension funds were dogged by inadequate investment returns. Part of the reason was that companies had taken pension contribution holidays in the 1980s because stock markets were booming and the funds had been able to meet liabilities out of existing resources. There have been a number of pension fund scandals, which we will cover in Chapter 22.

In 1998, Gordon Brown, the Chancellor of the Exchequer, removed the dividend tax credit on pensions, which was a blow to funds. Under changes to accounting standards, pension funds have been required to account for future liabilities on a current basis, which means that they must have assets to meet them. As a result, some companies have had sudden large pension fund deficits.

16

Pooled investments

Introduction

This chapter is about pooled investments. We will focus on investment funds, including unit trusts and open-ended investment companies, how you should select them, and how the charging structure works. We will compare investment trusts and focus on some of their unique features, including gearing capability. We will examine split capital investment trusts and how venture capital trusts work, as well as real estate investment trusts. We will cover exchange-traded funds (ETFs), and the mighty hedge funds.

Investment funds

Investment funds are designed to maximise portfolio diversification. Investors may invest a lump sum or regular monthly payments. They will gain access to a professional managed fund with a variety of assets, so diversifying risks and reducing dealing costs.

Investment funds cover both unit trusts and open-ended investment companies (OEICs). The EU member states, including the UK, originally developed the OEICs to make cross-border investing easier. The concept was introduced to the UK in 1997 and, of its 1,986 funds, 1,216 are OEIC.

The OEIC has some technical differences from the unit trust and, unlike the latter, is a legally constituted limited company. For practical purposes the two products are identical for the end-investor. Most funds are likely to become OEICs because this type of fund is more flexible than the unit trust, and can be marketed cross-border. Some OEICs are conversions from unit trusts.

Unit trusts and OEICs trade at prices derived from the net asset value and are open-ended, meaning that the fund may create or redeem as many further units for a unit trust, or shares for an OEIC, as are required to meet investor demand. You can view any fund's track record over recent years, but, as the regulator-driven mantra goes, past performance is no guarantee for the future.

In the case of unit trusts, there are two different prices for the units in existence: that at which you buy, which is the offer price, and that at which you sell, which is the bid price. The buying price is generally more than the selling price, and the difference between them, known as the spread, incorporates any initial charges and dealing costs. The OEIC has a single price which is linked directly to the value of the fund's investments.

Income paid out from an investment fund is net of income tax. Capital gains tax is payable on profits subject to the annual allowance (£8,500 for 2006–07). The trustee of a unit trust (the equivalent for an OEIC is a depositary) is usually a large bank and simply oversees the running of the fund. The trustee of a pension fund sets targets. In a unit trust, the manager appoints the trustee, but in a pension fund, the trustee appoints the manager.

Selection criteria

The risk profile and management style vary widely on investment funds and so does the five-year track record. You can find details of a fund's track record in the magazines *Money Management* or *Bloomberg Money*, or on a website focused on funds such as Trustnet (www.trustnet.com). See Appendix 1 for some useful sites. Let us now look at two factors that investors consider in selecting funds: charges and investment strategy.

Charges

Charges on investment funds have a significant impact on performance. There is likely to be an initial charge, also known as a front-end charge, part of which is the commission paid to the adviser or broker who sold you the fund. The charge varies. For a few funds, it will be as high as 6 per cent of money invested.

On a unit trust, most of the bid-offer spread consists of the initial charge. The OEIC has a more transparent presentation based on its single price, and it separately itemises the initial charge on the transaction statement. In addition, there is an annual management charge, typically between 0.75 and 2 per cent of the value of the investor's holding a year. Other fees are between 0.75 and 2 per cent and are not part of the annual management charge. They cover administration, custody, audit and some legal expenses including for trustees and registrars, and are detailed in the annual report and accounts.

A useful figure for the charges on a unit trust or an OEIC is the total expense ratio (TER), which enables comparisons across the industry. It is a single percentage figure showing fees as a proportion of a fund's average assets. The

TER reflects charges in a way that many find more useful than the widely quoted management charge, although it excludes commissions paid to brokers by fund managers.

Under simplified prospectus rules introduced in September 2005, the TER comparisons are like for like because the calculation is standardised. This affects all UCITS (Undertakings for the Collective Investment of Transferable Securities) funds, which are those marketable across the EU and registered within each EU country. Other funds may calculate the TER by their own methods.

Investment strategy

The actively managed fund tries to beat the market. There is investing for value, which seeks to buy stocks that are cheap in relation to underlying assets, and for growth, where you look for stocks that have good growth prospects.

The tracker fund aims not to beat the market but simply to track a popular market index such as the FTSE 100. Investors buy tracker funds because they are slightly lower down the risk spectrum than actively managed equity funds. Trackers may vary in their investment return, even when they are based on the same index, due to differences in both the fee structure and the tracking method.

Multi-manager funds have a strategy of maximising diversification. There are two main types: a *fund of funds*, where a manager invests in a variety of other investment funds, and a *manager-of-managers* scheme, where a number of fund managers are each given part of the fund to invest in the stock market. The manager-of-manager scheme costs less because it instructs managers rather than investing in an existing fund. In either case, the fund's performance depends on the skill of the stock selectors.

Investment trusts

The investment trust is a quoted company that invests in other companies' shares. It pools money from investors but, unlike an investment fund, it is not categorised as a collective investment scheme as defined by the Financial Services Authority (FSA). It may issue different types of shares and own subsidiaries.

Unlike an investment fund, which expands and contracts in size according to demand, the investment trust is a closed-ended fund, which means that it has a fixed number of shares in issue at any one time. For every buyer of an investment trust share, there must be a seller. The trust can issue new shares, subject to shareholder approval, and it can keep its assets in cash.

The share price of an investment trust fluctuates with supply and demand and market movement, and according to the value of the net assets, which are total assets less total liabilities. On balance, investment trusts are slightly riskier than investment funds because their discount or premium to net assets may vary and they are usually geared, although to varying levels. Unless the fund management is considered exceptional, the share price will tend to trade at a discount to net asset value.

Investment trusts are less well known than their younger, open-ended cousins, and as at 30 September 2005, had total assets of about £67.4 billion, which compares with assets just short of £300 billion for investment funds. But investment trusts have a more adventurous image, and their unique character-istics and flexibility, including the closed structure and freedom to gear up (borrow), make them sometimes very attractive. They make up at least 10 per cent of the FTSE 250 index, and invest significantly in, among other areas, unquoted stocks, and so provide money for financing. They are owned half by institutions and half by private investors.

Investors in an investment trust who want to make a complaint may not have the same access to the Financial Ombudsman Service as investors in an investment fund. But they do have access if the trust was purchased through a manager-sponsored wrapper product such as a savings scheme, pension, individual savings account (ISA) or through a financial adviser. There is also access to the Financial Services Compensation Scheme (see Chapter 22 for details of both). Investment trusts can be self-managed, but in most cases the trust employs a manager, who is answerable to the trust's board of directors.

Investment trusts vary by the type of stocks in which they invest. Some aim to generate high income while others go for capital gain, or a combination of both. Some invest in large blue chip companies and others in the riskier alternative of smaller companies. Also contributing to the risk profile is the geographical location; trusts that invest in emerging markets are more speculative than those that stick to Western Europe.

Any gains made by an investment trust on shares are not subject to capital gains tax, but investors may be liable if they should sell the trust, subject to their annual personal allowance (£8,500 in the tax year 2006–07), unless it is sheltered within an ISA, personal equity plan or personal pension. The trust distributes dividends after a 10 per cent income tax deduction but lower and basic rate taxpayers have no further tax liability. Higher rate taxpayers will suffer an effective tax rate of 22.5 per cent.

Investment trusts, unlike investment funds, do not have trustees or depositaries. Instead, they have an independent board of directors to oversee the management of the investment trust. In extreme cases, the board might choose to take the management contract elsewhere. Investment trusts have the flexibility to do this because they are companies in their own right.

Most investment trusts are available through monthly savings schemes, for which the managers may reduce or waive dealing costs. They are sometimes promoted as a flexible way of investing, enabling investors to stop and restart contributions without penalty. Advertising of investment trusts is allowed only in the case of wrapper products, and investors gain from the cost savings. But there will be a stockbroker's commission on trades, and buyers must pay stamp duty.

Many investment trusts have no initial charge, unlike investment funds, and the annual management fee tends to be lower although it can depend on the sector. The spread is usually narrower than on investment funds, although it can be wider, depending on the number of market makers.

Inclusive of all fees to the investor, investment trusts, in common with investment funds, often fail to beat the market average. Because of gearing, the trusts outperform in rising markets and underperform when markets decline.

Split capital investment trust

The split capital investment trust is a type of investment trust that has more than one class of share capital. Usually, one type of share is for income and receives all the income generated by the trust, and the other is for capital gain. The trust will have a fixed life span, perhaps seven years, as compared with the unlimited life of other investment trusts. At the end of its life, its remaining assets are distributed among shareholders.

In the bear market from March 2000, split capital investment trusts were highly geared and they saw their share prices plunge. When one fund collapsed in value, others followed because a number were linked by cross-share holdings and the funds had high levels of debt. By December 2003, 26 of about 95 split capital investment trusts were either in liquidation or had suspended dealing. The FSA conducted its largest ever investigation into the split capital trust sector.

All the fund management groups under investigation were dealing in zero-dividend preference shares. Some agreed to mediate with the FSA and it released details of the case against them in return for their agreement to keep the details confidential. On 24 December 2004, the FSA agreed a final £194 million negotiated settlement with 18 out of 22 firms under investigation, with no admission on their part. It was perceived as a climb-down from the £350 million that the FSA had originally demanded, although two firms had declined to participate. The FSA denied suggestions that it had released the news on Christmas Eve only so the press would not focus on it too hard.

The sentiment in the City, whipped up by parties with a vested interest, was that the FSA never had much of a case but relied on its authority as regulator to steamroller firms into a settlement. But the financial services industry learned that it needed, among other things, to check prospectuses and promotional marketing literature thoroughly, and to record calls.

The FSA itself made changes to the Listing and Conduct of Business rules, most of which took effect from 1 November 2003. It ruled investment trusts could not invest more than 10 per cent in any listed investment companies that did not have a stated policy that they would invest no more than 15 per cent of gross assets in other listed investment companies. The company's key risks were to be presented more clearly, and the board had to explain to shareholders annually why it had made any investment manager reappointments.

From 1 April 2005, the chairperson of the board has had to be independent of the investment managers. Any director of more than one company managed by the same investment manager will not be considered independent. Only one employee or adviser of the manager may serve on the investment trust board, and it will be subject to annual re-election by shareholders.

Venture capital trusts

Venture capital trusts (VCTs) are quoted companies that invest in small growth companies and aim to make capital gains for investors. They have been described as a form of investment trust. There is very little trading in the shares and market makers may offer a wide spread. The VCT manager has three years to choose companies in which to invest and may meanwhile put money in cash, bonds or funds. The VCT must hold at least 70 per cent of its investments in qualifying unquoted companies trading in the UK. The balance can be invested elsewhere, including in gilts or large company shares.

Investors receive 20 per cent (40 per cent in 2004–05 and 2005–06) income tax relief on their investment in new VCT ordinary shares, to a maximum level of £200,000. There is no longer capital gains tax deferral on investment. But if you have held your VCT shares for at least three years, your future gains (and losses) are exempt from capital gains tax and your future dividends received are exempt from income tax.

The annual charges on a VCT tend to be higher than for conventional investment trusts. The least risky VCTs are large, do not invest in too many start ups, have relatively low charges, and have experienced management, according to industry sources. Investors may spread the risk by investing in more than one trust.

The VCT plans an exit from its investments through a stock market listing or a takeover. If the company achieves a London Stock Exchange listing, it may remain a VCT investment for five years. Should the VCT be taken over, its investors will be entitled to a cut of the payment.

VCTs may be bought directly, or though a stockbroker or financial adviser. The range of buyers has broadened beyond high net-worth investors, sophisticated investors and corporates. Independent financial advisers may be keen to sell VCTs because of the high commission structure, which is typically five to seven per cent. They have been known to highlight the tax break and the FSA has expressed concerns that the risks are not being explained adequately.

Real estate investment trusts

In late 2005, the UK Government said it would proceed in 2006 with the creation of real estate investment trusts (REITs). These were created in the US in 1960 and are now popular in Australia, Japan, Hong Kong, France and the Netherlands. They buy, develop and manage properties and, over the past 30 years, have outperformed most benchmarks. REITs must distribute most of their earnings as dividends to shareholders. They have income and capital gains tax exemptions.

UK REITs are expected to have gearing restrictions, and may have to invest partly in residential property, which should help the Government to supply more rental accommodation. The government is considering allowing property investment funds, or PIFs.

Exchange-traded funds

Structurally, an exchange-traded fund (ETF) is an instrument that combines elements of a unit trust and an investment trust. You can buy your ETF on margin, and settle using the underlying shares instead of cash. Unlike with a unit trust, there are no set-up charges, and anybody completing a trade will immediately know at what price. The first ETF in the UK was launched in April 2000, and was called the iFTSE 100. The product had already existed for seven years in the US.

The ETF trades like an ordinary share on the LSE. Each unit tracks the movement of an entire index or sector, which provides the full benefits of diversification through a single instrument. There are ETFs based on both equity and fixed income indices. An ETF usually pays a dividend, and its price tends to be at a small discount to net assets. The price can change at any time during stock market opening hours. Like a unit trust, the ETF is open-ended, and can issue an unlimited number of units to meet demand. Because it is based offshore, there is no stamp duty on units purchased. You can technically sell it short, but there have sometimes been problems with borrowing stock to deliver.

Hedge funds (see below) increasingly use ETFs. The appeal is that it enables them to trade an entire index in a single transaction. Hedge funds may have a long-short strategy which involves shorting a stock and hedging the process by using an ETF to go long on the stock's sector. At the end of June 2005, there were more than 390 ETFs round the world, listed on 31 stock markets, of which Europe had 139.

Hedge funds

A hedge fund is a specialist type of pooled investment that is free to invest in all financial instruments or markets, including high-risk instruments, and may employ gearing (borrowings). It may be either an entrepreneurial start-up operation or part of a larger group. The fund is often structured as a limited partnership, and it has unregulated status, but its investments will not be promoted to the general public. In the UK, the fund manager is fully regulated by the FSA.

Many hedge funds are registered in the Cayman Islands where there is lighter regulation. But some funds prefer registration in Dublin or Luxembourg for the European exposure. Some French banks, for instance, will register hedge funds in Dublin because they know that French investors want a regulated jurisdiction.

The fund may be managed elsewhere. In Europe, funds are typically managed from London because of the commercial clout that derives from being regulated by the FSA. London is the largest hedge fund management centre in Europe, and second in size only to the US.

Hedge funds aim at absolute returns, regardless of market conditions, and tend to do much better than conventional funds. They are run by ex-investment bankers and other specialist financiers who give up highly lucrative jobs to set up a fund, and who know enough about markets to exploit a sophisticated tool book of modern investment vehicles.

The hedge fund managers invest their own money alongside that of investors, and will usually reveal how much. They are attracting the capital of sophisticated investors, including, increasingly, pension managers who are using hedge funds as a relatively new way to diversify their funds in a way uncorrelated to their equity positions. The lesson of the market decline from March 2000 is that the fund can lose value sharply if it is overloaded with equities.

The fund managers use increasingly diversified strategies. The best known of these are derivatives-related arbitrage, which means making money by exploiting small available differences in price, and long-short equity funds, which involve, for instance, buying Shell because you think it will go up and shorting BP because you think it will go down, so you are sector-neutral.

A variation is fixed income arbitrage. The strategy involves trading two bonds, both of which mature after a given time period, in the same currency, with the same credit and liquidity risks, but with different yields. The trader believes that the bonds should have *mean reversion* and that bond A will have a declining yield and so a rising price and, conversely, bond B will have a rising yield and falling price.

The trader will buy bond A, which is to go *long*, and will use it as collateral to borrow bond B, on which he or she will go *short*. In this way, the trader seeks to make a profit on the yield and price differences between the two bonds in the belief that it will be temporary. The trader will not worry if rates rise or fall, but will simply want the gap between the yields, and so the prices, to narrow to neutral. The trade will make a loss only if the gap widens. In practice, a hedge fund may take 40 or 50 such pairs, of which some will go wrong but a majority should go right.

Hedge funds do very little of pure short selling, which has unlimited downside. They often move markets at sensitive times, including during the book build for a securities issue.

A hedge fund can fail as well as succeed, and it may be on a spectacular scale. Long Term Capital Management (LTCM) demonstrated the point with its high-profile failure in 1998. It was a hedge fund headed by John Meriwether, who had previously run the bond trading operations of Salomon Brothers. The fund was highly geared and used derivatives, taking positions in bonds. The mathematical model on which the fund manager relied failed to take into account the flight to liquidity in the debt markets after Russia defaulted on its sovereign debt in August and September 1998.

LTCM had theoretical liabilities because of its high gearing, on one estimate as high as US\$1.25 trillion, and the Federal Reserve Bank intervened to persuade banks to provide extra support to the fund and so prevent a disruption in the financial markets. Since the LTCM collapse, the industry has become a lot more cautious. There has been less rigid following of mathematical models.

In its Financial Risk Outlook 2005, the FSA said that some arbitrage strategies of hedge funds were becoming *crowded* and achieving negative results, and that, if investors should withdraw their cash because of the poor investment returns, there could be price volatility and less liquidity in the market.

The FSA foresaw that hedge funds might move into new investment styles in which they had insufficient experience or that poor performance might lead to 'riskier behaviour' by managers and more aggressive position taking. It found there could be conflicts between hedge funds and traditional funds under the same management and between investment banks and hedge fund managers.

The FSA considers as slight the risk of systemic collapse as a result of the failure of a single large and highly exposed hedge fund or of a number of medium-sized hedge funds with significant and concentrated exposures. Similarly, the risk of any liquidity crisis brought about by hedge funds being forced to withdraw from the market is low.

There is pressure from the market not to over-regulate hedge fund managers. If the FSA required funds to be more publicly transparent, an issue often raised, the risk would increase that other investors would copy their trading positions, and the fund managers would lose the power of surprise. It could impact investment returns and cause investors to withdraw money from the funds.

The FSA has established *relationship managers* to deal with the largest hedge fund managers on a personal level and is watching the growth of retail involvement in the sector, which cynical stockbrokers attribute to the departure of the more sophisticated investors from some funds once the returns have declined. The FSA aims to improve its own data collection from managers and prime brokers.

Prime brokers provide hedge funds with settlement, custody and reporting services, for which they may not charge directly. They earn their main income from stock lending, which helps the funds to cover short positions, and from cash lending, which enables the funds to take more highly geared positions. Institutional stock and cash lenders are more willing to be exposed to the credit risks associated with the prime broker than to the hedge fund, which is usually domiciled offshore.

Some prime brokers provide start-up services for new hedge funds, including introductions to potential investors. They will help in implementing systems, gaining regulatory approval, and other areas. There are about 20 prime brokers, and, according to bankers, their future is under threat from moves to remove their intermediary role in stock lending by use of online networks and restrictions on shorting across continents.

Some large hedge fund managers may be subject to US as well as UK legislation. From February 2006, non-US hedge fund managers based anywhere with more than 14 US clients – regardless of the amount of assets under management – have been required to register with the US Securities & Exchange Commission (SEC). The move was in part a response to some fraudulent activity against retail investors by some of the smaller US hedge funds. Some managers resented this development, which meant that they had to get to grips with the detailed SEC rule book on top of FSA requirements. UK lawyers fear that the move, in time, could increase the SEC's reach and the severity of its oversight and rules for hedge funds and/or their managers.

Funds that prevent clients from redeeming their capital for two years or more will be exempt from US registration and some funds have increased their lock-up period, so that they exceed two years. Some funds considered pruning back their US client base, to keep within the maximum 14 investors permitted. US hedge fund managers with 15 or more clients but with less than US $25 million of assets under management will be exempt from SEC registration, although they will be subject to individual state regulation.

No doubt helped by the sensitivity with which they are regulated, hedge funds remain one of the City's greatest growth stories, providing liquidity and making the financial system more efficient. More than two-thirds of all European hedge fund managers are based in London. The funds have started attracting medium- to long-term investors who want to diversify their portfolios. The funds have shown that they can preserve investors' capital and achieve a real return, which is more than conventional equities investment has achieved across a span of recent years. Funds of funds, which invest in a variety of hedge funds, provide diversification, but not the same opportunities for outperformance.

One manager told me that he would not be surprised if, in ten years' time, institutional investors would put 10–15 per cent of their money into hedge funds. But every hedge fund has a different approach and managers will need to select carefully, he said.

17

Information merry-go-round

Introduction

The merry-go-round of information between listed companies, analysts, strategists and journalists is the basis on which the City grows and flourishes. In recent years, the regulations have tightened up to combat abuse of this information, but unofficial channels remain. In this chapter, we will examine how the communications process really works. We will highlight the main players and how they work together, including analysts, PR professionals, journalists and tipsters. We will focus on corporate information flow.

The analyst

Fundamental analyst

The analyst focuses on the dynamics of particular markets and makes trading and investment recommendations. He or she builds up an eclectic mix of analytical tools combined with subconscious thinking. The underlying aim is to understand the discount rate curve, which represents the market's expectations for interest rates projected into the future. This curve determines the average annual return, or yield, on bonds and other financial instruments. The analyst attempts to make an informed guess as to how it will behave. The prices of all financial instruments are strongly influenced by this unseen curve and all financial instruments trade around it, like gravity.

Pure expectation theory has it that the discount curve at the front end is an expression of projected rates from the Bank of England. The theory of market segmentation explains the longer end of the curve as reflecting interest rates focused on particular maturities. Such theories are never the full truth.

The analysts that focus on the stock market are the ones most likely to come to public attention, through media exposure. In the 1970s, stock market analysts were backroom boys in the stock broking community. They were better educated than their colleagues on the sales desk but less well remunerated. They were producing learned research and statistics and did not have to get their hands dirty selling shares to clients. Subsequently, with market deregulation, banks started acquiring stockbrokers, and analysts started playing a participating role in the marketing of new issues and sales of stocks while continuing their focus on research, which meant longer working hours. The work of analysts today is of value to various banking activities, including investment banking, trading and sales. An analyst typically follows six or seven large companies in a sector and backs up the salespeople with his or her specialist research.

Analysts often understand the specifics of the businesses covered, but less well than they should. Anecdotal evidence suggests that less than a quarter of them are qualified accountants. But they will have to consider company reports and try to forecast the future of a company. They indulge in informed guesswork which puts them, some would say, only a few steps ahead of tarot card readers. Even if they have worked in the industry they cover, their knowledge soon becomes outdated, and may not be equally applicable to every company. Analysts are outsiders looking in.

The analyst channels efforts into forecasting the ratios valued most in the City such as the P/E, earnings per share and discounted cash flow calculations (see Chapter 4). Fund managers have their own buy-side analysts coming up with the same sort of figures, but with no eye to selling shares or assisting investment banking interests. A company's basic figures may be culled from annual or half-year results. All listed companies in the EU have used International Financial Reporting Standards (IFRS) in their accounts since 1 January 2005, and this harmonisation enables comparability across Europe (see Chapter 19).

Once they have crunched the numbers, analysts prepare their reports. In the early days of IFRS, industry sources believed that analysts did not always make effective comparisons of reconciling accounting figures under IFRS with those of the previous year's published accounts. Regulators expressed fears that some information had not been revealed, whether by analysts or the companies themselves. (See also Chapter 18.)

Even in today's regulatory climate which is sensitive to bias and conflicts of interests, the hidden agenda remains that analysts make *buy*, rather than *hold* or *sell*, recommendations on most stocks because they are scared of upsetting the companies, some of which may be, or become, clients of their employer's lucrative investment banking division.

If listed companies give analysts a selective briefing or lead, they could be in breach of the part of the listing rules that deals with price-sensitive information and selective disclosure. The Listing Rules, issued by the UK Listing Authority, part of the Financial Services Authority (FSA), say that information that, if made public, could have a significant effect on the share price, must be announced to the market without delay. To stick to the rules, companies dole out the same bland information to analysts. Sell-side analysts who stumble on new information, which is what fund managers really want to hear, may have problems communicating it to their clients. Not all communication is official and analysts give big clients the best service they can.

Institutional investors know how to read between the lines, and perhaps glean from a telephone conversation with an analyst something extra. In keeping with this environment, fund managers rate analysts on quality of research as well as on forecasting record. But experience shows that an analyst who consistently makes ludicrous forecasts may not be taken seriously by salespeople within the analyst's bank.

The danger is when an analyst's report intended for the professionals gets into the hands of private investors, who may make the mistake of taking it too literally. Another danger is that, by this stage, it will probably be out of date. Research notes can need updating within hours or even minutes.

The Spitzer impact

The Spitzer settlement of April 2003 in the US arose because of the conflict of interests between research recommendations and investment banking activity from within the same firm. New York Attorney General Elliot Spitzer found that Henry Blodget, a Merrill Lynch internet company analyst, had in private emails disparaged an internet stock that he was recommending to clients. Spitzer found other instances of biased recommendations across the industry.

Ten leading global investment banks settled the matter with the Securities & Exchange Commission, the New York Stock Exchange, the National Association of Securities Dealers and with Spitzer. As part of the redress, the banks agreed to amend their practices. They would physically separate research and investment banking departments to prevent the passing of information. Senior management would decide the research department's budget without input from investment banking. Research analysts could no longer be compensated in a way that reflected investment banking revenues. Investment banking was to have no part in decisions on company coverage, and analysts were prohibited from participating in new business pitches and road shows.

The firms had to have firewalls that restricted interaction between research and investment banking. They would provide independent research to ensure that individual investors had access to objective investment advice. Each firm was to make its analysts' historical ratings and target forecasts publicly available. The firms entered into a voluntary agreement to restrict *spinning* – the allocation of securities in hot IPOs to certain company executives and directors.

The scandal focused on a hardly new phenomenon. The cosy cooperation between research teams and corporate finance has worked in bull markets, but there is a tendency for it to be exposed when markets suffer a downturn. There is a widespread feeling that the Spitzer settlement was politically motivated, and did not address the heart of the problem. Understandably, ex-investment bankers, academics and independent commentators have felt able to voice criticisms publicly more than those who held current positions in investment banking.

However it was criticised, the Spitzer settlement has set an international agenda. On both sides of the Atlantic, investment banks and brokers have been forced to reorganise their working arrangements to ensure greater segregation between analysts and corporate financiers. In early 2004, the FSA issued guidelines requiring those firms that held out investment research as objective to establish a policy for managing conflicts of interest. Significant in these are Chinese walls, which create a not always physical divide between analysts and investment banking. In mid-2004, the FSA introduced two new rules in which it narrowed the circumstances in which firms could knowingly deal ahead of published investment research, and required them to make it clear to clients whether the research was impartial.

In his latest book *The Greed Merchants*, published in May 2005, ex-investment banker Philip Augar said that because Spitzer and other regulators had allowed the banks to retain their business model, they appeared to have tackled only the symptoms and not the cause of the problem. Economist John Kay in an article in *The Financial Times* of 12 April 2005 said that there should be less equity research, of higher quality, and focused on strategic position and market position rather than earnings guidance and market tittle-tattle.

Technical analysis

Technical analysts tend to work independently or for large financial institutions and are far fewer than their fundamental counterparts. The technical analyst focuses on price movements, and makes forecasts. The cornerstone of technical analysis is trend theory, which is rooted in the idea of crowd psychology. If the share price is rising, everyone tries to jump on the bandwagon, establishing an up trend. On the same principle, panic selling can start a down trend. Technical analysts believe that the trend will stay in force until it is unequivocally broken.

Trend theory originated with Dow Theory, which financial journalist Charles Dow started developing in the late 19th century after he noticed that stocks tended to rise or fall together. Dow Theory says that the share price reflects *everything* that is known about a stock and that there are three trends in the stock market – primary, secondary and tertiary – and they may all be operating simultaneously. One way in which a trend will end is when the share price fluctuates for two to three weeks within a 5 per cent range, which leads to the breakout, and, by definition, a new trend, according to Dow Theory. Volume counts but is a secondary consideration, the theory says. Dow historians claim that the theory has an impressive track record. Critics say it is out of date and its signals come too late.

The chart patterns are based around trend theory. The famous *head and shoulders* pattern, for example, shows the trend breaking out through a support level and plunging. But it may not happen, and technicians are not slow to rationalise after the event. They describe their trade as an art not a science. Many who work in the City are sceptical about trend analysis. US speculator Victor Niederhoffer has queried whether the *trend* exists. In his experience, it is impossible to have a rational discussion with some trend followers because so many of these people have vested interests in perpetuating the myth.

After analysing price and volume, and related trends, the analyst may use indicators that focus on, among other things, whether the market is overbought or oversold, its relative performance and its rate of change. Many indicators are based around the moving average, which shows changes in the average share price over a given period. Others are based around volume. Technicians use cycles, which are based on regularly recurring price patterns within a specified period, to measure time.

Every technical analyst has favoured techniques, and some believe the simplest work best. But the variations are limited only by the imagination of traders and analysts and, a cynic would say, of software manufacturers. The types of charts in use vary. Short-term traders are increasingly drawn to Japanese candlesticks, which are an exotic alternative to conventional bar charts. For some, a line chart with its great detail may reassure, but others prefer to cut out the *noise* of intraday share price movement and use a point and figure chart. Computer software enables the technical analyst to switch from one chart type to another.

Technical analysis caters also for those who shun simplicity. William D Gann was a technician who is said to have made more money teaching his theories than practising them, but he has a unique, highly mathematical form of technical analysis linking price and time proportionately, with lashings of special numbers and astrological inferences thrown in. Courses in Gann theory have been marketed heavily and tend not to come cheap.

Elliott Wave Theory is another tough nut to crack. It finds that the market always rises in five waves and falls in three, and so assumes a perpetual long-term bull market. The proportional relationship of the waves is linked to Fibonacci numbers, which have a mathematical relationship claimed to be deep-rooted in nature.

Some in the City regard technical analysis as a somewhat fringe activity, but others take it more seriously. Some stockbrokers say it should be one tool for investors, but not the only one. Traders may use technical analysis in varying degrees, and it can be hard to get at the truth. Unusually for a fund manager, Anthony Bolton who runs Fidelity's Special Situations fund makes significant use of technical analysis. US equities trader Marty Schwartz has said that he spent 10 years trading on fundamentals and lost money before he started using technical analysis and became rich.

US fund manager John Train leads the pack of cynics. He once told me that, in his experience, no great investors have used the technique and that Wall Street firms had spent a fortune on state-of-the-art systems before they quietly shelved them. Fund manager Ralph Wanger has noted that technical analysis will always have a following because charts create patterns, and the human mind sees patterns, even in the clouds.

Others

The economist has the job of generating value-added research on the functioning of the economy, and will seek to understand why the Central Bank behaves as it does. The strategist is a broadly based type of analyst who sits between the analyst and the economist, and who makes broad calls on a number of asset classes and markets.

All three will focus on statistics that throw light on, among other things, trends in inflation, interest rates and currency movements. They understand that statistics are approximate but require them to have been reliably sourced from a genuinely random sample, taking into account any unusual factors. Statistics from some countries may not be of the same kind (or quality) as from the UK.

The numbers may be presented in fractionalised detail but this does not mean precision. Statistics such as Gross Domestic Output, a measure of a country's economic output, are frequently revised, and are a guide. A one-off figure could be a temporary blip and figures should be compared over a period. What counts is the trend. A rising GDP in a strong economy gives rise to inflation fears. If GDP rises by more than 3 per cent in each of four quarters in succession, the Bank of England will probably raise interest rates to restrain it.

Statistics, like financial ratios, may sometimes be calculated in more than one way. Unemployment is a good example. Economists consider more than one figure at once to get the broad picture. How far you can use macroeconomic statistics and events for forecasting the future is open to question. A recent government project focused on neural networks posed the question: what happens when you shoot a US president? It has happened three times, including once successfully, and every time the reaction was different.

The professional forecasters sometimes wisecrack that their most recent forecast is their best one. But their forecasts may be revised *ad infinitum* and, even if they are often wrong, may provide a thoughtful and valuable commentary on the market.

PR

PR agencies build the image of quoted companies to financial journalists and, in so far as they will listen, analysts. In choosing a PR agency, companies look for a track record, knowledge of the sector and proven delivery of results. In the event of a crisis, the company wants minimum impact on the share price. If it gets communication right, there could be a blip but not a disaster.

Companies assess the impact of PR on the business, and not just on the number of press cuttings. They use sophisticated measurement techniques. One insurance company, for example, knows it has its communication right when it delivers good results without provoking too many telephone calls from customers demanding a reduction in premiums on their policies.

Some companies will hire an agency on a retainer as a failsafe. For most of the year the agency will tick away at a maintenance level. But if a crisis arises, it will seek to protect the company's public image. At 5.00 pm in the evening, it will be ready to parachute a team in to help its client.

The agencies will represent companies during a takeover period, or for an initial stock exchange listing (see Chapter 5). The management of a company's communications during an IPO is best handled on a timetable, providing a drip of information in the market to colour perception, Matthew Hooper, managing partner, Shared Value, told a Moscow conference in March 2006. He said that investors looked for properly and accurately delivered news flow and that the press could eliminate speculation while remaining within legal reporting parameters.

Company results are normally published in March and September (based on a 31 December year end) and the PR agencies will have a major role to play in their distribution. The agencies have a billing structure which takes into account all time spent on client work and all expenses.

Some agencies also do investor relations (IR), which is about shareholder communications. IR reports to finance and PR to sales and marketing within the company but, in the open market, they must work together.

The skill of professional PR is to stay invisible, not to snatch the glory of the client, and to keep concealed how far the agency controls the agenda of the journalists. Signs of a PR agency's unseen hand are evident on a daily basis in the press. A handful of agencies are linked to all the main activity in the City, although there are rich pickings for other agencies in less high-profile businesses.

The large companies may have their own corporate affairs departments. These can be well informed and staffed by people who have the ear of the directors. But some in-house operations, not so well backed internally, 'just don't get it', according to industry sources.

Over time journalists have become more dependent on PR executives, finding them more accessible and more willing to explain basics than company executives. The relationship between journalists and PR could be described as symbiotic. Delve behind the headlines in the business or other financial press, and it is quite likely that the PR executive or PR agent had something to do with the placement of the story.

In the past, some PR agents have leaked price-sensitive information to the press with impunity. But regulations have tightened up and, under the market abuse regime, employees of PR agencies who do this may now be subject to civil or criminal action. From about mid-2005 industry fears have put an end to the 'Friday night drop' when PR agents would queue to give Sunday newspaper journalists exclusive stories of quoted companies. There is a feeling that the Sunday papers are now getting fewer scoops. In addition, the Takeover Panel has been known to censure PR agents for breaking the rules.

Journalists and tipsters

A good story is said to be one that somebody does not want you to print. But financial journalists, particularly on daily newspapers, often have little time to investigate and probe. They may rely heavily on PR input, including provision of news releases and, if they are lucky, free trips courtesy of a financial institution. The adage that you cannot bribe the British journalist may be true, but financial institutions know they can sometimes soften him or her up. Journalists use the basic information in a news release to build their own piece. Some will use chunks of it verbatim. One may argue that this is lazy journalism, but it shows the provider of the release understood the journalist's needs.

The news release may be slanted. If a company's sales are up but its profits are down, the press release may emphasise the first statistic. If net profits are down but pre-tax profits are up, the press release may focus on the latter. Journalists tend to be suspicious of PR agencies but not all will see through the angle. Some are arts graduates without any specialist business education, and may be hampered by a lack of in-depth understanding of economics, finance and company accounting. But many journalists, particularly on national newspapers, know their subject well and are highly respected for their professionalism.

Part of this professionalism may involve tapping sources who peddle only one side of the story and running with it in the newspaper, although later it may become clear that this is only half the story and that the source had an ulterior motive for providing the story. Andreas Whittham Smith, founder of the Independent, wrote in 1999: 'The iron law is that if information is to pass, both parties, not just the journalist, require a reward'.

Tipsters

The tip sheets and some financial websites, under the broad banner of financial journalism, may pride themselves as being contrarian, but it can translate into off the rails. At the height of the pre-March 2000 bull market, one financial website ran an online portfolio in which one of the main criteria for stock selection was that the conventional financial press had found the company valued too highly. The web site kept saying overpriced but popular stocks would soar higher. This approach turned out to be a disaster.

Individual share tipsters have an influence that is not always proportionate to their track record. They may lift their tips from secondary sources, rewriting them in their own words, combining material from several sources or carefully modifying a conclusion to make the whole thing appear original. The writer is not paid for how many recommendations will eventually turn out well. A track record can be glossed over, but the pages of the tip sheet must always be filled.

If the tipster wants to keep his or her reputation intact, it may pay not to be associated with one website or newsletter for too long. This way, his or her individual tipping record may never come properly under scrutiny. Many tipsters operate anonymously.

Others try to make their name. They may boast City experience but this does not in itself rubberstamp their investment advice. The old adage applies, if they know so much about stock-picking, why are they not investing their own money for a living?

Showmanship is another tactic of the tipsters, and one of the all time masters was US tipster Joseph Granville who, in his heyday, spoke to investors with his chimpanzee and a few bikini clad models in tow. He would wear blinking bow ties and play the piano or dress up as a chicken. He once dropped his trousers to read stock quotes on his shorts. He has been known to dress like Moses and deliver the 'ten commandments' of investing, and has purportedly walked on water.

When a small company tip is given prominence in a popular newspaper, the market makers increase the price. Other tipsters get wind and steal the idea. It is a spiral that can send up the share price all too briefly. Another big source of share tips is the internet bulletin boards. They are notoriously unreliable. Many who post on the internet have an ulterior motive. Their output, perhaps under several aliases, may slip untruths amidst a plethora of facts. Recently, the chief executive of a company criticised anonymously on the message boards tracked down the writer and sued him, and it led to a settlement. But writers who contribute to the bulletin boards from internet cafés have avoided identification.

Many tipsters have never invested directly in shares in their lives, and this tells its story. In today's regulatory environment, it is much harder for the tipster to hold shares in the company that he or she tips, but it happens. If the tipster buys through nominee holdings, or through a friend, in small amounts, it can be hard to detect.

In a landmark case, *Daily Mirror* journalists Anil Bhoyrul and James Hipwell in 1999 and 2000 made profits from buying shares ahead of tipping them in the *City Slickers* column of their newspaper and then selling them into the price rise. In 2000, the Press Complaints Commission (PCC) ruled on the case. The two journalists were dismissed for gross misconduct, including breaches of the parts of the PCC's Code of Practice applicable to financial journalists. The PCC exonerated Piers Morgan, then editor, from any breach of the Code, but found fault with how journalists had been allowed to operate.

The PCC has since issued editors with guidelines to enhance the code of practice and has described the *City Slickers* case as a victory for self regulation. In July 2005, the Treasury acknowledged that the PCC should be the competent authority for dealing with journalists making investment recommendations.

However, the slickers were also to face a criminal prosecution from the Department of Trade and Industry (DTI). In January 2000, the London Stock Exchange (LSE) alerted the DTI's companies investigation branch to a very significant rise in the shares of Viglen Technology. Eventually, the DTI started a criminal investigation and a criminal prosecution was brought for market manipulation, in breach of the Financial Services Act 1986, applicable at the time.

In early 2006, one of the slickers, James Hipwell, who denied misleading the market, was jailed for six months, of which three were suspended. The other slicker, Anil Bhoyrul, who had pleaded guilty, had received a 180-hour community service order. Terry Shepherd, a private investor, was sentenced to three months after having helped the slickers by publishing advance notice of their tips on the internet bulletin boards.

The national press covered the events in painstaking detail. If such a case were to arise now, the FSA itself could take enforcement action for market abuse. But criminal lawyers see this as unlikely because of the difficulty of proving the case.

Beyond tips

The press will highlight any perceived infringement or corporate failure and this will instil an 'apparent desire to place the blame on an individual or individuals', disguising the broader culpability of the organisation, according to risk management research by Dr Lynne Drennan at Glasgow Caledonian University. She has observed the process in the press treatment of Jeff Skilling as chief executive of Enron when the US energy company was hit by scandals in 2001, and in the scandals associated with Robert Maxwell, chairman and chief executive of Mirror Group Newspapers, and Nick Leeson, the trader on the Singapore Monetary Exchange for Barings Bank.

The press attracts allegations of bias. Martin Fridson, a managing director at Merrill Lynch, said in his book *Investment Illusions* that reporters had a tendency to obtain quotes from not necessarily the best authorities but those who could provide colourful quotes.

But if the press is not perfect, it often attempts to be impartial and, as former deputy City editor of the *Daily Mail* Michael Walters has said, it is for private investors the least slanted source of City information. It has far more impartiality than the press in less developed countries. In some ex-Soviet block countries, it is a criminal offence to criticise the government in the media and retribution is not always conducted through the legal process.

How far the press reflects City opinion in a rising or falling market, and how far it dictates it, is a matter of debate. Some believe that the press had talked up the high-tech stock boom ahead of the March 2000 market crash. Some journalists have felt flattered by such acknowledgements of their classic *power without responsibility*. Martin Dickson, as City editor at *The Financial Times*, told one compliance conference he felt his impact as a journalist was 'on the margin'. But the FSA has admitted that journalistic coverage of how it regulates the City can have significant impact.

The agenda of many publications is advertising driven, and the promotional material is subject to potential scrutiny by the FSA. The regulator focuses on adverts likely to have a major risk impact on customers, including specific risk areas such as spread betting and pensions, specific products, and the medium, including websites. Consumers think that by looking at advertisements for financial products, they are conducting research, but advertisers do not always make it clear what a product is, according to the FSA. It has fined some firms for misleading promotions.

Corporate information flow

LSE-listed and AIM companies must ultimately manage their own corporate information flow. They must establish systems to communicate with investors in a way that avoids the creation or continuation of a false market in listed securities.

The companies must first release information that might affect the price of their shares through a regulatory information service to ensure equal access. RNS is the largest of these services. It is provided by the LSE and is accessible through its website. On average, more than 500 regulatory announcements are disseminated every business day, according to the LSE.

If the news comes on a Saturday, it must still be disclosed, via press and news wires. At any meeting, however public, at which inside information is let out, there must be a prior or immediate announcement to ensure that the public has the information. The listed company must make a judgment on what information needs to be disclosed and when. The market tends to overreact to surprise news or rumours, which can take time to correct. The FSA has no benchmark level of share-price movement that triggers an investigation, and it will act proportionately to the risk, which suggests it may overlook market abuse leading to small price movements.

Companies must disclose related-party transactions, as by directors, and significant transactions, both of which require shareholder approval. There are half-yearly reporting disclosure options. To keep the market informed about the likely end-of-year results and to avoid a false market, companies may put out announcements on a more regular basis than is strictly required.

The information disclosed should be complete. In January 2005, the FSA fined Pace Micro Technology for misleading the market partly because when it stated its debt provision in an interim announcement it had failed to mention that it had withdrawn some of the trade debtor insurance described in annual reports.

Companies may delay disclosure of inside information if it is kept confidential and the non-disclosure does not mislead the market. This may be acceptable in negotiating mergers and acquisitions, where premature disclosure can scare away a party and make a deal not happen. If a journalist puts two and two together, and concludes that companies A and B are negotiating a merger, it will not necessarily trigger a breach of confidentiality. But if the journalist has the price of a transaction, this is specific information and disclosure is needed. A briefing of analysts in advance can also be a breach of disclosure rules.

18

Financial services regulation

Introduction

In this chapter, we will examine how financial services regulation has developed, and how it works today. We will see how the Financial Services Authority (FSA) regulates the City. We will focus on the influence of European legislation, and how fraud and money laundering are combated.

History of regulation

The Thatcher legacy

The City had enjoyed informal regulation until Margaret Thatcher became Conservative prime minister in 1979 and took steps to introduce a more formal approach to fit with the Conservative Government's master plan of nationalising private industry and introducing private pensions. The 'iron lady' believed that if London was to remain Europe's leading financial services centre, it had to lead by regulation.

In 1986, *Big Bang* ushered in reforms, which were part of a move to reduce the role of the London Stock Exchange (LSE) as a private club controlling its members by its own rules. (For details, see Chapter 1.)

The Conservative Government launched its privatisation programme, which encouraged wider share ownership. Small investors snatched a profit on new issues such as British Telecom and British Gas. It became the norm to *stag* new issues – buying and selling quickly on issue – and millions of people may have been left with the impression that investment in shares was a way to make a quick buck. Many lost heavily afterwards when they dabbled in the stock market outside the protection of the early privatisations. As some stockbrokers never tire of saying, the Government privatisations had not educated investors.

The Financial Services Act, 1986

Consumer protection was on the Thatcher agenda. The Conservative Government commissioned Jim Gower, a University professor, to prepare proposals for regulation. His recommendations led to the Financial Services Act, 1986, implemented in full in February 1998. The Act created self-regulation within a statutory framework. Firms and their key staff were required to obtain approval from the regulators as a condition of running their business. The Securities & Investment Board, known as the SIB, was responsible for overseeing self-regulatory organisations, known as SROs, which controlled authorised firms. The SROs created rules for member firms and policed their activities. Their authority was statutory in all but in name.

Among the SROs were The Securities Association, which authorised stockbrokers, and the Association of Futures Brokers and Dealers. They later merged into the Securities & Futures Authority. The Financial Investment Managers and Brokers Regulatory Association authorised share-dealing firms that were not stockbrokers as well as independent financial advisers. The other SROs were the Life Assurance and Unit Trust Regulatory Organisation, which authorised life assurance firms, and the Investment Managers Regulatory Organisation, which authorised fund managers; they later merged into the Personal Investment Authority.

Legislative changes extended across the financial sectors. The Insurance Companies Act, 1982 (see Chapter 3) was introduced to regulate general insurance companies. The Building Societies Act, 1986, was intended to make building societies more competitive.

Deficiencies in the new regime started to emerge. The spread of responsibilities among regulators for supervising financial conglomerates operating in more than one jurisdiction and across a variety of asset classes was not always clear and, as it turned out, it could lead to a lack of action. For more about this and on issues related to the Bank of England's supervisory role arising from the 1991 collapse of BCCI and the 1995 collapse of Barings, see Chapter 2.

The current regime

The Financial Services Authority

In Chapter 2, we saw how the FSA assumed responsibility for regulating whole-sale money markets and retail banking from the Bank of England in 1998. The regulator's powers and responsibilities were properly established at midnight on 30 November 2001, when the Financial Services and Markets Act came into force. The new legislation was comprehensive, incorporating 433 sections with 22 schedules, and it was the first to have ever straddled two parliamentary sessions.

The FSA became a single regulator for investment banking and insurance. The old SROs were abolished. Unlike the previous system, this was direct statutory regulation, and it placed much more emphasis on protecting consumers. It required the FSA to pursue four statutory objectives: to maintain confidence in the UK financial system; to promote public understanding of it; to secure an appropriate degree of protection for consumers; and to reduce the scope for financial crime.

The FSA recognises exchanges and clearing houses. In 2002, it started to regulate credit unions, which are savings and loan societies based on a common interest. Two years later, it was regulating mortgage advisers. The FSA authorises firms across the financial services industry, and approves individuals who work in it. Any firm undertaking regulated activity in the UK must be either FSA-authorised or exempt.

The FSA, like the SROs before it, has the power to withdraw approval for an individual that it considers not fit and proper to perform the controlled function to which the approval relates. It may impose a prohibition order that prevents any person from involvement in financial services activity and anybody who breached such an order would be committing a criminal offence. The FSA can apply for an injunction against any person or firm to prevent them from committing regulatory breaches.

In May 2003, the FSA assumed responsibility for vetting public companies for a full stock market listing, previously the prerogative of the LSE. The FSA must now approve prospectuses and other documents of companies that plan to start trading shares on the LSE.

More broadly, the FSA has the power to write rules and principles, codes and provisions. It is a private company, but it has statutory immunity from being sued from action taken in its official duties. The FSA is accountable, both to a committee of non-executive members, and to consumer and practitioner panels.

Once a year, the FSA must report to HM Treasury on how it has carried out its functions, and must hold a public meeting about it. The Treasury has the power to commission an inquiry into the regulator's operations, or a report on, for instance, a regulatory scandal. The Director General of Fair Trading may issue a report on any practice that it considers anti-competitive.

The FSA plans its rules in consultation with the industry and other parties. It publishes its consultation papers on its own website. The regulator has long been criticised for failing to understand the industry that it regulates. Critics say that the FSA has found it difficult to attract the right level of staff, given that it cannot pay the rates of the investment banks and brokers, some of whom have a strong demand for similar people in their own compliance departments. But a stint of working at the regulator has prestige, which can help in advancing one's career in the private sector.

Furthermore, the FSA has made some key senior appointments directly from the industry. In May 2004, it appointed Hector Sants as managing director, wholesale and institutional markets. He had previously been chief executive officer of Europe, Middle East and Africa at Credit Suisse First Boston. Compliance officers say that the lack of experience of the financial services industry remains an issue among some supervisory staff at a less senior level.

The principles-based regime

The FSA regulates the financial services industry through broad principles, although it also has rules. On the face of it, principles are all-encompassing enough to enable the FSA to present a case more easily against firms than by excessive reliance on rules, in which clever lawyers may look for loopholes. There has been debate on how well the principles-based regime has worked, and whether it will survive in its present form given rules increasingly foisted on the UK by EU directives. The US Securities & Exchange Commission works in cooperation with the FSA and has a tough rules-based approach.

The FSA puts an emphasis on management responsibility in interpreting its principles and rules and it has started to penalise senior managers for wrongdoing at a lower level in the firm. It has found it harder to prosecute individuals in the corporate sector because they are not subject to industry regulation. As part of the process, the FSA likes to seek industry solutions to problems. It was the financial services industry that introduced, on pressure from the regulator, new rules on unbundling from January 2006, in which investment managers must disclose to clients how much they have paid for execution and research respectively.

If the FSA makes a disciplinary decision with which a firm or individual is not satisfied, the matter may be referred to the Financial Services and Markets

Tribunal, an independent tribunal run by the Lord Chancellor's department, which will rehear the case afresh, listening to evidence from both the FSA and the appellant. The FSA has a mixed record of success in its enforcement actions against firms, which has demonstrated that the system of appeals has worked, but has also brought out the regulator's failure to prepare an excellent case, and some potential unfairness in procedure.

A turning point came when Legal & General was partially successful in its appeal against the FSA's £1.1 million fine for mis-selling of endowments. In January 2005, the Financial Services and Markets Tribunal found that the FSA had proved inadequate systems and controls but not mis-selling at Legal & General and it substantially reduced the fine.

In reaction, the FSA commissioned an independent review of its enforcement process, the Strachan review. It was published in July 2005 and suggested, among other things, a discounted fine for those who settled early with the regulator, and absolute transparency, so far missing, in all negotiations with the Regulatory Decisions Committee, an industry-led body which sat within the FSA and decided on penalties to be imposed. Some in the industry said an early settlement discount would make it more tempting to abuse the regulatory requirements, or that firms could be tempted to settle a case that might never arise. But the Strachan recommendations were implemented.

Generally, the FSA takes the view that the wholesale industry, consisting of financial institutions that deal with each other, needs less protection than consumers. In March 2006, it announced that it would abolish the *approved persons* list and mandatory examinations for the wholesale sector but on the basis that standards of competence should not be lowered. This followed a consultation where a number of industry views had been reflected.

Some large firms in the industry welcomed the move because it gave them a chance to develop their own training programmes well suited to wholesale needs. The smaller firms were less sanguine, although there was nothing to stop them continuing to use the same examinations as before. The Securities & Investment Institute had seen examinations as an irreplaceable benchmark and was disappointed by the decision. One of the wider ramifications of no mandatory examination for wholesale professionals is the potential adverse impact on transferability of individuals between firms, particularly across jurisdictions. The US has an examination culture entrenched in its financial services industry, and is unlikely to change it.

European legislation

European legislation, with its emphasis on bureaucratic regulation and consumer protection, is making substantial demands on the FSA's limited resources. The master plan is The Financial Services Action Plan (FSAP). It stems from the EU single market programme in the early 1990s and aims to create a single European market in financial services, with deeper, more liquid capital markets, a bigger pool of investors, and more choice for issuers and investors.

At the heart of the FSAP is the Lamfalussy process. This is a four-level approach to resolving shortcomings in the regulatory and legislative system for financial services in Europe. The Committee of European Securities Regulators (CESR) is active in carrying out some aspects of Lamfalussy. Regulators from various jurisdictions, including the FSA in the UK, have been making proposals through CESR to the European Commission.

At the European Council in Lisbon in April 2000, it was agreed that the FSAP should be completed by the end of 2005. In conjunction with the euro, the FSAP, through the Lamfalussy process, has enabled Europe to move closer to having a single capital market over the past five years. The first level of the process consists of legislative acts in the form of Directives, proposed by the EU Commission following consultation, and adopted by the Council and the European Parliament.

The parts of a Directive that are *regulation* impose wording from Europe, which cannot be individually interpreted, and the parts which are *directive* have more leeway because they are to be adapted in a country regulatory authority's individual rule book. Taken as a whole, there is limited flexibility. The UK tries to avoid gold plating, which would be to add its own requirements to those of a Directive.

Among the key Directives are the Market Abuse Directive, the Prospectus Directive, the Markets in Financial Instruments Directive, and the Capital Requirements Directive. Let us take a look.

Market Abuse Directive

Under the Financial Services and Markets Act 2000, the FSA has been able to impose financial penalties for market abuse which took place on or after 1 December 2001. Market abuse may include misuse of information, misleading statements and impressions, or market distortion, and the regulator has brought successful actions for all three. The UK, like the rest of Europe, is now subject to the Market Abuse Directive (MAD), part of the Financial Services Action Plan. It was implemented in the UK on 1 July 2005. Because the UK's regime previously in place had surpassed the Directive's requirements, the changes were not enormous.

Under the MAD, as before, the FSA is able to pursue market abuse, including insider dealing, as a civil case, requiring proof *on the balance of the probabilities*, or as a criminal case, with the much higher standard of *beyond reasonable doubt*. It has said that it will not pursue both types in a single case. The flexibility has made it easier to bring an action for insider dealing than before the market abuse regime existed, when a criminal standard of proof had been required.

The MAD is concerned with not just enforcement, but also prevention, including issues such as the disclosure of conflicts of interest and directors' dealings. For shareholders, the MAD aims to understand the expectations of the *reasonable investor*, a concept less familiar in some EU jurisdictions than in the UK. Information must be released to the market in a way that is timely and synchronised across jurisdictions. Delays in disclosure must not be detrimental to investors, potential and actual. There is a new requirement to keep insider *lists* of those who have insider information, which has given rise to uncertainties in some jurisdictions about who should be included on them, and what details should be provided.

The financial services industry has found teething problems in coping with the increased record-keeping requirements of the MAD. Cross-border implementation has led to inconsistent interpretations. The FSA has taken account of firms' requests for greater regulatory guidance.

Prospectus Directive

The Prospectus Directive aims to open up primary markets in equities and bonds. It was implemented in the UK on 1 July 2005, simultaneously with the MAD (see above). The Directive stipulates that issuers need only a single approval of their prospectus before they market the issue throughout Europe. Small companies are concerned about the cost of complying with the Directive, with reason. A company on the Alternative Investment Market (AIM) can no longer make a seamless move to the Main Market, but must produce a prospectus.

Markets in Financial Instruments Directive

The Markets in Financial Instruments Directive (MiFID) was first proposed in July 2001 as a replacement for the Investment Services Directive, and implementation across Europe is scheduled for 1 November 2007. It will establish EU-wide standards in some main areas of investment business. This Directive is widely reckoned to be the biggest piece of legislation to hit the financial services industry in recent years, and lack of early formulation of the details means that firms had to start preparing and budgeting for systems and controls, training and staff before they knew precisely what they would need.

The biggest expenditure is for large banks that have decided to become systematic internalisers, a move required if they are not to restrict order flow in securities trading. The Directive requires systematic internalisers to publish pre-trade quotes on *liquid* shares, with a prohibition on price improvement. There has been a lack of clarity on how to define systematic internaliser or liquidity. There is a new post-trade transparency requirement, by which the firm must make public the price, volume and time of the trade. As part of this, firms will have to start showing the sheer volume of over-the-counter business, including in bonds, a market considered by many to be sufficiently transparent.

There will be a best-execution requirement, from which only eligible counterparties acting as principals – trading off their own book – will be excluded. Best execution measures will encompass trading through to settlement. Asset managers and private banks will be required to obtain best execution when trading shares for their funds.

The requirement will apply to over-the-counter (OTC) derivatives, which are customised securities, and there will be a different route for each type of instrument. For less liquid securities, there will be a problem that will not arise in the case of, for example, liquid currency derivatives. In calculating best execution, there will need to be clarity on how banks charge the transaction costs both of constructing the instrument and hedging, and the arrangement fees.

The MiFID requires extensive maintenance and updating of records for any regulated activities involving conflicts of interest that may damage clients' interests. Firms must take a more proactive approach towards finding conflicts. Where no mitigation measures are possible, a firm for the first time must advise the conflict to the client so it can decide whether to proceed.

The MiFID will impact activity across European borders, where one of the benefits will be increased opportunities in capital flows. But lawyers have identified problem areas. If a firm opens a branch in another European member state, the host state's rules will apply. But if that branch then provides cross-border services, the group's home state rules will apply, and will create a problem in how to supervise the business. If, for example, a firm established in the UK puts a branch in Germany, which does business cross-border, this will be subject to the UK *conduct of business* rules.

The new customer classification under the MiFID will be retail, professional or eligible counterparty. The categories are comparable to the present customer categories of private, intermediate or market counterparty, but there are differences. A key concern has been that it will probably prove impossible to transpose old client categories onto the new without going through an expensive process of reclassifying each client individually. The lowest level of customer, which will be retail, will find it more difficult than before to upgrade to the next level, which will be professional, where less protection will be required. In early 2006, the Treasury said it intended to lobby the European Parliament on this issue.

At its annual general meeting on 22 July 2005, the FSA expressed concerns that the MiFID would cost more than the benefits it brings to the UK. FSA chairman Sir Callum McCarthy called it 'deeply unsatisfactory' that the Directive had been subject to no comprehensive EU cost-benefit analysis. Draft level 2 measures published in early February 2006 were a maximum harmonisation directive, which meant that there was a little, but no more, wriggle room for country regulators such as the FSA to add rules. It was more prescriptive than UK firms were used to.

In a speech to the PEP & ISA Managers' Association shortly after the level 2 draft was published, Stephen Hanks, economic adviser to the Treasury, said it was likely that some European states, but not the UK, would miss the 1 November 2007 deadline for implementing the MiFID.

Capital Requirements Directive

The Capital Requirements Directive (CRD) was approved by the European Parliament in September 2005. It is to introduce a supervisory framework in the EU which reflects the Basel II rules on capital measurement and capital standards (see Chapter 3). The CRD updates the Capital Adequacy Directive (1993) and the Consolidated Banking Directive (2002), which contained the old EU rules.

The CRD is designed to have significant impact on prudential regulation of firms across the EU, particularly in terms of relating capital levels much more closely to risks, according to the FSA. It is intended to harmonise standards and make it easier for firms to do business. At the time of writing, an earliest opportunity start date of 1 January 2007 had been proposed for the simpler approaches to credit and operational risk, but the UK preference is for a *Big Bang* start date of 1 January 2008 for the full range of approaches.

Fraud

The financial services industry is a playground for fraudsters. One of the growing frauds is phishing, which is to trick people into revealing their bank account details and passwords, or similar sensitive information by email or via the internet. Another internet scam is the advance fee fraud, a spurious loan offer presented as conditional on payment of an upfront fee. The promoters take the fee but do not pay the loan. They sometimes claim to be banks based in Guernsey, Jersey or the Isle of Man. Their only presence is on the internet and when they have stolen enough money through advanced fees, they disappear.

A few claimed that internet-only banks are fronts for fraudulent capital-raising activities. One scam worked repeatedly is to launch a non-existent

IPO. From the fraudsters' perspective, the aim is to rake in fast money, and it does not matter which of various methods is used. Once the regulators have closed a dubious website, another one will pop up, probably run by the same fraudsters under a different name. The site may have a giveaway similar logo. The stopping and starting process may continue indefinitely, raking in money in between.

The fraudulent sites tend to have a slick design with bold colours and hard selling copy in US English. They provide email addresses and telephone numbers for queries, but telephone approaches will reach an answer phone. If a call is returned, it will be from a boiler room in an unknown jurisdiction to which there will never be direct telephone access. The punters will be unable to track down the operation in a hurry once they realise that they have been ripped off. The salespeople will often use false names, so if there is trouble and they need to flee they will not be easily traced. If an operation has collapsed, a secretly linked outfit may approach fleeced victims and claim to offer debt recovery services for an upfront fee. Many fall for what turns out to be a second scam.

The FSA publishes on its website (www.fsa.gov.uk) a list of unauthorised firms targeting UK investors. Check the *Investors Chronicle* chat rooms at www.investorschronicle.co.uk for stories of embittered investors. The UK Government is reviewing the whole issue of fraud and in May 2005 introduced the Fraud Bill, which defines fraud for the first time in the legislation. The Bill includes new measures for modernising the law to equip investigators and prosecutors with the necessary tools to keep pace with the changing world of fraud, including phishing and internet fraud, according to a Home Office statement.

Serious fraud

The City of London police has increased its fraud investigation activities and takes on simpler cases such as that of Joyti De-laurey, who was sentenced to seven years in June 2004 for stealing almost £4.5 million from her employer, Goldman Sachs. The police works increasingly with the Serious Fraud Office (SFO), which takes on some large complex cases, and both cooperate with the FSA.

The SFO is an independent government department with up to 300 permanent staff, and is part of the UK criminal justice system. It started operating in April 1988 and has jurisdiction only over England, Wales and Northern Ireland. The department investigates and prosecutes serious or complex fraud cases exceeding around £1 million in value. It selects cases on such criteria as whether they have a significant international dimension, give rise to widespread public concern, or are complex and require specialist input.

The SFO has a mixed track record. It has had some high-profile successes, including the BCCI investigation, which led to six convictions, the latest in April 1997, and the Barlow Clowes case, where the principal defendant Peter Clowes was sentenced to ten years in February 1992. In the Guinness case, following an SFO investigation, the four principal defendants were convicted in September 1990. The failures have been no less publicised. One was the Blue Arrow trial, which cost taxpayers an estimated £40 million. Another was the 1996 indictment of Ian and Kevin Maxwell, sons of Robert Maxwell. They were found not guilty of fraud charges after a trial that had lasted eight months and cost taxpayers £25 million. This is one of the cases that led to Government proposals to scrap jury trials in complex fraud cases on the basis that juries do not understand complex fraud. The House of Lords has so far rejected them.

Cases tend to have a four-to-five year gestation period, and so annual results are not an accurate barometer of the SFO's output. The number of defendants has been under 80 a year, and typically under 50, so a few successes or failures have varied the annual conviction rate significantly. The cumulative conviction rate stands at about 70 per cent a year. In recent years, the SFO has become better resourced, although critics say that it still does not attract the best investigative staff because it cannot afford to pay private-sector rates.

Money laundering

Money laundering is closely linked with fraud, and it takes place when criminals try to conceal and disguise the origin and ownership of the proceeds of their crimes with the aim of avoiding prosecution. There are three stages in the process of laundering money. The first is placement, in which the launderer introduces dirty money, the proceeds of crime, into the legitimate financial system; the second phase is layering, by which he or she attempts to separate the proceeds in time and space from the original acquisitive crime by moving them through a series of financial transactions; the third stage is integration, at the end of which the launderer has created a legitimate explanation for the source of these funds, allowing him or her to use them openly as an individual would use honestly acquired assets.

Money laundering takes many forms and is multi-jurisdictional. Cocaine production in South America, oil production in Africa and terrorism in the Middle East are all fertile sources of dirty money that ends up getting *washed*. London's financial services industry provides opportunities for money launderers, as do foreign exchange bureaux, casinos and estate agents. 'The best place to hide a tree is in a forest', says Chris Hamblin, money laundering consultant at Complinet, a regulation and compliance consultancy service.

The Money Laundering Regulations came into force in the UK in April 1993. Since then, the financial services industry has had to put procedures, controls and training in place, and there has been a lot of regulation. Following the 11 September 2001 terrorist attacks on the World Trade Centre in New York, governments worldwide have focused more on the prevention of money laundering than ever before and most countries have reviewed their existing laws or enacted new ones. Cynics say that much of the impetus for this has been political and that most sophisticated money launders are still not being caught.

Anti-money laundering regulations, and their efficacy, vary wildly between countries. The US imposes draconian criminal penalties on those caught for money laundering, but plea bargaining is allowed. The enlargement of the EU, with its single currency, and the development of technology give greater opportunities for organised crime. In the UK, the Treasury has estimated that £25 billion of criminal money passes every year through the economy. If the figure is right – something that nobody can confirm – it is uncertain whether it represents fresh money, or simply £5 billion circulating through the system five times. Law enforcers, including Customs, recovered £85 million in 2004–05 and, at the time of writing, were targeting £100 million in 2005–06. It may not sound proportionately much, but the target is rising, and these recent figures are a considerable improvement on the £44 million seized in the 10 years to 2002, according to law enforcement sources.

Financial services companies in the UK have long been required to report transactions that may be deemed suspicious to the National Criminal Intelligence Service (NCIS). Under the Proceeds of Crime Act 2002, a person may go to jail for not filling in suspicious activity reports (SARs). In recent years, there has been much concern about the backlog of SARs, which came in great quantity from firms, particularly divorce lawyers who were trying to cover their backs. The reporting system improved towards the end of 2005, however, by which time all law enforcement agencies had direct and immediate online access to the SARs database. On 31 March 2006, NCIS will have closed.

From 1 April onwards, the Serious Organised Crime Agency (SOCA) will have started up, bringing together the responsibilities of NCIS and the National Crime Squad. It will have taken control of the organised crime investigations previously conducted by Customs and Excise and the immigration service. The SOCA claims a new concept of intervention to reduce 'harm' to the UK, and unlike the NCIS, it can give any information to anybody from its database if this would be consistent with its aims of targeting organised crime. The SOCA is expected to have more private, but more interactive, relationships with regulators.

In October 2005, the FSA closed a consultation with the industry over proposals to replace its Money Laundering Sourcebook with a two-fold emphasis: first, on the Money Laundering Regulations 2003 and on Joint Money Laundering Steering Group guidance; and second, on high-level standards and management responsibility. A key message was that it would not be retreating from money laundering, but it required firms to take a proportionate, risk-based approach in addressing the problem, and a holistic view. The consultation draft of Steering Group guidance, provided from the industry and backed by the FSA, stresses the need for a more risk-based approach and a stronger role for senior management in mitigating risks.

The FSA has supported the Treasury in its negotiations over the Third Money Laundering Directive, to be implemented by the end of 2007. The Treasury has said that a lot of the requirements of the Directive are already in place in the UK. There will be some new definitions, including one for politically exposed persons, and more detail, including a distinction between enhanced and simplified due diligence. The Directive has an explicit risk-based approach written into it, which means that firms must apply a proportionate approach, focusing more on areas of greater risk. Some in the financial services industry fear that the legislation may lack teeth, and that some continental European jurisdictions may take advantage of the flexibility of the risk-based regime. The Treasury acknowledges a potential problem, but believes that good regulation rather than more EU legislation will provide the answer.

If a firm has inadequate systems and controls to ward off money launderers, the FSA has shown it has teeth. As an early example, in December 2002, the FSA fined the Royal Bank of Scotland (RBS) £750,000. It was a first penalty against a financial institution for failure of money laundering controls since the FSA assumed regulatory control in this sphere in December 2001. RBS was found to have weaknesses in its anti-money laundering controls across its retail network but – as is the case with all other FSA fines in this area so far – there was no evidence that money laundering had happened. The fine had been low because the bank's management addressed the shortcoming promptly and took an open and constructive approach to the regulatory investigation, according to the FSA.

19

Corporate governance

Introduction

This chapter guides you through how corporate governance works and has developed in the aftermath of the Maxwell scandal and the Enron collapse. We will look at, among other things, the Cadbury Code, the Combined Code and the Myners Report, as well as revision to the Listing Rules. We will scrutinise the Sarbanes-Oxley Act in the US, and its broad impact. We will see how International Financial Reporting Standards (IFRS) have tightened up accounting.

The concept

Corporate governance is about how a company conducts its corporate affairs and responds to stakeholders, employees and society. It covers ethical, legislative and other rules specifying how a company should act. The concept is not new. In 1776, Adam Smith said in his book *Inquiry into the Nature and Cause of the Wealth of Nations* that managers could not be expected to manage other people's money with 'the same anxious vigilance with which the partners in a private copartnery frequently watch over their own', and that 'negligence and profusion, therefore, must always prevail'.

Today two models of corporate governance are acknowledged. The stakeholder model places the interests of shareholders alongside those of employees, suppliers and the local community. Western companies and governments prefer the agency model, where shareholders, as owners of the company, delegate authority to its managers, who are their agents, and stewards of their assets.

Corporate governance has made enormous strides forward since the business excesses of the late 1980s, including collapses such as that of Polly Peck, and frauds such as when Robert Maxwell, chairman of Mirror Group Newspapers, plundered the pension funds of his companies (see Chapter 22).

The Cadbury Code

To prevent such abuses in future, the Committee on the Financial Aspects of Corporate Governance was set up in 1991. It was also known as the Cadbury Committee after its chairman Sir Adrian Cadbury, and was backed by the Financial Reporting Council (FRC), the London Stock Exchange (LSE) and the accounting profession. In 1992, the Committee produced the Cadbury Report, and with it codes of best practices applicable to UK listed companies.

The Cadbury Code, as these codes of best practice became known, set a direction and standards for corporate governance. The Code addressed the doubts of investors, the public, and the media about the effectiveness of boards, and whether non-executive directors or auditors could stand up to dominating chairmen and chief executive officers.

The Code proposed that the board should run the company and be held accountable, that the role of chairperson and chief executive should be separated, and that at least three independent non-executive directors should be on the board. Audit remuneration and nomination committees should comprise mainly non-executive directors, and there should be independent communication between non-executive directors and the auditors through an audit committee.

The reforms were mostly for listed companies, but were considered good governance guidance for any organisation. The Code was not legally binding, but companies listed on the LSE were expected to *comply or explain*, ie either to follow the provisions of the Code or to explain why they had not done so.

The Greenbury Committee

The next focus of attention was on the high earnings of company directors in companies with a mediocre performance, an anomaly often highlighted in the press. The Greenbury Committee, led by Sir Richard Greenbury, was set up in early 1995 and, in July of that year, produced a code on directors' pay. The Committee set out to link pay and performance. It focused on transparency shortcomings, including in share options. But it recognised that high calibre directors needed to be paid properly.

The Combined Code

In 1998, the Hampel Committee, under the chairmanship of Sir Ronnie Hampel, reviewed Cadbury and Greenbury. It put the case for continued self-regulation in corporate governance and against legislation. This gave rise to the Combined

Code, which set out the main guidelines for UK corporate governance, and the LSE issued it in 1998 as an appendage to the UK Listing Rules. Companies are required under the Listing Rules to include a statement in their annual reports on how they have applied the Code.

The Code consisted of principles of good governance and a code of best practice. Unlike Cadbury and Greenbury, it concentrated on a principles-based approach but, like those earlier codes, operated on the basis of *comply or explain*. It required boardroom practice to be clearer and more formal and took corporate governance to investors.

The Turnbull Report

Internal controls were next on the agenda, and The Turnbull Report, 1999, provided guidance in this area to listed companies, superseding the Rutterman Report, 1994, which had focused on internal controls and financial reporting. Turnbull said that internal controls should be both embedded in an organisation's operations, and responsive to changing risk inside and outside the company. In October 2005, minor revisions to Turnbull were announced.

Accounting scandals

Corporate governance received a push from relatively recent accounting scandals. Enron, a US energy company, went bankrupt in December 2001 and was accused of share ramping and fraud. In June 2002, WorldCom, a US telecoms group, revealed a US $11 billion accounting fraud and, a month later, made a Chapter 11 bankruptcy protection filing.

In December 2003, the Italian food and milk products company Parmalat almost defaulted on a small bond issue. Shortly afterwards, it was discovered that the group had falsified its accounts to conceal losses and that up to €800 million had been embezzled, mainly by Calisto Tanzi, the group's former chairman and chief executive.

OECD Principles of Corporate Governance

The OECD Principles of Corporate Governance had been created in 1999 by the Organisation for Economic Cooperation and Development, a Paris-based organisation of industrialised countries. The Principles were loosely based on the Cadbury Report and others, and represented the lowest common standard acceptable to OECD members. They were widely accepted as a benchmark. In

2002, the Principles were revised after consultation between representatives of OECD and non-OECD governments, businesses and other bodies. The basic ideas had not been queried, but OECD ministers had considered that there was a need for further guidance.

For example, the Principles required that an independent auditor should annually audit a company's accounts, but this was not always heeded. They required a company board to monitor and manage potential conflicts of interest of management, board members and shareholders, including misuse of corporate assets and abuse in related-party transactions, but this was not easy since the conflicts extended beyond the companies to financial analysts, institutions and rating agencies.

The revised Principles, approved in April 2004, aimed to rebuild and maintain public trust in companies and stock markets and advocated greater transparency. They asked governments to ensure effective regulatory frameworks, companies to be accountable, institutional investors to become more aware, and shareholders to have an effective role in determining executive compensation.

Directors' Remuneration Report Regulations

In August 2002 the Directors' Remuneration Report Regulations came into force. They aimed to improve disclosure and accountability to shareholders, and to enhance the competitiveness of listed companies by clarifying the link between pay and performance.

Under the Regulations, listed companies are required to publish a report on directors' remuneration with their annual report and accounts. The report must contain details of individual directors' remuneration packages, the company's remuneration policy and comparative company performance graphs.

Directors have a personal obligation to provide relevant information, and must prepare, circulate and file the remuneration report correctly, failure of either being a criminal offence, punishable with a fine. Auditors must confirm that auditable information has been properly prepared. The company must put an annual resolution to shareholders on the remuneration report. The result of the shareholder vote is advisory.

Higgs and Smith

The role of non-executive directors within a company came under particular scrutiny after the Enron fraud. The government asked Derek Higgs to report on the role of non-executive directors. Higgs liaised with the Smith Committee, established by the Financial Reporting Council (FRC) under Sir Robert Smith, which focused on the audit committee's role and the relationship between external auditors and the company that they audited. The Higgs and Smith reports were published together in January 2003.

Higgs said that non-executive directors should support the interests of shareholders, and have stronger communication lines with the company's main shareholders; at least half the board members, excluding the chairperson, should be non-executive directors; and non-executive directors should meet at least once a year without the chairperson or executive directors.

The Higgs report was controversial. Some non-executive directors have complained that it did not encourage investors to be sufficiently flexible towards corporate governance, and that it required non-executive directors to be assessed regularly, but not the same of executive directors. Higgs suggested an expanded Combined Code, incorporating amendments on audit committees suggested by Smith, and the FRC started consultation.

Revised Combined Code

The revised Combined Code was published in July 2003, and applies to reporting years starting in or after November 2003. It made the Combined Code still more principles-based, and encouraged more transparency and greater shareholder accountability. It says that all listed companies should have a nomination committee, whose members are mostly independent, non-executive directors; before a chairperson is appointed, his or her time commitment should be assessed, and no individual should chair more than one FTSE 100 company; the chairperson must ensure that directors receive timely information; and disclosure in the annual report is compulsory.

Executive directors should not have more than one non-executive directorship in a FTSE 100 company and should not chair one, according to the Code. The chairperson and chief executive should have separate roles: non-executive directors should be independent; and appointments to the board are made on merit. Directors' pay should be linked to corporate and individual performance, based on a formal and transparent procedure, and directors must not help to decide their own pay.

In financial reporting, the board is required by the Code to present a balanced and understandable assessment of the company's position and prospects. A system of internal controls should be maintained and reviewed annually. The audit committee should consist only of independent directors, and make recommendations on the appointment and removal of external auditors.

Most of the revisions to the Code were in the detail. Probably the most significant new element was a requirement that the Board should formally evaluate its own performance and the chairperson should act on results. Some directors believed that there was not enough evidence of a connection between evaluation and greater effectiveness, and that too much attention was given to simplistic aspects of board performance, such as attendance at meetings, and not enough to less easily assessable aspects such as commercial ability and ethics of directors.

There is evidence of less scepticism today. In 2005, Edis-Bates Associates conducted a survey of company secretaries on their views on the Combined Code. The aim was to help the FRC in a review it was undertaking on implementation of the Code. The survey, published in October 2005, found that 71 per cent of company secretaries who responded believed that the rules on evaluation were working, although in smaller companies they were less inclined to agree. Company secretaries gave their boards 6.5 out of 10 for rigour in their last board performance evaluation. Over three-quarters of survey participants believed evaluations would, over time, improve their own board's performance.

In January 2006, the FRC published the results of its review. It found that, since the introduction of the revised Code, there had overall been an improvement in the quality of corporate governance among listed companies, and a more constructive dialogue between boards and their main shareholders. This showed a lot more support for board evaluation than might have been expected in 2003, according to an FRC spokesman. The FRC recommended some minor changes to the Code and, if agreed, they were to take effect later in 2006.

Not everybody is in agreement. In late 2005, researchers for a survey by Hanson Green interviewed 20 chief executives and chairs about corporate governance. Most of them said that the revised Combined Code had led to very little return in relation to time and money spent. A separate survey by Russell Reynolds interviewed nearly 60 company chairs about the revised Code and 65 per cent of them thought it had little impact on performance.

The Myners Report

Pension funds came under individual scrutiny after the Maxwell pension theft and subsequent legislative changes. In 2001, the Myners Report, commissioned from Paul Myners by the Chancellor of the Exchequer, recommended a voluntary code of practice for the pension fund industry. The report highlighted the need for still greater transparency in how pension funds were used. It found that many pension fund trustees lacked the investment expertise to assess services sold to them by investment consultants and fund managers, and relied on a small number of investment consultants supplying bundled actuarial and investment advice.

Myners found that pension funds devoted insufficient resources to asset allocation, and that unclear contractual structures created unnecessary incentives for short termism in investment. He said there was insufficient focus on adding value through shareholder engagement, and that pension fund trustees should voluntarily adopt best practice principles for investment decision making on a *comply or explain* basis. Only individuals with the right skill and experience should take decisions. The performance of all advisers and managers should be measured, and trustees should assess their own performance. Trustees should engage with investee companies when it was in the interest of their fund members, and investment strategies and returns should be reported annually. Fraud compensation provision should be extended.

The government agreed that the principles would benefit pension funds, consumers, industry and itself. The Myners recommendations went ahead. In December 2004, the government reported that implementation had achieved only partial success.

The US and the Sarbanes-Oxley Act

Accounting has come under scrutiny in the US, which has had impact on the UK and the rest of Europe. In 1987, the Treadway Commission Report found audit committees important for combating fraudulent financial reporting. In 1988, the Securities & Exchange Commission (SEC), the US regulatory body, ruled that regulated companies should have an audit committee with mainly non-executive directors. In the Enron accounting scandal, the Arthur Anderson team in charge of the company audit was found to have destroyed documents to conceal the truth. The case showed a need for stricter controls and The Sarbanes-Oxley Act 2002 was an emergency piece of legislation phased in by US Congress, based on reforms agreed with the New York Stock Exchange.

The Act, named after its authors, democratic senator Paul Sarbanes and republican congressman Michael Oxley, mainly affects a company's external auditors, internal accounting professionals and IT providers. It applies to companies that issue securities in the US, including about half those included on the UK's FTSE 100 index, and to those that own a US subsidiary or are required to file reports with the SEC. The company's physical location is not significant, but the national rules of a non-US country will prevail should they conflict with the Act.

Sarbanes-Oxley aims to reinforce the independent status of external auditors and requires procedures that stamp out creative accounting. Financial reports should be auditable and supported by data, as well as proof against alteration, with systems in place to detect this.

Accountants cannot mix auditing with certain activities, including actuarial or legal services, and bookkeeping. Auditors are supervised by a Public Company Accounting Oversight Board that is answerable to the SEC. They are required to maintain audit records for five years. Failure to comply may be punished with a fine and up to 10 years' imprisonment. The company's audit committee must pre-certify all other non-audit work.

Under the Act, significant extra disclosure is required in the report and accounts, as well as ethical guidelines for senior financial officers. Guidelines are required on analysts' conflicts of interest. There is a ban on personal loans to executive officers and directors. Accelerated reporting of trades by insiders is required, with no such trades allowed during pension fund blackout periods. The Act increases corporate responsibility for any fraudulent actions taken, and there are criminal and civil penalties for securities violations.

The chief executive and chief financial officer must sign off financial statements to confirm compliance with the provisions of the Securities & Exchange Act, 1934. If the statements turn out to be incorrect, the signatories could be held criminally liable under Sarbanes-Oxley, even if they had not intended deceit. They could receive a fine of up to US $1 million and up to 10 years' imprisonment. If they certified the inaccurate statements wilfully, the fine could be US $5 million, and the prison sentence 20 years.

Sarbanes-Oxley requires organisations to introduce adequate IT systems and assess their adequacy annually. To assist the process of justice, whistleblowers are protected. Civil penalties are added to disgorgement funds to relieve victims.

US listings have become less attractive to foreign companies as a result of Sarbanes-Oxley, and the LSE has benefited from greater interest in a London quotation from, among others, Russian and Chinese companies.

European auditing rules

On 16 March 2004, the European Commission published draft proposals on auditing rules with the aim of enabling investors to be more confident that company accounts were accurate. This was part of the update of the 8th Company Law Directive on statutory audit, which the Commission tabled in 2003 to avoid auditing scandals such as Enron and Parmalat. In September 2005, euro MEPs in Strasbourg backed the proposal, which would guarantee the independence of auditors in relation to the management of major listed companies. The proposal would also require listed companies to have an audit committee or a body with equivalent functions to oversee the auditor's work, and to rotate audit partners regularly.

The European Commission has said it sees no need for a single EU-wide corporate governance code and that, in most cases, rules should be left to each member state. But it has proposed some common requirements. If agreed, revisions to the 4th Company Law Directive will require all companies listed in the EU to include in their annual reports a statement on how they have complied with the relevant national code, and to describe their internal controls related to financial reporting. This Directive is at the time of writing with the European Parliament.

Operating and financial review

In 1992, the Cadbury Committee concluded that shareholders needed a coherent narrative of a company's performance and prospects, including the factors likely to influence a company's future progress. It said this narrative could be met by the provision of an essentially forward-looking operating and financial review (OFR), on which the Accounting Standards Board (ASB) issued a first best practice statement in 1993. The ASB statement was updated in 2003 to reflect developments in narrative reporting.

The Company Law Review, put in place by the Government in 1988, recommended that most public companies and large private companies should be required to publish an OFR. In May 2004, the government proposed that quoted companies only should be subject to this obligation. It singled them out because, as a class of entity, they had dispersed shareholdings and a market in their shares.

The Department of Trade & Industry commissioned the Radcliffe Group, an independent body led by Rosemary Radcliffe, to prepare guidance for company directors on *materiality* in the context of the OFR. In 2003, the EU Accounts Modernisation Directive required large and medium-sized companies to include an enhanced review of a company's business in the directors' report, which was part of the annual report.

The government dovetailed the requirements of the OFR and the Directive so that quoted companies did not have to provide the same information in both. As a result, the reference to *materiality* was dropped, and the final report of the Radcliffe group set out practical guidance for directors on what should be included in their OFRs.

In 2004, the DTI put draft regulations in place, and the OFR became a statutory requirement for all UK-listed companies to publish for financial years starting on or after 1 April 2005. It was to provide a balanced and comprehensive view of how the company is developing, its performance, its position at the end of the year, and of trends and factors affecting the company. It was to analyse recent performance and statistics, and describe potential risks and liabilities.

Some directors had difficulties with the judgemental reporting style, although others welcomed the open and flexible structure. On 28 November 2005 Chancellor Gordon Brown made a surprise announcement in his speech to the Confederation of British Industry annual conference that he intended to remove the requirement to publish the OFR. He presented this planned move as evidence of the Government's deregulatory credentials.

Many felt that the OFR had been a sensible move towards corporate transparency, and listed companies had invested a lot of time and money into meeting the publication requirement. But businesses will still have to adhere to the Accounts Modernisation Directive, which – for quoted companies – was to have been enforced through the OFR. The business review required by this Directive puts less of an onus on firms to give information about the future and it is less clear on how far it requires owners to understand the strategy of the business, but many of the requirements remain the same.

The DTI has estimated that to remove the requirement to produce the OFR and have it audited saves UK-listed companies £33 million a year. Some consider this a small sum relative to the overall expenditure of the companies and the importance of transparency.

International Financial Reporting Standards

For financial years beginning on or after 1 January 2005, harmonised accounting standards came into force for the consolidated accounts of all listed companies in the European Union. UK-unlisted companies could at this stage choose to continue using the UK standards. International Financial Reporting Standards (IFRS) is to be adopted in 90 countries.

Under IFRS, the cost of stock options estimated at the date of grant will be expensed to the profit and loss account as the benefit is earned. Goodwill must be recognised and tested for impairment. Dividends are no longer accrued, unless they are declared before the year end. Deferred taxes are calculated on revaluations as well as on timing differences. There are more choices for accounting for actuarial gains and losses. The classification of leases into operating or finance must be reassessed. Hybrid securities such as preference shares are classified as debt rather than, like before, as equity because there is a focus on the substance of the transaction, which, in this case, may resemble a debt instrument. Derivatives must be put on the balance sheet at fair value and marked to market through the profit and loss account.

As a result of IFRS, company accounts are likely to be longer than before, and with greater disclosure, perhaps inclusive of commercially sensitive information. Any material error discovered in previous statements during the conversion process must be corrected.

Regulators hope that IFRS means fewer accounting scandals. In April 2005, the Financial Services Authority (FSA) said that IFRS information should be published as soon as it was reliable and no later than the publication of interim financial information, and that price sensitive information about the transition should be published immediately. (See also Chapter 17.)

There are discussions ongoing about divergence between IFRS and US GAAP, which lends support to the view that the UK rules-based approach to regulation is gathering momentum on this side of the Atlantic. For details of how IFRS has affected the work of analysts, see Chapter 17.

Listing Rules

Under the Listing Rules, new applicants for listing must ensure that directors are free from conflicts of interest between corporate and personal interests, unless the company has arrangements in place to manage these conflicts. The FSA dropped a proposal made from October 2003 for an equivalent continuing obligation because the Combined Code and company law adequately covered these requirements.

The Model Code, an appendix to the Listing Rules, is a code of conduct imposing restrictions beyond the law. It aims to stop directors or employees of listed companies, and linked parties, from abusing, or placing themselves under suspicion of abusing, unpublished price-sensitive information. It applies especially in periods shortly before results are reported. In July 2005, the FSA simplified the Model Code as part of its revisions to the Listing Rules, extending it to persons discharging 'managerial responsibility'.

The future

The FSA is focusing on principles and management responsibility, as discussed in Chapter 17, which makes corporate governance a bigger issue than before. Regulators, senior management, listing authorities, analysts, and investor-related trade bodies have an interest. Rating agencies take account of corporate governance when they give companies a credit rating. Governance and senior management is a frequent theme on FSA supervisory visits to financial services companies, and the regulator has suggested that non-executive directors have a role in watching how the companies operate, according to PricewaterhouseCoopers.

Over time, there will be pressure from the stock market, environmental and other groups and league tables to promote good standards, according to corporate governance consultants. But how far companies see corporate governance as red tape, and how far they apply it in spirit, remains to be seen. Much of this relates to how far companies believe they can benefit from corporate governance.

In a December 2004 paper, *Corporate Governance and Performance*, Hermes Pension Fund Management noted that even when research had established a correlation between corporate governance and performance, it was notoriously difficult to prove causation. But Hermes considered that it had sufficient evidence to support its view that good corporate governance improved the long-term performance of companies. In coming to this view, Hermes took into account opinion-based research; focus-list research and performance of shareholder engagement funds; and governance-ranking research.

The most widely quoted opinion-based research into the link between corporate governance is McKinsey's *Global Investor Opinion Survey* (2000, updated in 2002), which found that 80 per cent of respondents would pay a premium for well-governed companies. The size of the premium varied by market, from 12 per cent in the UK, to around 40 per cent for companies operating in countries with a less certain regulatory environment such as Egypt, Morocco and Russia. Other studies have supported McKinsey's finding that investors favour well-governed companies. But Hermes noted that opinion-based research relied on circumstantial and inevitably subjective data.

Investors issue *focus* lists with the aim of inducing company management to address performance or governance-related problems by publicising them. CalPERS issues the best-known focus list. Until 2004, the companies included in the CalPERS focus list had substantially outperformed in the five years after their listing. Hermes said that, on balance, the focus-list studies supported the view that publicising company problems and actively engaging with the companies, where appropriate, to address their failings identified could improve their performance.

Hermes found further evidence that active ownership improved performance in the success of shareholder engagement funds, which invested in under-performing companies with potential for improvement. Hermes' original UK Focus Fund has outperformed the FTSE All-Share Total Return Index by 4.5 per cent on an annualised basis since its inception in 1998.

Governance-ranking research aims to establish a link between factors or standards that objectively measure a company's governance quality and its performance. But any single governance standard may be unrelated to the performance of companies in a particular market during a given period of time, according to Hermes.

Whichever direction corporate governance takes, there are issues over which approach is best for the UK. The US approach to corporate governance is rules-based, and this has been making increasing inroads into the UK principles-based culture, much as in the field of financial services regulation. How far the UK can avoid being unduly influenced by the US rules-based approach over the next few years may depend partly on how far it can align its corporate governance principles with those of continental Europe, which has both rules and principles, according to PricewaterhouseCoopers.

20

Insurance – the London companies market

Introduction

In this chapter, we will take a broad look at insurance and the London market. We will see how London is split between companies on the one hand and Lloyd's (covered in Chapter 21) on the other. We will focus on how underwriting works, and the intricacies of reinsurance. We will examine the impact on insurance of world events such as terrorism, as well as regulatory developments.

The concept

Insurance is a service that offers financial compensation in return for a premium payment should an adverse event occur. In an insurance transaction, one party, the insurer, undertakes to pay another party, the insured, money if a specified form of financial risk should arise. For this service, the insured pays the insurer a fee, known as a premium.

The UK has the largest insurance market in Europe, and third largest in the world behind the US and Japan, accounting for £295 billion in premium income, which is 9.1 per cent of the global total, and of which £45 billion is from overseas business. It employs 325,000 people, which is a third of all financial services personnel.

Insurance may be categorised under three broad headings: general insurance; life and pensions; and health and protection. Of the 772 insurance companies authorised to carry on insurance business in the UK, 568 do only general business, as defined below, and 159 are authorised specifically for long-term business (such as life insurance and pensions). The remaining 45 insurers are composite, which do both.

General insurance is defined by the Association of British Insurers as insurance of non-life risks where the policy offers cover for a limited period, usually a year. It is covered in this chapter and the next. For discussion of the remaining two categories, see Chapter 22.

Insurers limit exposure to risk by passing their liability to a reinsurance company, a procedure known as reinsurance. It is effectively how insurers insure themselves, and we will see how it works in this chapter.

London

The London market consists of the international insurance and reinsurance business, mostly non-life. It has only about 3 per cent of worldwide non-life premiums, but it includes a high proportion of very large or complex risks. It accounts for 10–15 per cent of industrial insurance business, and 40 per cent of the marine market, according to a recent Swiss Re report. London represents 25 per cent of internationally available reinsurance. It is, furthermore, a *leading* market, setting the rates and providing the intellectual capital for risks that are written elsewhere.

The London market is split between the company market, which consists of insurance companies, and Lloyd's of London, which consists of syndicates, and which we will examine in detail in Chapter 21. The insurance company market grew in the 1970s as foreign insurers opened City offices. Most London market companies are members of the International Underwriting Association. London has both non-Lloyd's brokers, and 164 Lloyd's brokers. Most of the larger brokers are in both categories.

There are 39 protection and indemnity associations, known as P&I clubs, in the London market. They were set up to cover marine risk, and provide much higher levels of cover than available commercially because they buy substantial pooled reinsurance. Some clubs are now used by doctors and lawyers to provide professional indemnity cover. The UK's share of this market was close to 70 per cent between 1997 and 2004, according to data compiled by Standard & Poor's.

Types of business

There are three main types of business in the London market: marine, aviation and transport, known as MAT; home-foreign; and non-MAT treaty reinsurance. The London market's MAT business developed from Lloyd's marine underwriting, and Lloyd's does more than half of this business. The London market has about a fifth of global premiums for the marine and aviation business. Home-foreign business covers writing risks from London that are outside the UK. This type of business is roughly split two thirds from Lloyd's and the rest from insurance companies. Non-MAT treaty reinsurance is general risks, ie non-transport, of which insurance companies do around two thirds, and Lloyd's the remainder.

The underwriting process

The London market, whether the insurers are companies or Lloyd's syndicates, works as follows. A broker seeks insurers for specific risks, and must find a *lead* underwriter who will accept the first share, perhaps 25 per cent of the risk, and so establish the policy terms, and then find *following* underwriters who will subscribe on this basis. This risk syndication can be spread across anything from one or two to ten or more companies or syndicates on each risk, with great variations across different classes of business.

Some underwriters will take more risks than others. The quality of underwriting may vary according to information received, advice taken and risk modelling, as well as the type and amount of business taken on, premiums payable and reinsurance terms. Market conditions also play a part.

In the part of the insurance cycle called a hard market, insurance rates rise because demand exceeds supply. Profits tend to accrue in a hard market, attracting extra capital into the market. As the supply increases again, it tends to create a soft market, in which lead insurers focus on market share rather than profit.

A major disaster leads to a hardening of rates, particularly in the classes of business that are most affected by the disaster, which may be welcomed by the industry. After the 11 September 2001 terrorist attacks on the US, aviation rates particularly hardened, and after Hurricane Katrina in August 2005, energy reinsurance rates hardened. Classes not directly affected may also see a hardening because the relationship between supply and demand changes, but the change is less pronounced. There are usually other factors in play. If rates are softening in any case, a major event may slow the trend, but not entirely reverse it.

Underwriting profit for a non-life or reinsurance company is measured through the combined loss expense ratio, known as the combined ratio. It is the sum of the loss ratio, which is losses paid or reserved as a percentage of premiums received, and the expense ratio, which consists of the expenses for the insurance business other than claims, as a percentage of premium income. The claims, expenses and premium are net figures, which means that they are what is left after taking into account all relevant cash inflows and outflows.

If the combined ratio is 99 per cent, the insurance company will have made a 1 per cent underwriting profit. But if it is higher than 100 per cent, non-life insurance policies may still be profitable after allocated investment income has been taken into account.

Insurance companies need to ensure that they manage the underwriting cycle. In really good years, they may make a profit on their pure underwriting but, more often, they make a loss. If interest rates are high, the companies may set insurance rates at a relatively low level to attract funds and invest the premiums for a maximum return. By such cash flow underwriting, insurers can cover underwriting losses out of interest payments. If interest rates prove volatile, the strategy is risky. Insurers need to be cautious not to cut prices beyond their means, which is what led to the high-profile collapse of Independent Insurance, a liability insurer, in June 2001.

Reinsurance

To offset its own exposure, an insurance company will use reinsurance, which works as follows. The insurer passing on the liability is known as the ceding office. It pays a premium to the reinsurer, which is the company that accepts the cession and assumes responsibility for claims. Any of the business that the insurer keeps rather than passing onto the reinsurer is known as retention. Reinsurance solutions can be generic or bespoke.

Let us look in more detail at how the reinsurance contract works. It can be proportional or non-proportional. In the case of proportional reinsurance, also known as participating reinsurance, both the premium received from the insured and the cost of the claims are split equally between the ceding office and the reinsurer. Property insurers prefer this arrangement because the sum insured is usually known, making proportional divisions practical.

Proportional reinsurance may be treaty or facultative. If it is surplus treaty, the reinsurer must accept any surplus risk above that retained by the ceding office. If it is quota share treaty, the ceding office must reinsure a stated portion of every risk. If the business is facultative, the ceding office chooses whether to reinsure and, if so, how much, and the reinsurer similarly chooses how much to accept.

Non-proportional reinsurance is where losses are split disproportionately, if at all, between the ceding office and reinsurers. It is commonly excess-of-loss reinsurance, where the ceding office pays the initial layer of every claim. The reinsurers pay the balance up to a set figure, beyond which further excess-of-loss cover may apply.

Excess-of-loss cover may be arranged on a treaty or facultative basis. Liability insurers use this type of cover because the extent of any payout is based on the value of claims. Marine insurers sometimes use excess-of-loss cover, and, at other times, proportional, reinsurance. In excess-of-loss reinsurance, many contracts need syndication, and so the broker plays more of a role than in some proportional insurance. Excess-of-loss reinsurance needs more analytic and quantitative input, and brokers have developed this.

Excess-of-loss-ratio, or stop loss, reinsurance is a variation on the theme. It does not insure individual events, but it prevents excessive fluctuation in the net claims ratio, which is the average of net claims to net premiums. For example, a company might be covered for 90 per cent of any excess beyond 60 per cent.

For excessively large risks, reinsurance pools can operate. They enable insurers to reinsure 100 per cent of their risk into a pool. Profits and losses will be shared equally between participants. There are specialist types of reinsurance, including financial reinsurance, which aims to spread the incidence of losses over a number of accounting periods and not just one. Subsequent comparable products include the securitisation of insurance risk, and insurance derivatives.

Terrorism has given rise to a specialist focus on reinsurance. On 10 April 1992, an IRA bombing campaign led to an explosion in the financial centre of London which threatened to make insurance cover for acts of terrorism unavailable. Following extensive discussions between the Government and the insurance industry, Pool Re, a mutual reinsurance company, was created in 1993. It is owned by participants in UK commercial property insurance, and the Government is its reinsurer of last resort. In 2002, Pool Re cover was extended from only fire and explosion to all risks related to terrorism, including nuclear contamination. The 11 September 2001 terrorist attacks on the US, among other things, triggered insurers into closer inspection of their reinsurance arrangements, including the quality of their reinsurers.

In recent years, insurers have become less inclined than before to use reinsurance arrangements as a substitute for good underwriting. They are giving brokers less discretion in choice of reinsurer, particularly for long-tail business, where the liability may be discovered and claims made many years after the loss was caused. The £200–300 million insurance payouts to those who claimed on long tail asbestosis-related diseases have served as a warning.

Some cedants want collateralised structures, and others spread their credit risk by having more reinsurers on the programme. There is an increasing use of downgrade clauses, by which if a reinsurer's rating falls below a trigger level, the primary insurer may be permitted to void the contract or require collateral to be posted. The existence of this trigger limits the reinsurer's ability to attract new business.

As part of the same reaction, credit rating agencies have lowered the financial strength ratings of some reinsurers, although they rate the sector outlook as stable. Many reinsurers feel that the rating agencies have too much power, and use outdated methodologies. The agencies say that the reinsurance market sometimes makes ratings the scapegoat for its own failings.

When reinsurance rates have declined, it means smaller broker commissions. But the broker may recommend more cover or a lowering of the deductible for the same outlay.

Dispute resolution

When disputes arise between insurers and their reinsurers, the usual way to resolve them is through arbitration. The process of arbitration is acknowledged as time-consuming and expensive, and, although every case is supposed to be confidential, parties involved sometimes leak details. There is growing interest in alternative methods outside the courts, such as mediation, which are known collectively as alternative dispute resolution, or ADR.

Regulatory developments

Today the Financial Services Authority (FSA) regulates and supervises the UK insurance and reinsurance industry, including brokers, along with the rest of the financial services industry. It takes a much more proactive approach to insurance regulation than its predecessor, the Department of Trade & Industry. To improve solvency requirements, from 31 December 2004, the FSA introduced requirements for insurers to have capital that more closely matched the risk of business written.

The need for *contract certainty* was highlighted by the events of 11 September 2001. In December 2004, John Tiner, chief executive of the FSA, said that he was concerned about the 'deal now, detail later' culture of the London insurance market. Shortly afterwards, the FSA gave the London market two years to find a solution.

The London market had already taken a significant step towards the achievement of contract certainty with the development of a standardised London Market Principles, or LMP, slip format to record submissions. In October 2005 it published the Contract Certainty Code of Practice & Checklist to offer practical guidance to market organisations regarding how they can meet the further requirements of contract certainty. These require all terms and conditions to be agreed at inception, and for an evidence of cover to be issued within 30 days. Brokers and insurers are now implementing the Code of Practice.

Contingent commissions are where insurers pay commissions to brokers depending on profit or volume and are another area of regulatory focus. In April 2004, New York Attorney General Eliot Spitzer launched an investigation into contingent commissions and subsequently alleged that certain brokers had taken pay offs from insurance providers in return for introducing clients, with the result that the clients were denied best prices for policies required. During 2005, a small number of brokers agreed to pay substantial fines to settle charges initiated by Spitzer, including bid rigging, but many neither admitted nor denied the allegations. Spitzer said that there would be further investigations across the industry.

Within weeks of Spitzer's allegations, seven global insurance brokers announced that they would stop contingent commissions and, by early 2005, they were presenting revised business models. Spitzer focused on primary insurance, but reinsurance is likely to be restructured as a result, according to industry sources. It could be separated more clearly from other insurance within holding companies, and there could be more price disclosure to cedants, they said.

The EU Reinsurance Directive is a component of the European Commission's Financial Services Action Plan and was approved in June 2005. Its aims are to simplify the European reinsurance market, make it more transparent, and harmonise its legislation. The Directive enables companies supervised by a home state regulator to write business across the EU on a single passport.

The future

As an insurance centre, London has significant underwriting expertise, diversity of business and a reputation for innovation. It has access to backup specialists such as lawyers, consultants and claims adjusters, and provides the best expertise in interpreting contractual clauses for settling claims. More commercial aviation insurance is underwritten in London than anywhere else.

For such reasons, London constantly attracts new capital. But its market share of the global growth in non-life premiums has declined since the 1990s. London is strictly regulated, which has obvious commercial benefit, but it is harder to obtain an insurance licence there compared with some competing centres such as Bermuda. Technology weakness is seen as likely to have impacted adversely on London's growth, but the market is now addressing this.

Many accounting and settlement procedures have been based on a message format which is not transferable internationally and, by 2006, the London market had planned to have introduced a new standards model that would enable the creation of portable data.

21

Insurance – Lloyd's of London

Introduction

In this chapter, we will focus on how Lloyd's of London works. With the companies market (covered in Chapter 20), it makes up the London insurance market. We will examine the history of Lloyd's, how syndicates work, and the chain of security and past problems, as well as recent developments.

Lloyd's explained

Lloyd's is part of the London insurance market. It is not a company but a market. Lloyd's members accept insurance business through annual ventures known as syndicates but are not responsible for each other's losses. The members included companies, which may underwrite through only one syndicate, and individuals, known as Names, which typically underwrite through a number of syndicates. The 62 syndicates in the market cover speciality areas such as marine, aviation, catastrophe, professional indemnity and motor.

The syndicates compete for business, cover all or part of the risk, and are staffed by underwriters, on whose judgement the market depends. The managing agent employs underwriting staff and manages one or more syndicates on members' behalf, and may not carry out any other function. Accredited Lloyd's brokers place risks at Lloyd's for clients. Other insurance brokers can access Lloyd's through an accredited Lloyd's broker.

According to Lloyd's, the market has a good track record of paying claims that dates back over 300 years. But some market sources suggest that the record became truly unblemished only in 1925 when mutualisation began.

The mutualisation process is where members of Lloyd's pool resources in the Lloyd's Central Fund, which is available as a fund of last resort to the syndicates. In this section, we shall look in more detail at how Lloyd's works.

History

Lloyd's started as *Edward Lloyd's Coffee House*, a 17th-century coffee house where timely shipping news was made available and marine insurance could be obtained. In 1769, a breakaway movement of customers set up the rival *New Lloyd's Coffee House*. In 1774, as business increased, rooms were hired in the Royal Exchange. In this way, merchants, underwriters and brokers started the Society of Lloyd's.

In 1811, Lloyd's gained a constitution, regulating admission more strictly, and the market was incorporated as the Society of Lloyd's and Corporation of Lloyd's under the Lloyd's Act of 1871. In 1887, Lloyd's issued its first non-marine policies and, 17 years later in 1904, a first motor policy, followed in 1911 by an aviation policy. In 1958, Lloyd's moved to Lime Street.

Capital support

The capital support from members, known as syndicate capacity, dictates how much business a syndicate can write in a year. The capital that backs the syndicates comes from corporate and individual members. Corporate capital was introduced in 1994 and now makes up 89.5 per cent of the market capacity. In 2005, corporate members provided £12,277 million of capital and 1,625 individual members provided £1,445 million of capital to the Lloyd's market.

Where the corporate member is part of the same group as the managing agent or owned by the same company, it is referred to as an *aligned* member. If the syndicate consists entirely of a single corporate member aligned to the managing agent, it is an *integrated Lloyd's vehicle*.

Chain of security

Premiums and other monies received by members are held for the benefit of policyholders in premium trust funds at syndicate level or in overseas regulatory deposits funded from them. These are to pay claims, reinsurance premiums and underwriting expenses and are the first link in the 'chain of security'. Moneys are invested, with availability when required.

In case the premium trust funds do not have enough resources to pay policyholders, every member, corporate or individual, must hold additional capital at Lloyd's, which is held in trust and is the second link in the chain of security. Other assets of Lloyd's members are available to meet claims and are the third link. The fourth link in the security chain is the Central Fund, available to back Lloyd's policies issued after 1992. The Council of Lloyd's has discretion to use it.

As at 31 December, 2004, there was £21,873 million in premiums trust funds and overseas deposits to ensure policyholders' claims would be met if members were unable to meet their underwriting liabilities. There were also members' funds at Lloyd's of £9,622 million, with additional declared assets of members of £219 million. The Central Fund had £556 million in net assets, mainly cash and conservative investments. In aggregate, the value of Lloyd's central assets amounted to £1,184 million.

Past problems

To sign up as Names in the 1980s, members of the public needed only £100,000 in assets.

Some of the business included London market excess of loss (LMX) cover, which led to the LMX spiral. Syndicates and insurance companies would be responsible for paying an initial slice of a loss, with a next slice passed on to a reinsurer, and the next to another, sometimes winding back down to the original insurer or reinsurer who would take another slice, effectively reinsuring itself. This way, Names' risk was recycled, concentrating rather than spreading exposure.

The LMX business contracted and the cost of cover became more expensive, but a few syndicates were left with most of the reinsurance claims and made cash calls on Names to pay the claims. Members' agents placed new Names and some old Names on what turned out to be high-risk syndicates. New US pollution legislation was introduced in the 1980s, and US courts were awarding damages to workers exposed to health risks. The asbestos and chemical companies started claiming against insurance policies and, in their turn the insurers claimed from their reinsurers, often Lloyd's syndicates. This was long-tail business, so named because claims could arise up to decades after the policy was written.

Disasters hit Lloyd's insurers. In 1988, the Piper Alpha oil platform caught fire and fell into the North Sea. In 1989, Hurricane Hugo struck Puerto Rico, St Croix, South Carolina and North Carolina and, in the same year, oil tanker Exxon Valdez ran aground off the Alaskan coast. In 1990, there were storms across Europe.

Names backed one year venture syndicates, and closing syndicate years passed their portfolios of policies and reserves covering claims forward to future years. The process was known as reinsurance to close (RITC). As a result, a closing syndicate had liabilities not only from policies written during the year in which it accepted business, but also from policies acquired by reinsuring to close the previous years of account.

It was old US general liability risks, including asbestosis claims, as well as reinsurance catastrophe claims related to the LMX spiral, that in the late 1980s and early 1990s caused large losses to Names. In 1988–1992, losses in the Lloyd's market totalled £8 billion and some respected commentators queried whether the market could survive. By 1988, active Names on Lloyd's syndicates numbered more than 32,000, up from about 6,000 in 1970.

In 1991, up to several thousand Names resigned from Lloyd's, and others reduced or stopped their underwriting commitments. Many refused to pay cash calls. Some took legal action against members' and managing agents for negligent advice, negligent underwriting or closure of years of accounts, and against auditors.

David Coleridge, then chairman of Lloyd's, appointed a task force under David Rowland, chief executive of broker Sedgwick, which in January 1992 recommended many changes to the Lloyd's market, including new governance arrangements, but keeping the essential form. Among the changes introduced, smaller Names were given the option to pool their limits into Members' Agents Pooling Arrangements, which spread their resources into large lines of underwriting and so reduced their risk. Corporate members with limited liability, but also higher deposit requirements to support underwriting activity, were introduced.

Rowland created the Hardship Committee to help Names pay their debts. It was headed by Lloyd's council member Dr Mary Archer, wife of best-selling novelist Jeffrey, and enabled some in proven financial hardship to pay up in stages or by a deferred arrangement. For the 1992 year of account, 22,162 Names were actively underwriting at Lloyd's. Insurance companies were formidable competition for the syndicates, but they faced major claims by building societies against mortgage guarantee policies issued in the burst 1988 housing bubble, and on some marine insurance, not reinsured at Lloyd's.

In 1993, David Rowland became Lloyd's first full-time paid chairman. In 1996, he completed a market-wide reconstruction and renewal (R&R) settlement plan. The main part was to form Equitas Reinsurance Ltd, a government-approved insurance company whose reinsurance would have the effect of closing all the 1992 and prior years of account of Lloyd's syndicates writing non-life business. It closed all open years of account and gave Names what Lloyd's described as 'affordable finality'. But it was not within the power of Lloyd's at the time, and is not within the power of Equitas now, to grant an absolute release to Names from their liabilities to policyholders. There was, and still is, a residual risk for Names if Equitas should fail to pay liabilities in full.

Lloyd's had calculated that the premium required to reinsure the losses incurred on the 1992 and prior years of account amounted to £14.7 billion. In comparison, the syndicate assets available to meet these liabilities amounted to £9.9 billion. A significant part of the balance was believed to be irrecoverable from the many Names who had incurred significant losses.

The Lloyd's R&R plan made an early estimate of a £2.8 billion settlement offer to help fill the gap, and this was increased to £3.2 billion. It consisted of £1.1 billion of litigation settlement funds from the underwriting agents, auditors and their respective Errors & Omissions (E&O) insurers and £2.1 billion of debt credits. The debt credits were funded by a special contribution from the Lloyd's Central Fund, contributions from the agents and brokers, contributions from Lloyd's following sales of assets, and a loan facility that would be repaid through a premium charge on the 1997 and subsequent years of account. To help Names pay their share of the remaining shortfall, special arrangements were made that allowed for the early release of anticipated surpluses from the 1993, 1994 and 1995 years of account.

In March 1996, the Department of Trade & Industry authorised the formation of Equitas, subject to certain requirements, including an agreed level of surplus assets over liabilities. Lloyd's sent out its settlement offer to all 32,000 plus Names at the end of July 1996 and by the first closing date, 28 August 1996, acceptances were sufficiently high for the Council of Lloyd's to declare the offer unconditional. Equitas accepted the reinsurance obligations and proceeded with the run-off of the business. Ultimately about 95% of Names accepted the settlement offer and more than nine years on, Equitas is still in business paying off the Names' liabilities on their behalf.

Recent developments

Since 30 November, 2001, the Financial Services Authority has been responsible for direct regulation of the Society of Lloyd's and Lloyd's underwriting agents. In 2003, Lloyd's implemented a new franchise model.

Since 1 January 2005, Lloyd's main market-financial-reporting regime has been on an annual accounting basis under UK GAAP. This means that syndicate annual accounts are required to recognise a profit or loss for the financial year in question and give a true and fair view of that result and of the syndicate's financial position at the end of the financial year.

The accounting difference between the annual accounting basis and the three-year fund accounting basis can be considerable. Under annual accounting, the Lloyd's loss from the 11 September 2001 terrorist attacks on the US was accounted for in the 2001 financial year, when the loss occurred, but under three-year accounting, it was split between 1999 (a very small proportion), 2000 and 2001, the years in which the relevant insurance policies incepted.

On the international front, Lloyd's has a large global licence network and Lloyd's underwriters write business in 200 countries. Lloyd's has licences in over 73, the latest being a reinsurance licence in China, which it sees as an investment in a future in which insurance is becoming more international. Lloyd's also plans a representative office in India.

But Lloyd's is calling for a level playing field. Like other European reinsurers, Lloyd's finds it hard to understand the US *credit for reinsurance* rules. These rules mean that US reinsurers reinsuring US insurance companies are not required to provide any collateral to cover their liabilities, whereas all foreign reinsurers, including those from the UK, must post collateral equal to 100 per cent of their gross liabilities to US insurers. Lloyd's is pressing for reforms in this area to recognise the strength and security of the reinsurer and not to differentiate based on where the reinsurer is located.

The current rules have helped to increase the cost of reinsurance – Lloyd's costs are estimated to be in the region of US$150 million per annum – and to restrict much needed critical capacity. Immediately after the 11 September 2001 terrorist attacks on the US, Lloyd's was required to provide more than US$3 billion to top up funds at a time when money was needed to make immediate claims payments. The 2005 hurricanes – Katrina, Rita and Wilma – also required Lloyd's to top up its funds to over US$10 billion.

22

Personal finance

Introduction

Personal finance is not a business practice of the City, but it overlaps with its activities. Banks and stockbrokers sell personal finance products, some of which are investment backed. Fund managers, seen as part of the City, run the funds in which the investments are placed.

Over a lifetime, most people save and borrow money, buy or rent a property, and use a bank account. To reduce the overall risk, people are advised to diversify their investments by putting money into various assets, including shares, bonds, cash, commodities and property. At any one time, one asset class may be doing well and another badly.

In this chapter, we will give you a brief overview of personal finance, including property, life policies and personal savings, as well as complaints and compensations. We will look at the different types of adviser. Personal finance includes pooled investment schemes, as covered in Chapter 16, which you should read with this chapter.

Financial advice

There is more than one way to buy personal finance products. You can respond to press advertisements. If you are willing to do your own research and forfeit advice, you can buy from an internet supermarket or a discount broker and receive a discount on initial charges at least.

The traditional way to buy is through a financial adviser. Until December 2004 and up to six months later, the choice was between appointed representatives, who worked for one financial services company and only offered its products, or independent financial advisers (IFAs) who could advise across the market place. A 1999 report by the Director of Fair Trading had found that the

Get a great deal online

David Jeal from The Share Centre highlights what to look for in your online share dealing service

You don't have to be an ardent 'ebay-er', 'silver surfer' or budding Bill Gates to know just what an impact the internet has had on our everyday lives. And that's just as true when it comes to investing. Nowadays, the private investor has access to information, news and views like never before – and it's all down to the internet.

Any investor knows that reliable information and market knowledge, coupled with a good sense of timing, makes for better investment decisions. Whether that's historical information gleaned from studying a company's track record, up-to-the minute knowledge about trading patterns that come from looking at 'live' prices and trading information, or getting your timing right from being able to deal 'there and then', it's all part of the online mix.

But don't imagine online trading is a new fad – it's been with us for over 8 years now and has come a long way: latest figures suggest some 650,000 private investors carry out some or all of their dealing online, and many brokers report over half of all 'execution-only' trades are completed online. Nor it is a case of 'take it or leave it' – most brokers combine the many advantages of online trading with more traditional telephone, post or even face-to-face facilities, letting you decide when and how you use which service.

Useful places to get details about broker's services include the industry's trade body, APCIM's website (**www.apcims.co.uk**) and the LSE's own website, (**www.londonstockexchange.com**). Other ways to start your search include some of the comparison and directory sites, like **www.find.co.uk** or **www.moneysupermarket.com**

What most brokers will also have in common is the need for you to hold your shares in nominee name. This simply means that instead of your name appearing on the share register, your holdings are clustered together in the broker's nominee name. But don't worry – you remain the beneficial owner, and your shares are 'ring-fenced' from the brokers own assets, so they are safe and secure. Some offer personal membership of CREST, the market settlement system, so you can still have your name on the register; typically this will incur an extra fee. Either way, it's still a good idea to take a look behind the website – how long have they been around; what's their track record; are they properly regulated and members of the appropriate market organisations.

As with many things, the nominee system has pros and cons. It means your chosen broker can carry out your trading for you when you want, with little, if any, paperwork. They'll look after corporate actions, like takeovers and mergers, and collect your dividends. And they'll usually send you regular reports detailing your activity, the value of your investments, etc. On the other hand, if you like working your way through a company's Annual Report, voting on shareholder resolutions or attending the AGM then do make sure you choose a broker who will arrange all this or you – because your name isn't on the register you won't receive information direct from the Company. Watch out for shareholder 'perks' too – a few companies won't let Brokers pass these on to their investors, and some Brokers won't pass them on even if they did.

When it comes to choosing your online Broker there are a few other things to consider too. Start with what you want from them. Most online services are 'execution-only' so make sure the site is easy to use, that there's telephone back-up if you can't use it for any reason, and that there the right level of information and research tools to support your likely trading needs.

Some services do offer more, so if you are likely to want some advice, investment tips or someone to talk over your ideas with, you'll want to be happy that's readily available, covers the types of investments you'll want advice about and, most importantly, that they 'talk your language'. In effect, that you feel 'at home' with them.

Then there's the question of costs. Online competition has driven down the cost of dealing commission and there's a variety of different charging methods to be found. In broad terms, commissions split into two types: 'flat' (a fixed cost per trade, often tied to doing a particular number of deals in any specified period) and 'variable' (a percentage of the value of the deal). Comparison sites like Money Supermarket let you input your typical trade and show you how prices compare. Once again, do make sure you've got the complete picture. Are account fees payable and, if so, how much and what do they cover? Can you change your trading tariff if your dealing pattern changes? Are there 'safe custody' fees if you don't trade for a while? What are the costs if, at a later date, you want to transfer your account elsewhere? And, most importantly, are all their charges clearly visible?

Some broker's sites enable you to open an account online, others will require some paperwork, but don't jump at the first site you come to, have a look at what's on offer, call them for a chat, then decide. After all, your online broker's not just for your next trade but will be an important part of your investment life!

polarisation in service choice had not delivered the expected consumer benefits and it prompted depolarisation.

Under today's regime, there is still the appointed representative and the IFA as before, but there is also the multi-tied agent, often a bank, which can sell products from a select number of companies. Many customers do not properly understand the distinction between the three, according to financial advisers. Since this system started, some smaller IFAs have closed down their business, or merged, and many customers use multi-tied agents without fully understanding that they are receiving a more restricted service than provided by an IFA, although it is no cheaper. Some banks are multi-tied in investment products but not in insurance products, and they sell their own brand of insurance only, which can be expensive. Some firms are a combination of IFA and multi-tied.

Customers now receive clearer information about the service that the adviser is offering including, for the first time, an upfront indication of the cost. The information is given through terms of business, and a menu document which explains the cost of the firm's services and the different payment methods. The IFA must now offer customers a choice of paying either a commission on sales or a fee. In the past, some companies had offered fee-based services, but many had worked only on commission. As before, most people prefer to go down the commission route.

The menu compares the *maximum* sales commission of the adviser concerned with the market average for each product type. If for instance there are 100 funds of a particular kind, and 99 pay 3 per cent commission, but one pays 5 per cent, it is the latter that will be compared with the average. Many customers go away with the wrong impression that the IFA is charging a commission that is 2 per cent higher than average, even if it is not recommending this product.

Property

People often invest in funds where a main asset is commercial property. Domestic property is rarely included in funds, but the biggest personal investment most people make is their home. If you use your property as security on a loan, you will take out a mortgage. It means that you are borrowing to buy, which is the most usual way to acquire your home. The decision to take out a mortgage that you may not be able to afford is risky. If you are unable to make the agreed repayments, the lender can sell the property to repay your debt.

There is now no tax relief on mortgages for the purchase of your home. Stamp duty is payable on properties priced above £120,000, on a rising scale according to the cost of the property. A mortgage may be repayment, interest only, or a combination. The repayment mortgage requires you to pay your lender a monthly sum that combines repayment of capital borrowed with interest on the loan. If you make all your payments, the loan will be repaid at the end of the mortgage term.

If you have an interest-only loan, you will pay only interest to the lender every month. Only at the end of the term will you pay back the original debt in a lump sum. You will need a savings vehicle, perhaps a pension, ISA or endowment to build up enough money over the years to pay off what is left of the loan at the end of the term, but you can also pay as you go throughout the life of the loan. You will need to review your investment regularly to make sure it is on track to pay off what is left of your debt.

Some mortgage providers offer lower rates for a certain period. It may be through a fixed rate mortgage, which guarantees the level of monthly payments, a capped rate mortgage, which sets an upper limit, or a discount mortgage, where the rate is set at a margin lower than the lender's standard variable rate for an initial specified period. Another type is a tracker mortgage, where the interest is set at a certain margin above or below the Bank of England's base rate.

An offset mortgage is where the credit that you hold with the lender is offset against what you owe on your mortgage. The main advantage is that it is tax-efficient because your savings can be used to pay off parts of the mortgage rather than earning interest at a taxed rate. Another advantage is flexibility, meaning that you can make such repayments when you have the cash to do so, but withdraw from your mortgage when you need the cash for something else.

Life policies and pensions

Life and protection

Let us take a brief look at the type of non-investment life and protection products available. The two key protection life products are whole-of-life and term insurance.

Whole-of-life policies will pay out when you die. You will pay regular premiums to build up a pot of money, which is invested, and the cover is not limited to a period. The premium will generally go up, typically every 10 years, although you can get it guaranteed. Returns on the life funds within the policies, inclusive of bonuses, will have been taxed. Gains on a qualifying policy are free of any further tax charge. To qualify, the policy must be held for 10 years, or three-quarters of the policy term, whichever is shorter, and premiums must be paid at least annually.

The product is useful for inheritance tax purposes. If your children will be beneficiaries of your estate and would have an inheritance tax liability of £100,000, you can get a whole-of-life policy, write it in trust for your children and it will provide a lump sum to pay off that liability. But if you fail to use a trust, you will inflate the estate by £100,000, giving rise to a potential extra £40,000 inheritance tax liability. This is an area in which you need specialist advice.

Term insurance is cheaper and the premium is guaranteed. It pays out a tax-free lump sum only if you die within a specified period and, if you do not, the cover will end. It could instead pay out a family benefit income under these circumstances, which is useful for a spouse whose partner has died during the term. Lots of people use term insurance in conjunction with a mortgage.

The key protection products are private medical insurance, critical illness cover, income protection insurance and long-term care insurance. Let us consider each.

Private medical insurance

This aims to cover the cost of private medical treatment of acute conditions, defined as illness or injury, where treatment will lead to recovery. Premiums increase with age.

Critical illness

This pays a tax-free lump sum if you suffer from any illness or condition, or have any surgical procedure, covered by the policy. Sales of critical illness insurance have been down since the cost of guaranteed premiums started to rise steeply in 2002.

Income protection

This pays a tax-free monthly income for an agreed period if you are unfit to work because of sickness or accident, resulting in a loss of earnings.

Long-term care insurance

This covers the cost of long-term care in your home, or in a residential or nursing home. It includes a wide range of care services.

In the lucrative area of protection insurance, the fastest-growing sector has been the non-advisory, including through web sites, supermarkets and similar channels. Customers do not always understand that if they buy a product without advice and complain about its suitability to the Financial Ombudsman (see later in this chapter), the complaint is unlikely to be upheld. Financial advisers say that to treat customers fairly, non-advisory sellers should be forced to provide a lot more information about the products than they do. The Financial Services Authority (FSA) has been regulating most sales of general insurance and pure protection insurance from 14 January 2005, and was to have conducted an effectiveness review in April 2006.

Investments

In this section, we will refer to products which are primarily investment, not protection, but include an element of life insurance. These are either endowments or investment bonds. In simple terms, the endowment is a regular savings version of the investment bond, but is more tax efficient because, unlike the bond, it requires no further tax payment, regardless of circumstances.

Endowments

Investment-type insurance is based around endowments, which have the same tax treatment on gains as whole-of-life policies. An endowment policy will pay a fixed sum on death during the period of the policy, unless the policyholder survives the term, at which point the accumulated value of the policy will be paid out. The endowment can be tax-efficient. There is no tax deferred but, when the policy matures, no higher rate tax is payable.

The sales of endowment products have dwindled drastically partly from the impact of mis-selling in or around the late 1980s and early 1990s. Financial salespeople, particularly in banks and building societies, frequently recommended interest-only mortgages with an endowment policy.

The expectation was that once the term was over, the policy proceeds should at least repay the mortgage, but there were no guarantees of the required investment returns and the risks were not always made clear. As it turned out, declining stock markets and overall returns were lower than expected and it led to a predicted shortfall in the value of the capital sum to be repaid at the end of term by some endowments purchased alongside an interest-only mortgage.

All mortgage endowment providers must regularly write to their customers to update them on the performance of their investments and the projected value of their policy. While the existence of a projected or actual shortfall is not, in itself, grounds for complaint, those letters set out how policyholders may complain if they believe that the nature of the endowment and its risks were not properly explained to them, and if they have suffered financially as a result of buying this sort of mortgage. If customers have proven their case, companies have been paying compensation, although the process can be lengthy.

For customers facing a shortfall on an endowment with an interest-only mortgage who have not been eligible for compensation, additional action has been advised. It may take the form of saving more money in another vehicle or the total or partial conversion of the interest-only mortgage into the repayment kind.

The insurance companies that had sold endowments switched out of risky equities into bonds under regulatory pressure, which means that endowment holders have failed to benefit as much as they might have done from a subsequent rise in the stock market. There is no longer any real market for new endowments, according to financial advisers.

Investment bonds

The investment bond is a savings vehicle. The key benefit is that it enables you to defer, or possibly to avoid, any additional higher rate tax on gains and income generated by the bond.

The product is useful for those who pay higher rate tax but, in the future, will no longer be doing so. Financial advisers can receive a high commission to sell this product, and so have often been known to recommend it above cheaper and more tax-efficient alternatives.

Pensions

Your pension is a tax-efficient savings vehicle designed to provide you with a tax-free sum on retirement followed by a taxable income for the rest of your life. The main point to understand about a pension is that it is a wrapper, in which you can put any funds, and you can get tax relief on contributions. The funds will grow in a tax efficient environment. They are no longer tax-free because tax is paid on dividends, but no additional personal taxation is payable.

As you are essentially investing in funds, these may do well or they may do badly. The best performer can produce more than three times the annual pension of the worst, according to industry sources. The poor performers significantly outweigh the good. Investors tend not to switch out of them. This is mainly through lethargy or inability to follow the performance of the fund, according to financial advisers. Older pensions may have penalties for switching funds or stopping contributions. It gives the fund manager little incentive to improve performance.

The main types of pension are state (basic and second), personal (including the stakeholder) and occupational.

State

The UK Government provides a full basic state pension to women aged between 60 and 65, depending on when they were born (to become 65 from 2010) and men at 65 who have paid enough national insurance contributions.

The state second pension was introduced in April 2002, and provides an additional state pension. It replaced the state earnings-related pension scheme, or SERPS, which was an earnings-related part of the basic state pension. If you are an employee, you can pay into the state second pension, or opt out and have partial rebates of your national insurance contributions paid into a personal pension instead.

Personal

Individuals who are self-employed, or are not on a company pension scheme, may take out a personal pension. It is usually provided by insurance companies and is in addition to the state pension.

Stakeholder pension

The stakeholder pension is a cheap and flexible form of personal pension which was introduced to address the shortfall in pension provision. It meets Government standards for fair value and, by the end of December 2004, about 2.3 million had been sold. The pension is run by trustees or an authorised stakeholder manager. It is a popular option to use a stakeholder pension when leaving (contracting out of) the second state pension. Every employer with five or more employees must offer them a stakeholder pension, or a suitable alternative.

Sipp

The self-invested personal pension, known as Sipp, is the premier option for those with a reasonable pension, perhaps of tens of thousands of pounds upwards, according to Justin Modray, independent financial adviser at Bestinvest. The Sipp's unique facet is the investment freedom it gives, enabling the holder to choose from a wide investment universe, including investment funds, shares and commercial property. Charges are levied on the underlying instrument, and there are also charges on the Sipp wrapper although these have recently become much lower.

The Sipp used to be the preserve of the rich. It has spread its net, but for those with very small pensions, or who don't want the risks and rewards associated with greater freedom of investment choice, a stakeholder pension may be a better bet.

In a briefing paper accompanying the late 2005 pre-budget statement, the US Treasury said that the Sipp would not attract tax advantages from investing in property and alternative investments from 6 April 2006, as expected. The financial services industry was infuriated because it had spent large sums preparing to promote Sipps in anticipation. But in retrospect, the feeling was that many would not have been able to afford to buy a property for a pension fund. If they had, the property would have been owned by trustees of the pension fund and, if it had been their only investment in the pension fund, would be insufficiently diversified.

Occupational

The occupational pension is a company scheme that an employer makes available to members of its staff. The employer may match employees' contributions with its own, or make none. Employees may supplement their own payments by additional voluntary contributions, known as AVCs, or by personal pension contributions. In many public sector schemes, the employer makes all the contributions.

There are two main types of occupational pension. In a *final salary* scheme, employees will receive a proportion of their final salary on retirement, but many companies are phasing out these schemes because they are expensive to maintain. In a *money purchase* pension, cash is invested in a fund to create for the employee, on retirement, a pot of money.

The pensions crisis

There have been pension scandals, but they are not about performance. They are more to do with mis-selling or mismanagement. Between 29 April 1988 and 30 June 1994, many firms sold personal pensions to individuals who would have been better off if they had stayed in, or joined, their employer's scheme. It led to compensation payments.

Two pension scandals

Pension fund scandals have had the unfortunate effect of tarnishing the industry's reputation even for years later, and have made the public distrust the industry. Let us take a look at two.

Maxwell

The Maxwell scandal was a watershed that led to major reforms of pension regulation. In November 1991, tycoon Robert Maxwell, owner of Mirror Group newspapers and the Labour Party's biggest backer, died in mysterious circumstances. He vanished from his yacht off the Canary Islands. The most popular theory was that he had jumped off the deck into the water and drowned to escape from his business problems. Another theory is that he was pushed, and the facts remain unresolved.

After the event Maxwell's business empire, including Maxwell Communications and Mirror Group Newspapers, floundered amid substantial debt and parts of it collapsed. It became clear that Maxwell had illegally *borrowed* more than £400 million from the Daily Mirror's own pension fund to support the price of Maxwell Communications. He had switched funds between his businesses to expand his empire. About 32,000 pensioners were left facing financial insecurity.

The Department of Trade & Industry (DTI) launched a vigorous investigation into the Maxwell scandal and, in 2001, it published a report that was critical not just of the tycoon's business but also of those in the City who had profited from it and who had not made proper checks.

The DTI report found that Maxwell had taken cash regularly and on an unsecured basis from the pension fund since 1985. He had disclosed minimal financial details relating to his companies and pension funds. 'Maxwell had always regarded the pension funds as his own and ran his companies and the pension funds as if they were one', it said.

In future, the DTI recommended that pension trustees should be trained, and sanctions imposed on companies that did not report fraud. It said there should be more guidance on the audit of business empires, and that auditors should be discouraged from cross-selling services to their audit clients. The report sought to disabuse the public of the idea that fraud and market manipulation could be eliminated.

Since the Maxwell scandal, pension legislation has tightened up, and pensions must now be sufficiently well funded to keep a minimum balance. The Pensions Act, 1995 established the Occupational Pensions Regulatory Authority, which supervises the establishment of required legal set-ups to protect people's occupational pensions. The Pensions Compensation Board was established in April 1997 to pay compensation to individuals whose money had been stolen from occupational pension schemes when the employer had become insolvent. It was dissolved on 1 September 2005 and the responsibility for fraud compensation passed to the Pensions Protection Fund.

The Equitable Life saga

Equitable Life established a solid image with the public, not least through its television campaigns with the famous line, delivered in a warm, soothing tone: 'It's an equitable life, Henry'. Between 1957 and the late 1980s, Equitable Life wrote pension policies with generous guaranteed annuities. But in the 1990s, interest rates declined, and the Society asked some of its policyholders to take a cut in bonuses.

The policy holders took legal action against the Society for an alleged breach of contract. The Society appealed, ultimately to the House of Lords, but was required to pay out. Equitable Life had a £1.5 billion hole in its balance sheet and was almost ruined. It stopped accepting new business and drastically reduced the value of investments belonging to the 800,000 shareholders for whom it had not guaranteed returns.

In 2001, Halifax bought Equitable Life's sales force and non-profit policies for £1 billion. In March 2004, the Penrose Report, based on a government investigation, accused the Society's management of dubious practices. The Serious Fraud Office launched an investigation that, at the time of writing, remains unresolved.

Industry insiders reckon that pension fund scandals are a good part of the reason for the £27 billion annual savings gap between the amount being saved and that needed to fund a comfortable retirement, as estimated by the Association of British Insurers in 2002. The gap is likely since to have risen.

In November 2005, Lord Turner's Pension Commission published a final report with a prescription for pension reform. It recommended a gradual rise in the state pension age and, in return, an increased basic state pension, linked in value to average wage growth rates rather than inflation. The state pension would become based on UK residence rather than on years worked. For private pension provision, Turner suggested a new National Pensions Savings Scheme (NPSS), in which you would be automatically enrolled on joining a new company, but with a right to opt out. Turner wanted an independent commission established to take an overview of pensions.

Some consumer groups welcomed the Turner proposals. Critics focused on, among other things, the potential cost of the new state pension to the taxpayer. The Association of British Insurers (ABI) took the view that the NPSS would bring significant start-up costs and new risks for the taxpayer, and that defensively managed funds backed by a new state bureaucracy would be out of place. It favoured a private sector-led alternative. The ABI said its own initial research showed that automatic enrolment would be popular with employees but not always with employers.

Following the report, John Hutton, Secretary of State for Work and Pensions, said that the government's response would be based on five tests: whether the proposals promoted personal responsibility, were fair, were affordable, would simplify the system and were sustainable in the long term. Industry sources suggested this response meant that the government would not act quickly, if ever. Of more immediate interest are the *A Day* pension reforms, which will have started by the time this book is in your hands.

A Day – New opportunities

Under rules introduced from 6 April 2006, known as *A Day*, the maximum allowable pension of two thirds of final income will have been replaced by a lifetime allowance, which for 2006–07 will be £1.5 million. Any pension fund size above this level will be subject to an effective 55 per cent tax rate. Anybody may contribute up to 100 per cent of their earnings to any pension scheme, subject to an annual allowance of £215,000.

Under the new regime, employees may take pension benefits while they remain at work and accrue a further pension. From 6 April 2010, the earliest age at which you can withdraw a pension will rise from 50 to 55.

Annuities and unsecured pension

Annuity

An annuity is a contract from an insurance company that converts your pension fund into income that you will be paid for the rest of your life. On retirement, the bulk of the pension fund has in the past had to be used to buy a traditional annuity. Since April 2006, it has been optional.

If you take this route, you can take up to 25 per cent of the pension money saved as a tax-free sum, and use the rest to buy your annuity from an insurance company. Based on your annuity, the insurer will make regular income payments to you and the capital becomes its property. The income paid by the fund depends on the annuity rate at the time of conversion and varies between providers. It is derived from the long-term interest rate on government bonds and the average life expectancy of an individual.

Unsecured and alternatively secured pension

Since April 2006, if you are a member of a money purchase pension scheme, and you are aged between 50 and 75, you have been able to take an *unsecured pension*, previously known as income drawdown, at up to 120 per cent of the income available if the fund had bought an annuity. The figures must be revised every five years. Unlike before A Day, investors are not required to draw an income.

Such schemes have not always been a wise alternative. Research commissioned by Annuity Direct for the 10th anniversary of the plans and published in November 2005 showed that investors who used income drawdown to delay buying an annuity until 75 were far worse off than if they had bought an annuity 10 years earlier.

If you are over 75, you can continue drawing income from your pension plan rather than having to buy an annuity, but must use an *alternatively secured pension*. It is slightly more restrictive than the unsecured pension, and a figure of 70 per cent replaces the 120 per cent, representing the percentage of the income that would be available if the fund had bought an annuity. The figures must be revised every 12 months. Investors still need not take an income.

Savings

Bank and building society accounts

Bank and building society accounts vary in flexibility and the interest rates that they pay. Savings are becoming increasingly complicated. In past years, the savings account was either instant access, which paid a bit of interest, or was a notice account, which paid more. In today's more competitive environment, some accounts have high rates, but there can be lots of catches. For example, the rate may fall away after six months or an even shorter time. There may be restricted withdrawals, meaning that if you make more than a certain number of withdrawals within a set period, there is less, or no, interest payable.

ISAs

If you have savings and are not using the Individual Savings Account (ISA) in other ways, you should use a mini-cash ISA to put away up to £3,000 a year. It is a wrapper in which your cash can grow without paying income or capital gains tax and is available without charges through your bank or building society. The ISA can also be used for other investments. Every year the public has invested consistently about £28 billion in ISAs, but there has been increasingly more investment in cash and less in shares. In early 2006, the Treasury was considering ways of simplifying the ISA regime. If you want to know more about the ISA or other financial services products, refer to my previous book *The Times: How to Read the Financial Pages*, published by Kogan Page.

National Savings and Investments

National Savings and Investments started life in 1861 as the Post Office Savings Bank. As the UK's second largest savings institution, it has more than 26 million customers who have invested more than £66 billion. It promotes secure, sometimes tax-free, government-backed savings products, but the returns tend to be fairly uncompetitive. Interest rates may be fixed, variable or index-linked.

Will

You should take steps to organise a will, which is a formal arrangement to distribute your assets after your death. To be valid, it must be in writing, signed by the testator, and witnessed. If you do not make a will, your estate will be distributed under the laws of intestacy. Should your estate be worth more than £285,000 (tax year 2006–07), it will be subject to rules on inheritance tax.

Complaints and compensation

The Financial Ombudsman Service

The Financial Ombudsman Service (FOS) was established under the Financial Services and Markets Act 2000 as an independent organisation with statutory powers to address and settle individual disputes between consumers and financial services companies. The service is financed by a levy on financial institutions. Consumers and small businesses use the FOS as an alternative to the court system, which is also available.

If a financial services firm, including a stockbroker, has operated incompetently or dishonestly, private investors should first complain to the firm. If this does not get a satisfactory result within eight weeks, there is in most cases access to the FOS. The FOS will look at initial advice on pensions but not at ongoing administration, and does not cover consumer credit away from banks or building societies.

The FOS may use mediation or adjudication to resolve an issue. In the year to 31 March 2005, the FOS investigated 110,963 cases, of which two-thirds were on mortgage endowments, and it gave 55 per cent of them to guided mediation, 39 per cent to formal adjudication, and 7 per cent to a final decision by the Ombudsman. The length of time a case takes to resolve depends on its complexity, but most are resolved within six months, according to an FOS spokesperson.

In early 2005, the FOS and the FSA issued a joint consultation. They agreed to make existing complaints procedures transparent and to make access to experts more formally available.

Financial Services Compensation Scheme

This is the UK statutory fund of last resort for customers of authorised financial services firms. The scheme is an independent body that can pay compensation if a firm is unable, or likely to be unable, to pay claims against it. The FSCS is funded through levies on the industry.

The future

On a practical level, the Government is seeking to encourage a savings culture. It has, for example, introduced child trust funds. But how far the public can come to trust promoters of pensions and other savings products in the aftermath of the various scandals remains to be seen. The financial services professionals accept that their industry is not perfect but see it as worrying if people prefer to take investment advice from their mate down the pub than from themselves.

On the bright side, the internet is enhancing personal awareness of how savings and protection products work, and financial advisers notice a feeling among young people that it is cool to know about finance. Personal finance has started to appear on the school curriculum, and education may well prove the way forward.

Final word

The book is over, but this could be a new beginning. The City is always developing and I hope what you have gained from this reading will help you to keep up with it. The websites listed in Appendix 1 will broaden your knowledge and the books recommended in Appendix 2 will deepen it.

Do not stop there. Read the business pages of *The Times* and, for intraday developments, *Times Online* (www.timesonline.co.uk). You will soon gain extra knowledge and understanding that you can put to practical use. Good luck!

Appendix 1

Useful websites

Here are some of the financial websites that have helped me. Use this list as a starting point.

Accounting

Financial Reporting Council, www.frc.org.uk

Banking and building societies

Abbey National, www.abbey.com
British Bankers' Association, www.bba.org.uk
British Venture Capital Association, www.bvca.co.uk
The Building Societies Association, www.bsa.org.uk
Egg, www.egg.com
European Central Bank (English site), www.ecb.int
First Direct, www.firstdirect.com
Nationwide Building Society, www.nationwide.co.uk

Bonds

Debt Management Office (gilts), www.dmo.gov.uk
International Capital Market Association, www.icma-group.org

Complaints

Financial Ombudsman Service, www.financial-ombudsman.co.uk

Derivatives and commodities

APX Group, www.apxgroup.com
Baltic Exchange, www.balticexchange.com
Euronext, www.euronext.com
Ice Futures, www.theice.com
London Metal Exchange, www.lme.co.uk
Numa Financial Systems, www.numa.com
Onewaybet.com – an excellent website about spread betting, www.onewaybet.com
World Gold Council, www.gold.org

The economy

Bank of England, www.bankofengland.co.uk
Samuel Brittan – economic commentator for *The Financial Times,* www.samuelbrittan.co.uk
HM Treasury, www.hm-treasury.gov.uk
National Statistics, www.statistics.gov.uk
Organisation for Economic Co-operation and Development, www.oecd.org

Factoring and leasing

Factors and Discounters Association, www.factors.org.uk
Finance and Leasing Association, www.fla.org.uk

Insurance

Association of British Insurers, www.abi.org.uk
British Insurance Brokers' Association, www.biba.co.uk
Chartered Insurance Institute, www.cii.co.uk
International Underwriting Association of London, www.iua.co.uk
Lloyd's of London, www.lloyds.com

Interdealer brokers

GFI, www.gfi.com
ICAP, www.icap.com

Investment funds

Hemscott, www.hemscott.com
Morningstar.co.uk, www.morningstar.co.uk

Standard & Poor's – funds website, www.funds-sp.com
Trustnet – a particularly good website, www.trustnet.com

News, data and research

Advfn, www.advfn.com
AFX News, www.afxpress.com
AWD Moneyextra, www.moneyextra.com
Bloomberg News, www.bloomberg.co.uk
Breakingviews, www.breakingviews.com
Citywire, www.citywire.co.uk
Compeer, www.compeer.co.uk
Digital Look, www.digitallook.com
The Economist, www.economist.com
FT.com, www.ft.com
Interactive Investor, www.iii.co.uk
Investors Chronicle, www.investorschronicle.co.uk
Mergermarket, www.mergermarket.com
MoneyAM, www.moneyam.com
The Motley Fool UK, www.fool.co.uk
Reuters, www.reuters.co.uk
ShareCast.com, www.sharecast.com
Times Online, www.timesonline.co.uk
Trustnet, www.trustnet.com

Pensions

Financial Services Authority pension website, www.fsa.gov.uk/consumer/pensions

Post-trade services

CREST, www.crestco.co.uk
LCH.Clearnet Limited, www.lchclearnet.com

Regulation, trade bodies and similar

Alternative Investment Management Association, www.aima.org
Association of Investment Trust Companies, www.aitc.co.uk
Association of Private Client Investment Managers and Stockbrokers, www.apcims.co.uk
Committee of European Securities Regulators, www.cesr-eu.org

Competition Commission, www.mmc.gov.uk
Complinet.com, www.complinet.com
Corporation of London, www.cityoflondon.gov.uk
Department of Trade and Industry, www.dti.gov.uk
Ethical Investment Association, www.ethicalinvestment.org.uk
European Union, www.europa.eu.int
Federation of European Securities Exchanges, www.fese.be
Financial Services Authority, www.fsa.gov.uk
International Organization of Securities Commissions, www.iosco.org
National Association of Pension Funds, www.napf.co.uk
Office of Fair Trading, www.oft.gov.uk
Press Complaints Commission, www.pcc.org.uk
Securities & Investment Institute, www.securities-institute.org.uk
Serious Fraud Office, www.sfo.gov.uk

Stock market

Aimquoted.com – discussion on AIM stocks, www.aimquoted.com
London Stock Exchange, www.londonstockexchange.com
OFEX – official OFEX website, www.plusmarketsgroup.com
OFEX stocks are discussed at www.unquoted.co.uk

Appendix 2

Further reading

Here are some of the books that have worked for me. You can obtain some of these online or by telephone, often at discount prices, through Global-investor. com at www.global-investor.com, which is my favourite bookshop because it has a high level of personal service, and delivers quickly and reliably. Otherwise, try Amazon at www.amazon.co.uk.

General guides to the City

The sequel to this book, although written before it, is *How to Understand the Financial Pages* by Alexander Davidson, Kogan Page, 2005.

You will find a lucid if concentrated overview in *The Money Machine: How the City works* by Philip Coggan, Penguin Books, 5th edition, 2002. The City has changed since when it was last updated, but this book remains a valuable guide.

There is greater depth and a more international perspective in *An Introduction to Global Financial Markets* by Stephen Valdez, Palgrave, 4th edition, 2003.

For an uncritical, but clear bird's eye view, read *How the City Works, An Introduction to its Financial Markets* by William Clarke, Sweet & Maxwell, 6th edition, 2004.

How to Read the Financial Pages by Michael Brett, Random Books, 2000, is a readable reference guide that has particularly clear explanations.

For details of how the markets work, read *The Economist Guide to Financial Markets* by Mark Levison, Profile Books, 3rd edition, 2000.

For a historical account of how the City has developed and the biggest players were formed, read *The Death of Gentlemanly Capitalism* by Philip Augar, Penguin Books, 2001.

A very lively read is *City State: A contemporary history of the City of London and how money triumphed* by Richard Roberts and David Kynaston, Profile Books, 2002.

For a thinking approach, including detailed coverage of institutional investors and capital markets, read *The City: Inside the great expectation machine* by Tony Golding, Pearson Education Ltd, 2001.

Analysts

On how analysts work, read *The Super Analysts* by Andrew Leeming, John Wiley, 2000. It contains interviews with named analysts and investors.

Investor's Chronicle Guide to Charting: An analysis for the intelligent investor by Alistair Blair, Financial Times/Prentice Hall, 2002, is a cynic's introduction to technical analysis. It is entertaining and informative.

Corporate finance

The Greed Merchants by Philip Augar, Penguin 2005, is an ex-banker's critical account of investment banking.

The Penguin Guide to Finance by Hugo Dixon, Penguin Books, 2000, is a journalistic primer on corporate finance.

Derivatives

For details on how derivatives work, try *The Investor's Toolbox* by Peter Temple, Harriman House, 2003. It is packed with clear explanations for private investors.

To understand how derivatives trading can go wrong, read *Rogue Trader* by Nick Leeson, Warner Books 1999. It is the autobiography of the trader who brought down Barings Bank.

Economics

To get to grips with economics, read *The Investor's Guide to Economic Fundamentals* by John Calverley, John Wiley, 2003. It is a clear overview from a chief economist and strategist at American Express Bank.

Also read *Free Lunch* by David Smith, Profile Books, 2003. This an easy-to-read beginner's guide to economics from the economics editor of *The Sunday Times*.

For details on how economic indicators work, try *First Steps in Economic Indicators* by Peter Temple, FT Prentice Hall, 2003.

A useful reference guide is *Guide to Economic Indicators* by Richard Stutely, Economist Books, 2003.

Discover how economic statistics are manipulated and be entertained in *How to Lie With Statistics* by Darrell Huff, Penguin, 1991.

Regulation

Dealing with Financial Risk by David Shireff, Economist Books, 2004, is a journalistic trot through the basics of financial risk management.

The Laundrymen by Jeffrey Robinson, Pocket Books, 1998, is a cracking primer on money laundering. It offers provocative, liberal solutions.

Stock market

The Naked Trader by Robbie Burns, Harriman House, 2005, is a tongue-in-cheek beginner's guide to trading written from experience and largely based around the ADVFN website. It contains more than a few new rules alongside the old.

The UK Trader's Bible by Dominic Connolly, Harriman House, 2005, is a lucid guide to the mechanics of how share trading works in London.

For a readable introduction to shares and other investments, try *The Motley Fool UK Investment Guide* by David Berger, David Gardner, Tom Gardner, edited by James Carlisle, Boxtree, 2002.

One of the best books on the UK stock market is *The Zulu Principle* by Jim Slater, Texere Publishing, US, 2000. It is now a little dated.

One Up on Wall Street by Peter Lynch, edited by John Rothschild, Simon & Schuster Inc, 2000, provides an expert fund manager's view of Wall Street.

The Disciplined Trader by Mark Douglas, New York Institute of Finance, 1990, shows you how the secret of successful stock market trading is in the mind.

Forecasting Financial Markets: The psychology of successful investing by Tony Plummer, 4th edition, Kogan Page, 2003, explains the mass psychology behind stock market rises and falls from a technical perspective.

Index

Index of advertisers

ALSO AVAILABLE FROM KOGAN PAGE

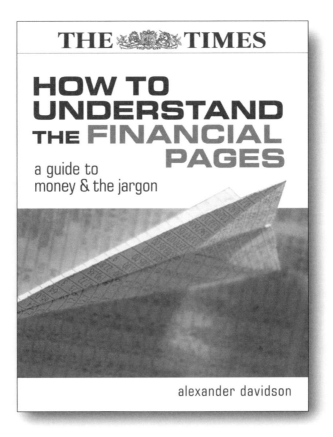

ALSO AVAILABLE FROM KOGAN PAGE

0 7494 3885 1   Paperback   2002

ALSO AVAILABLE FROM KOGAN PAGE

0 7494 4577 7   Hardback   2006

ALSO AVAILABLE FROM KOGAN PAGE

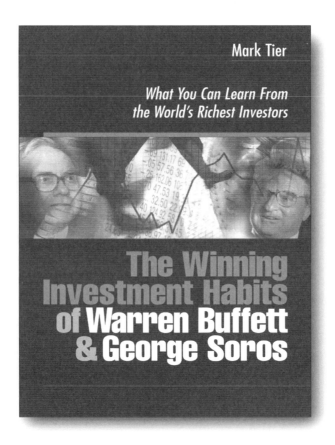

0 7494 4503 3   Hardback   2006